C0063 01451

D0551351

In 1979, Liz Pryor, a good girl from a privileged Chicago family, discovered that she was pregnant. At only 17 years old, her parents were determined to keep this shameful event secret from everyone, even her siblings. One snowy January day, after driving across three states, her mother dropped her off at what Liz believed was a Catholic home for unwed mothers, but was in fact a locked state facility for delinquent pregnant girls.

Over the next six months, alone and isolated from everyone she knew, Liz developed a surprising bond of friendship with the other girls, which led her to question everything she once held true. Told with tenderness, humour and candour, *Look at You Now* is a deeply moving coming-of-age story that pays tribute to the triumph of the human spirit in times of adversity, and the transcendent power of friendship in the toughest of times.

also by liz pryor

. . . .

WHAT DID I DO WRONG?

LOOK AT YOU NOW

look at you now

look at
you now

ONE GIRL'S JOURNEY
FROM SHAME TO STRENGTH

liz pryor

Atlantic Books
London

Glasgow Life Glasgow Libraries	
GoMA	
C 006301451	
Askews & Holts	11-Jan-2017
306.8743092/LL	£12.99

First published in the United States in 2016 by Random House,
an imprint and division of Penguin Random House LLC, New York

Published in e-book in 2016 and hardback in 2017 in Great Britain
by Atlantic Books, an imprint of Atlantic Books Ltd.

Copyright © Liz Pryor, 2016

The moral right of Liz Pryor to be identified as the author of this work has been
asserted by her in accordance with the Copyright, Designs and Patents Act of 1988.

All rights reserved. No part of this publication may be reproduced, stored in a
retrieval system, or transmitted in any form or by any means, electronic,
mechanical, photocopying, recording, or otherwise, without the prior permission
of both the copyright owner and the above publisher of this book.

10 9 8 7 6 5 4 3 2 1

A CIP catalogue record for this book is available from the British Library.

Hardback ISBN: 978 1 78649 046 9
E-book ISBN: 978 1 78649 0476

Printed in Great Britain

Atlantic Books
An Imprint of Atlantic Books Ltd
Ormond House
26–27 Boswell Street
London
WC1N 3JZ

www.atlantic-books.co.uk

To Peter, thank you for convincing me
to be brave

No legacy is so rich as honesty.

—William Shakespeare

author's note

This work is a memoir. It reflects my experiences and memories as accurately as possible. Aside from references to members of my family, names, locations, and identifying details have been changed, and some individuals portrayed are composites. For narrative purposes, the timeline of certain events has been altered or compressed.

look at you now

chapter 1

My mom hadn't uttered a single word in the two hours we'd been driving. Clearly, nothing in the world feels as quiet as the silence of a mother. There were no other cars on the Indiana interstate that day. Snow was pouring out of the sky and the road was slick. I thought about offering to drive but when I looked over, I dared not speak.

It was early January 1979. "Baby, I Love Your Way" was playing on the car radio. I had just turned seventeen and was a very young senior in high school. Young, not because I was smart and skipped a grade, but probably because my parents wanted to get me off to kindergarten as soon as possible. There were a lot of kids in our house: I was born number five out of seven children in nine years. My brothers were the oldest and then came the five girls. Our mom called us her army and sometimes her crowd, and maybe most fitting, her herd. Being a part of an army, crowd, herd, had great value as a little kid. There's a sort of mob identity thing that goes on in big families, a free pass that you can take advantage of.

Other parents, older siblings, neighbors, teachers, coaches, *people*, give a nod when you're one of so many. A nod that says, "Oh yeah, you're okay, you're one of them." It's like having a little something extra inside that reminds you you belong somewhere in the world, and it never goes away. I'd grown up my whole life knowing I was loved. Knowing I would always have a place I belonged.

I didn't think much about the way we grew up; it was just my life, and up to that point almost all of it had been spent in our hometown of Winnetka, Illinois, a small community thirty minutes north of Chicago, perched like a Norman Rockwell painting on the edge of Lake Michigan. We lived in a gigantic house with three stories, eleven bedrooms, four fireplaces, and a killer basement. In the winters we made snow forts in our backyard, and our tree-lined driveway covered with snow looked like a fairy-tale wonderland. But the best thing about that great house was how perfectly it fit our army of family: seven kids and two parents.

My dad grew up the son of a naval captain and went to boarding school in Connecticut before heading off to college. He worked for IBM after graduation, and then came the Pryor Corporation, a business he started on his own in our garage before I was born. Our mom, well, she was the president of *us*. She did everything that had anything to do with the seven of us and our home. She drove, fed, nursed, looked after, scolded, praised, and kept the ship running, every day. Our mom spent her entire life within the protected walls of the North Shore. Her parents still lived just a mile or two away from us. After Catholic high school, she went down the street to college at Northwestern University, where she majored in theater and starred in most of their musical theater productions. She met and fell in love with my dad at Northwestern and married him soon after graduation. They settled in the area, and quickly we kids arrived, one after another.

Northwestern University was a beautiful sight. Every time we drove past the ivy-covered brick buildings, set back on the edge of Lake Michigan, our mom pointed out the sorority where she'd lived and the fraternity where my dad had lived. I'd watch the college kids walking with their backpacks, holding hands and being young, and found it near impossible to imagine that could ever have been our mom and dad—that they could have ever been young, ever been anything other than our parents.

. . . .

We finally pulled off the interstate to get gas. It was late morning, the sky was dark, and the snow still hadn't let up. My mom uttered her first words in hours.

"Are you hungry?"

"No, thank you, Mom."

She stepped out of the car and closed the door hard. I leaned over to change the radio station. Frank Sinatra came on singing, "I've got a crush on you." This was the music my mom loved and had been singing my whole life. My grandfather, her dad, was our mother's most cherished confidant. We called him Papa and he was the quietest, kindest man I'd ever know. He and my aunt and my mom sang and played music in our living room after family dinners sometimes. I'd hide behind the drapes, when we were all supposed to be sleeping, and watch my grandfather play the tiple; it sang straight through my heart the first time I heard it. It had ten strings and looked like a baby guitar. As Papa played, my mother would sit on the couch, her big brown eyes wide and alive. She'd tap her high heel on the living room carpet, stand up, arms stretched in the air like she was talking to God, and belt with a voice that thundered through the house. Her beautiful face lit up the room, but it was her verve that was so impossible to ignore.

On one of those nights when I was about six years old, I found the courage to come out of the drapes and ask my grandfather if he would teach me to play that tiple. He answered with a bent little smile, "No, this is a useless instrument. It won't exist by the time you grow up. You need to learn to play the guitar."

"Okay, where's a guitar?"

"We don't have one, and you're too young, Liz. I'll teach you when you're eight or nine."

What? That was a hundred years away. I committed the rest of that year to campaigning for a guitar, declaring on a daily basis that I could not live without it. I put notes all over the house; in drawers, in the fridge, in the bathrooms, in their cars. All of them read, Please, please, please get Liz a guitar, any guitar will do! And then the following Christmas, under the tree, like magic, there sat a guitar bigger than me with a note that read, Here you go, Love, Papa.

The guitar became like an appendage. It gave me the greatest access to myself I would ever discover. It was like finding a key to the place inside that could help me understand what mattered most in life. The music helped me through and around the things that lived inside me. Once I began, I didn't stop. I wrote, played, and sang for everyone and anyone who would listen. And ultimately, I got a seat with the grown-ups in our living room. Singing along just like my mom did.

* * *

I watched as my mom crunched her way back through the snow and ice from inside the gas station, carrying a small bag and a cup of coffee. Our mom didn't go anywhere without her high heels. She had heels for every occasion. On that day, she wore her three-inch-heeled, fur-lined, zip-up black leather boots. She navigated the winter ground like a seasoned professional—a lifetime of Chicago winters gave her the practice. She handed me a small carton of milk and a travel box of Ritz crackers. She carefully placed her hot coffee on the floor and then leaned over and flipped off the radio. I knew things were bad, I mean radically bad; that was the first time she'd ever, ever turned off Frank Sinatra.

She made her way back on to the toll road. The quiet was killing me. I wasn't used to *this* kind of quiet. My mom had been a consummate communicator my entire life; you always knew where you stood because she couldn't stop herself from telling you how she felt. I watched the sad, beaten-looking farmhouses outside the car window along the interstate. I watched the cold-looking farmers and their kids bundled up, walking in the fields. For the first time in my life it dawned on me how lucky I was. How incredibly fortunate our family was. We were the people who didn't need or want for things. I had an extraordinary life. I was watching the snow fall in sheets onto the farmhouses when I noticed a little boy riding a snowplow with his dad. I thought back to the time my dad first taught me to ski. I was a tiny kid. We were in Aspen, Colorado, just after Christmas on a perfect, crisp, sunny day. I was gliding along the snow in my new red skis, between my dad's legs. I remember hanging on to his knees for dear life, trying not to fall, listening over and over again to his strong, knowing voice, "Bend your knees, Lizzie, and lean forward." With my dad around, I felt like I could do anything. I glanced over at Dorothy, driving in silence, and realized, life wasn't mostly a struggle for our family; it was mostly a ride, a really good ride, actually. But that day in the car, life was doing what it does: It was changing, and there was nothing I could do to stop it. I wanted all of this to be a horrible dream. I prayed for that, but I kept opening my eyes to find myself still sitting in the passenger seat as Indiana passed us by.

The seat was uncomfortable. I reached over to move something nudging me in the side—my mother's black patent leather purse. She'd had it ever since I could remember. It was packed full to the brim. Her initials, DPB, were monogrammed in shiny gold thread on the outside flap. Dorothy Bennigsen Pryor. No one said her first name quite like our mom. It was as though there were three syllables when she said it, and only two when anyone else said it. "Dorr-o-tthy," she'd say, long and slow. She said a lot of words long and slow. Her hello, particularly on the phone, was the longest hello in the history of the world. "Hhhheeeellllooooo?"

She insisted that I answer the phone, "Hello, Pryor residence, this is Liz speaking." It's just good manners, she'd say, but I couldn't do it. I usually answered with a benign "Hello?" Dorothy would quickly correct me. "Lizzie, do you realize, when you say hello you sound as though you are grunting, or ill? That sound you make isn't a word; the person on the other end couldn't possibly understand you. The word is pronounced *Heellloooo*; say it as it is supposed to be said, please." This was the stuff that moved her. I never tested it, but I'd guess using the word *fuck* or *shit* would have elicited less conflict with our mother than ending a sentence with a preposition, or using a word incorrectly, or failing to enunciate the "beaaauuuuttiifffuulll" words of the English language. Dorothy didn't just have certain rules or thoughts about life. She *lived* them, passionately, and acted as though we couldn't exist without truly understanding and living them ourselves. She was unlike any other mother I'd ever met, and everyone noticed. It wasn't just her curiously dramatic manner and expression. It was the fact that you could feel when she spoke how much she believed what she was saying. That was the powerful part. There was a sense of plea behind everything she said. A plea you couldn't ignore, because her belief was so potent. Find the good in people; go to church; laugh; be kind; read books; say thank you; look your best; kill them with kindness; you only have *one* shot to make your first impression—those were the front-running lessons in our mom's book on life. But none of them were expressed or taught in the usual way. Everything came at us in a *Dorothy* way, a way that forced itself inside and became a part of us forever.

. . . .

The heat in the car was blasting hard, but Dorothy was always cold, and I wasn't about to ask to turn it down. I leaned my cheek against the glass window. Indiana looked like a winter paradise outside now, white and gray and strangely beautiful. The silence in the car was intermittently broken by the clanking sound of my mom's forgotten coffee mugs rolling beneath our seats. I leaned over and looked underneath the seat. Everything in the car reminded me of what I was about to leave behind: my life, my mother, my family, our home, my friends; everything that made me feel like me. The worn, musty carpet smell brought back all the times I'd hidden on that same car floor many, many years earlier.

"If a policeman comes, smile and tell him your mom will be right back."

"Mom, no, we can't park here."

"Mom, you have to find a spot like everyone else."

"Mom, come back!"

Inevitably a policeman would approach the car.

"Hello, kids. Wow, how many of you are there?"

"Our mom will be right back."

"Okay, but where is she?"

"She'll be right back."

"Well, she can't park in the middle of the street and leave you kids in the car."

"We told her that."

"We know."

"Is that a real gun?"

Every time a policeman came to the window of our car while our mom was double-parked doing errands, I'd grab my stuffed dog Henry. My aunt Bev had sent me Henry for Christmas when I was seven years old. The instant I saw Henry, I loved him. I'd dive to the floor, Henry under my arm, and hide. I'd cover myself with my coat, hoping to look like a blob on a messy car floor instead of a kid with a stuffed dog. But mostly I wondered if they put little kids in jail for being left in a car without a mom. I was glad I threw Henry in the side of my suitcase that morning. He'd been everywhere with me since I could remember. Maybe he would help remind me of all the things I would need to remember.

* * * *

I glanced over at my mom and cleared my throat. "Could we pull over so I can use the restroom, Mom?"

She lifted her eyebrows, but didn't say a word. We pulled over a few minutes later. The roadside diner we found was called the Roadside Diner. I wanted to laugh—it was something Dorothy would think was funny and stupid—but that wasn't going to happen. Not today. I hopped out and ran to the restroom. As I made my way back to the car, I could feel my mom watching me. As soon as I got in, she turned the car around and pulled up next to a funky-looking man standing by a truck. She rolled down her window and asked, "Sir, how much longer until the Greenfield exit?"

My mother had a very strange habit of arbitrarily acquiring a mid-Atlantic accent that somehow sounded British, in the same way Katharine Hepburn did. It drove us all batty. It was so completely random—you never knew when it would emerge. Really? You're from Chicago, and two seconds ago you sounded like you're from Chicago, but now suddenly you're Katharine Hepburn?

The trucker guy responded, confused, "What?"

She lost the Katharine Hepburn accent and said, "Forget it!"

I felt her look over at me. If things were normal, I might have rolled my eyes and said something sassy or funny, but I stayed quiet. My mom was doing the tapping thing on the steering wheel, which I'd seen her do before. Methodically tapping each finger a few times on the wheel, waiting a moment, and tapping the next. What was she doing? Singing in her head? Counting something? Saying the rosary? Our family was Catholic, and Dorothy loved, loved, loved to pray. She told us every day that we should pray as often as possible. I remember praying like crazy in third grade when I was waiting for her to pick me up after CCD class. Dorothy called it catechism class, its purpose was to *further my religious teachings*. I called it Sunday school on Wednesdays, and I really didn't like having to go. Every Wednesday when I was eight years old, I had to go after school to Saint Mary's Church for CCD and get ready for my first Holy Communion.

On one of those Wednesdays my mom was late picking me up—really late. She'd been late before—in fact, she was always late—but that day I had a feeling she might actually truly forget me. The other kids were long gone and as I waited, I began to worry about how long it would take my family to notice I was not there. Would it take a few meals, a few days, maybe even weeks? There were a lot of people in our house, maybe no one would notice one kid missing. . . . I decided, while thinking on it, to roll my white kneesocks all the way up as far as they would go, and then all the way back down to my ankles. *Up, down, up, down, up, down, up, down, up, down, up down,* until one of my socks lost its tightness and dropped on its own to my ankle. I had half a peanut butter and jelly sandwich and some raisins in my lunch box. I didn't know if the priests would mind if I lived on their steps, but maybe they wouldn't; they were very generous people. I noticed a bunch of trees in the parking lot across the street and decided it would help me not to panic if I counted something. I counted all of the trees.

One, two, three, four, five, six, seven, eight, nine, ten, eleven, twelve, thirteen, fourteen, fifteen, sixteen, seventeen, eighteen, eighteen trees exactly, not counting the ones on the sidewalk. I decided to click open and click closed my yellow Tweety Bird lunch box fifty times. *Click open, click closed, click open, click closed, click open, click closed, click open, click closed.* The sun was getting lower by the second. I looked over at some kids crossing the street and noticed their Catholic school uniforms. Although we were Catholic, we didn't go to the Catholic schools because my dad would not allow it. He was not a Catholic, he was nothing—that's what he said. I felt lucky that I could wear whatever I wanted to school every morning. I had on my favorite blue-and-white seersucker skirt and my white turtleneck with the duck on the neck. It was getting cold and I wished I'd brought my yellow sweater, but at least I had long sleeves. I looked all the way up at the church steeple bells and then heard the rectory door at the side of the steps creak open. I turned to see Father Joseph making his way toward me. My mom, and her parents before her, had known him a long time. Dorothy had lived in this area her whole life, and it felt like she'd known everyone a long time. He smiled, and I smiled back. Finally, a person, even if it was a priest.

"Hello, Lizzie Pryor."

"Hi, Father."

"This is a surprise."

"Yes. . . . My mom is late."

"The other children have long gone. Are you sure she's coming?"

"I think so, I mean, I hope so." I studied his long black robe as he sat down on the step next to me. It was like a dress.

"Do you like thumb wars, Liz?"

"Yes, I do."

"Do you want to play?"

I stuck my thumb out and beat him six times in a row. He looked carefully at his watch after the thumb wars and said, "Do you think we might give your mom a call?"

"446-7737, that's our number. Yes, thank you, Father. I think that's a great idea. It will be busy, it's always busy, but we'll just have to try again and again till they answer, okay?"

Just as we were about to go inside and call, I saw my mom's car pull up. I was crazy with relief. I frantically gathered my things and almost bonked the priest on his head with my book bag.

"Sorry, Father, but you see? There she is, you see her? That's our car, see it? Do you see it? She's here. Thank you for keeping me company. I'm going to be all right, Father, and have dinner with my family and live at my house, isn't that great?" I flew down the steps and into the backseat of my mother's messy car. Father Joseph made his way to the car window equally quickly.

"You're really late, Dorothy."

Her Katharine Hepburn voice surfaced. "I am well aware of how late I am, thank you, Father."

"I see. Well, I do have the authority to caution you: This should not happen again."

She looked right at him. "I am doing the best I can, Father. I have six other children at home and my husband is traveling for work."

"God has millions of children, Dorothy. Your best was not good enough today. I'll pray for you. And you, Lizzie, come find me if she happens to be late again, okay?"

"Okay, I will, Father. Practice at thumb wars so you can beat me." He waved as my mother pulled off. I decided I would pray for my mother too, to not be late so much.

* * *

Hours later, the day was ending, we were still driving, and there was nothing to see but darkness. My mom was messing with the wipers, trying to get the snow off the windshield. There were piles of papers, school flyers, books of stamps, and lipsticks strewn across her dashboard. It was a wonder she could see out the windshield at all. She never did fit the image people had of a woman with seven kids. She didn't own an apron and never baked a pie or cookies in her life. She wasn't a line-the-lunches-up kind of lady; she was more of a fly-by-the-seat-of-her-pants, hope-like-hell-she-makes-it lady.

A lot of our life was left to chance, and by what seemed so often a miracle, things ended up working out most of the time. It might have been her unwavering belief in positive thinking. My mom was a fanatic about finding the good in people and in life, and she was a believer in hope. Whatever the situation, she could find the pinhole of greatness. It was a gift. She pounded phrases like *see the glass half full, smile and the world smiles with you, turn the other cheek, rise above it, expand your horizons, reach for the moon* into our young minds until she was *sure* we would look and find the good first.

I suddenly thought about all the things in life my mom had so seamlessly taught me by simply being who she was. Her faith in life was lodged inside me in a way I could never really explain.

What I imagine Dorothy was placed on the planet to do was to love people. Strange as that may sound, she was a master. Being loved by our mother was one of the most important things that would happen to any of us. No matter the other ways she fell short, she effectively taught seven people the single greatest thing life has to offer: She taught us how to love and how to be loved.

· · · ·

I hadn't seen a thing, not even a billboard, for miles. We were in the middle of nowhere. Then finally a lone building appeared ahead. As we drew closer I could see it was a small hospital. There was a big square cement building behind it on a little hill. I saw a faded green wooden sign out in front of the cement building that read, Gwendolyn House. The sign had a large crucifix on it, with a dented Jesus lying sad and suffering. We pulled into a spot in a small parking lot outside of the cement building. My mom dropped her head onto her hands, which were still holding the steering wheel. I felt my guilt all the way through to my bones. I was the reason for all of this. It was on me. I wondered in that moment if it was true that God only gives you what you can handle. I'd heard that saying a thousand times. When I was really little, I remember hoping that God knew I couldn't handle losing the tetherball tournament, and that I couldn't handle not getting a guitar. I hoped God wasn't taking a break that day in the car. I hoped like hell he was watching and would make sure I could handle what was happening.

Dorothy finally lifted her head off the steering wheel and faced me. "Lizzie, I need you to pay very close attention to what I am about to say. It is extremely important, do you understand me?"

"Okay, Mom."

"We're here, and there are a few things you need to know." She shuffled around in the seat as she spoke. "We've decided we are not going to tell your brothers and sisters, nor your grandparents, a single word about this. Neither your friends nor anyone you know can *ever* know you were here. They will all be told you are sick and at the Mayo Clinic in Rochester, Minnesota."

What? This was the first I'd heard of this.

"I'm sick? What am I sick with, Mom?"

"I don't know yet."

"What's the Mayo Clinic?" She looked almost annoyed.

"It's a medical diagnoooosticcccc clinic in Minnesota, one of the best in the country."

I looked at the dark vastness outside the car. I was trapped. Trapped in that car, in my body, in my life—and about to be trapped in a cement building in the middle of nowhere, Indiana.

Dorothy continued, "They will take care of you here and that's what you need." She began to sound like the incoherent mumble of Charlie Brown's parents. "I'll try to visit, but I have to take care of your sisters, *wa wa wa waaa.*"

I wanted to ask her if it would be better if I *were* sick, maybe even dying, if that would be easier, but I didn't because somehow, in that very moment, my mom looked different to me. For the first time in my life I saw her as a person. I remember once seeing my third-grade teacher out at a restaurant and thinking, What the heck is Mrs. Beckwar doing *eating*? Teachers don't go to restaurants. And moms aren't people, they're moms. But that moment in the car, Dorothy was just a person, racked with worry, defeated and overwhelmed. It scared me. *I* was the cause of this. I'd shamed my parents to the point of having to lie to my brothers and sisters, and to all their friends. And on top of that, they were asking me to lie to everyone who meant anything to me, for the rest of my life. I wasn't taught to lie. I guess someone forgot to tell me that lying was *indeed* acceptable, if life got bad enough, and if your kid was truly terrible. I looked at Dorothy—the devout practicing Catholic, the firm believer in "all things will work out"—and I was suddenly terrified. I didn't see hope or faith or any good in this; all I saw was despair. Watching terror besiege the person who had continually given me strength throughout my life was like someone reaching over and pulling out my own power cord.

"Mom, I'm sorry, more sorry than I've ever been in my life." I could barely get the words past the rising mountain in the back of my throat. "I know how disappointing I am. I even know that you may never be able to love me the same."

She stared straight ahead and said, "Love doesn't work that way, Liz. I'll love you as I've always loved you forever. Mark my words, that will never change."

My entire body began to tremble. "Mom, I really don't want to go in there."

"I know you don't, but it's what we have to do." My chest felt as though it was going to come up through my throat. "I don't know what else to do. There weren't a lot of options. If you're here I can at least drive up to visit you."

We both sat quietly, both terrified, in different ways. She sat up straight, as though she were gathering her own courage, and turned off the car.

"We have to go in. Get yourself together." It was still snowing. I got my bag and my guitar out of the trunk and followed the click, click, click of Dorothy's heeled boots across the icy path toward the entrance. The building was set back on a small hill, surrounded by a lot of land and what looked like an endless amount of trees. It was mostly concrete, and I couldn't see any windows. There were very few lights on, so I couldn't see very well. The first thing I noticed as we made our way to the entrance was a small sign to the right of a big door that read Locked Facility. My mother pushed the red button marked Entry and a loud buzz sounded. We walked into a small hall lit by fluorescent lights above. We went through another door and into a stark entranceway. The floor was tiled and the walls painted brown. A large black woman with unfriendly eyes was sitting at a desk behind a wiry chain link–looking fence barrier, almost as if she were in a cage. I peered through the fence into the small room where she sat. I saw a little TV and some file cabinets. The woman ignored us. My mother leaned toward the desk and said in her slightly hushed Katharine Hepburn voice, "Pardon me, we are here to see Ms. Graham."

I whispered, "Why does it say Locked Facility, Mom?"

There was a ball of terror churning inside me. Before she could answer, another woman approached, a petite white woman wearing a gray wool suit, with short black hair and wire-rimmed glasses resting on her head. She looked to be in her forties, around my mom's age. She said hello and led us into her office. There was a framed plaque that read,

Even though I walk in the dark valley
I fear no evil for you are at my side
With your rod and your staff that give me courage

The woman took off her coat, folded it just so, and sat down on the wooden desk chair. She looked at me and said, "I am Ms. Graham, welcome to the Gwendolyn House." She said it without a lot of welcome. She looked down at the papers in front of her as she continued. "I am the resident social worker and will be here for Liz in any way she might need me. Beginning with the mandated weekly sessions she will attend here in my office . . . Tuesdays are her day, one o'clock, and she may never miss." She wasn't a warm person, but she wasn't mean either, she was just kind of cold and sterile. My tears were falling out of my eyes like rain off a roof, but there was no sound.

My mother spoke. "I am Dooorrrooothy Pryor, and as you know this . . . is Liz. We are grateful for the accommodation on such short notice." The woman looked at me curiously over her reading glasses for a long moment and then asked my mother, "Why is she crying?"

Dorothy, in the way only she could, said in a matter-of-fact tone, "She's pregnant." She said it long and slow, making her point.

The woman paused. "Well, yes, that *is* why she's here. But why is she crying?"

Dorothy paused, and then, "I would guess she's crying because she's terrified, Ms. Graham. She just turned seventeen years old, she has to leave her friends and family, she has to hide from everyone she knows, miss her last months of high school, and of course she will have to labor and *biiiiiirth* a child." The Charlie Brown–muffled-parent voice had disappeared. I could hear my mother again, loud and clear.

Ms. Graham appeared miffed. She looked at me over the edge of her glasses, sitting low on her nose now, and handed me a tissue. She went on to explain what I could expect for the next several months. Ms. Graham described the "facility" as a place where unwed mothers, some "in trouble," some just "unfortunate," come to receive the care and assistance they need during pregnancy. It was now a government-run facility.

"Many of the girls in this facility are wards of the state," Ms. Graham said. "They've come from juvenile detention homes and/or foster care. They all come from households surviving below the poverty line, which allows them to come in for the care they need for the duration of their pregnancies. This is a locked facility; the girls cannot leave the premises. They have specific times when they can go outside, but we have worked very hard to make it a place where they feel welcome."

The silence was deafening as we both absorbed Ms. Graham's words. Was this a prison? Was that how badly I'd messed up my life? My mother finally asked, "Can you explain to Liz what we spoke about on the phone?"

Ms. Graham began. "Yes. Here is how it will work: You will have access and free rein to go anywhere at all times. You will have a badge that gives you this access but you must show it to the guards. Your parents have been clear about not revealing your last name to anyone; therefore, no matter what happens, do not reveal your last name. You will be Liz P. while you are here. It is not often—actually, never have we had a resident such as yourself—someone who is in hiding from her community and family—so we are working it out as we go along. You obviously will be the only resident to have access, meaning you are not technically on lockdown. Your father has provided money you might need while here, although there are not too many places to spend it. There are beautiful grounds, which you cannot see at night, but in the morning you can look for the paths we have through the surrounding grounds outside. There is also a schoolhouse up the hill, which the girls walk to and from daily. They attend school for a few hours in the mornings. The cafeteria is in the basement; the food is not great, but you will find things to eat. There are vending machines at the end of the hall. You also have pay phone privileges. You will be in a single room for as long as we can offer that to you. At the moment we are clear, but we may have to allow a roommate in, as the girls filter in and out all the time. There is a doctor on the premises, with whom you will meet every week for your OB checkups. The hospital where you will deliver your baby is right next door, easily accessible, through a secure hallway under the building."

Ms. Graham kept talking. She sounded strict, like a boring high school history teacher, but there was something else about her. I could feel little drops of kindness, maybe even a softness as she spoke. "There are chores required for the residents who live here, and you will not be exempted from them; it felt wrong not to have you participate. They involve sweeping, emptying garbage, cleaning bathrooms, things like that. Your name will be on the white chore board in the lounge area—with a television, couches, et cetera—on the wing where you will stay. It is not much but the girls spend most of their day there. I am the social worker here; you will report to me once a week to let me know how you are doing. There is a woman in charge of your wing with whom you can consult if you have any issues. There is a chapel behind the facility that is open all hours. There is also a discipline system on your wing for girls who don't fulfill their responsibilities or who partake in any sort of violence or harm to fellow residents. These girls have had challenging lives; they are also emotional and they're pregnant. Some of them have had altercations, but for the most part they are well-adjusted and grateful to be here where there is a warm bed and food to eat. Smoking is allowed in the lounge and cigarettes can be bought in a machine in the basement. When is your baby due?"

My mother answered, "Her baby has to be delivered before her high school graduation date, which is June first."

"I see. Well, let us hope that happens for her."

The Katharine Hepburn voice was gone. The hardcore, end-of-her-rope Dorothy had emerged. "That has to happen for her," she said. "It took a lot of cooperation to get her high school to agree to the school credits transferring and to keep all information off the records. The only unbending requirement is that she be physically present for graduation. Liz will be going off to college in the fall, but not without showing up to receive her diploma. Her high school was incredibly accommodating. Liz, you should feel very grateful."

I was having trouble breathing. I whispered, "I'm grateful, Mom."

"When the time comes, Mrs. Pryor, we will see if inducing labor for Liz would be something the doctor can recommend."

The Katharine Hepburn voice returned. Dorothy was back in control. "I thank you, Ms. Graham, thank you again for *everything*. This will be an adjustment, but we have no choice. Please call if she needs anything, day or night. And, Ms. Graham, as I told you on the phone, Liz will be giving this baby up for adoption immediately after the birth. In fact, she has made a promise that she will not look at, touch, or ask about anything other than the sex of the child. We need to make sure she follows through on that; in the end, it will make it easier for her."

Ms. Graham looked over at me, as though she needed confirmation. I nodded, and then watched as my mother reached for her white cashmere scarf. As she wrapped it around her neck she said something else, but her voice sounded muffled and far away. I was sinking underwater and had nothing to grab on to to stop myself. She was leaving, I was staying, and I'd never ever been more terrified. It was the same feeling I'd had as a young kid, when she dropped me at school in kindergarten. And then again in the beginning of the year in first grade, second grade, and third grade. I had cried and whimpered my way through school in the early years away from my family, away from my mom. Something inside me couldn't seem to catch hold of myself.

"Lizzie?" my mother was saying. "I have to go; your sisters are at home alone. I have a lot of people with a lot of questions that I have to somehow figure out a way to answer. And a long drive back." I sank further and further down to what felt now like the bottom of the black sea.

"Can you show her to her room and help her set up, Ms. Graham?"

Ms. Graham nodded as my mom grabbed her purse and her camel hair coat. I followed the click, click of her heels out of the office and into the hall. With her back to me, she pressed the handle of the steel door that led to the outside world, to the snowy night and the long drive home. When she turned to face me I saw her eyes well up.

"You'll be okay, sweetheart. I'll come back this weekend and we'll go somewhere nice. I feel terrible leaving you here, but I know it's the right thing. Remember to pray, Liz. Ask God to help us through this."

She hugged me close; we stayed like that a long time. I was sobbing hard until she finally backed up and took my face in her hands.

"I love you, Liz."

"I'm sorry, Mom, I'm sorry about all of it," I said. She squeezed me tightly. "You'll be back Friday?" I asked.

"Friday it is."

The door slammed shut behind her. I stood in her wake for what felt like an eternity, and then made my way back to the woman's office. Ms. Graham asked me how long I'd been playing the guitar. She was trying to be nice, but I couldn't answer; I was still crying.

One hallway led to another, then down a few stairs to another heavy door with a lock on it. Ms. Graham took a ring of keys out and opened the door. We entered a corridor that had an odd odor and flickering lights. She turned to me and said, "You will be fine here; you just have to give it some time."

We turned and entered a good-sized room with paneled walls and a thumping ceiling fan going round and round. This must be the lounge. There was another door on the opposite side of the room leading out to what looked like a hall with rooms. The hall in this wing must have made a U shape, and the lounge was in the middle with two doors. There were several young pregnant girls sitting around, most of them smoking cigarettes. The room was thick with smoke. A TV with an antenna held together by tinfoil sat crooked against the main wall. There were two shabby couches, a recliner, and several chairs scattered around. There was one lone window oddly placed in the wall in the back, mostly covered by a dreary-looking curtain.

As Ms. Graham began trying to get the girls' attention, I noticed a very young girl with a horrible scar running down the entire side of her pale face. All the girls looked up at me, except for the girl with the scar. Ms. Graham pointed at each girl as she spoke.

"This is Nellie, Tilly, Amy, Hadley, Marina, Elaine, Doris, Wren, and that over there is Deanna." A few of the girls waved. "This is Liz; she is a new resident."

The white chore board on the wall had my name on it. The other girls had their first initials and last names, but mine was my first name and last initial. One of the girls was sitting in a beaten leather La-Z-Boy chair reclined all the way back, a big girl with dark brown skin wearing huge red hoop earrings that looked like bracelets. Her pregnant belly hung heavy over her jeans. She was eating a bag of Doritos while holding a cigarette and a can of Orange Crush. Ms. Graham stepped away to fix the TV, which the girls were all saying was broken. I took another look at the black girl in the recliner. She caught me and said, "What are you looking at? You stay the fuck away from me." I nodded and then looked down at the floor.

I followed Ms. Graham through the room, out the other door, and down the hallway. Mine was the last room at the end of the hall, on the left. Ms. Graham turned to me. "Remember, your day to see me is Tuesday, Liz. Every Tuesday you will come to my office at one o'clock. But I'd like you to come by tomorrow and we can see how you are getting on. If you need me for anything, you can ask Alice how to get ahold of me; she is your resident supervisor."

"Okay."

"Do you think you're going to be okay tonight?"

"I don't know."

She was gone, and I was alone. The room had two beds, two dressers, and a long window along the wall at the head of the beds in the room. The bed frames were steel, the room mostly cement and brick. I couldn't bring myself to open my suitcase. It would be like opening the doorway to hell, and I knew I wouldn't survive. Crying had become like breathing. I took off my long winter coat. It was a full-length gray wool cape coat my mother had given me for my birthday the year before when I turned sixteen, which felt like a long time ago. I laid the coat out on the bed and sat on it. The cinder-block walls were painted a dirty cream color, and the floor was gray linoleum. The dressers were built into the wall and had several drawers. I took a long time deciding which side of the room I should use; maybe the side you couldn't see when the door opened would be the best. My mom had put a jar of peanut butter and a box of Wheat Thins in my tote that morning. I pulled them out and placed them on the dresser on my side of the room. I pushed my suitcase and guitar to the side I'd chosen. I saw my stuffed dog Henry's ear hanging out of the outside pocket of my suitcase and pulled him out. I'd brought him along at the last second early that morning. Henry had the same goofy look on his face he'd always had. I thought about all the places that silly dog had been with me and wondered if I should put him back in the suitcase to spare him from this place, but instead I placed him on the bed and looked at him. And for just a moment, everything felt like it was going to be okay. Henry was the one reminder of life before this place.

Maybe it was all a dream, a horrible nightmare, and I was going to wake up in my room at home to see my Madame Alexander dolls on the shelf and hear my little sisters, the twins, fighting in the next room. But you always know it's not a dream when you find yourself hoping it's a dream, again and again and again.

I got sick to my stomach later that night. I threw up several times in the bathroom that was attached to the room. It was clean and sterile-looking, like one in a hospital. It had those steel handles mounted on three walls, the ones you see in homes for old people. I caught a glimpse of myself in the mirror as I splashed water on my face; it was hard to look at myself. When I did, the voice in my head reminded me that I was a horrible person, and I could think of nothing to defend that. I *was* a horrible person.

I had no idea what time it was, but time was meaningless anyway. My tears wouldn't stop no matter how hard I tried. I looked out the window at the cold trees in the darkness, and then noticed the lock latch. I unlocked and opened the window about a foot and took a deep breath from the freezing cold outside, as though I'd discovered a secret place from which I could steal oxygen. The cold tore through me and stayed in the room. I curled up like a baby on the bed, looked out at the tree nearest the window, at the way the snow sat so perfectly on each branch, and wondered if anything was ever going to look beautiful again, and finally fell asleep.

chapter 2

The morning was trying to trick me into believing a new day could make things better. As the bright sun filled the room, I closed my eyes hard, pulled my coat over my head, and tucked into a small piece of dark. My mind flooded with thoughts, memories, and images of everything I'd just left behind, until it stopped on the familiar face of my father. I remembered only the quiet steady comfort of his voice when I was little, waking me up in the morning at home.

"Get up, Diz, I'll meet you in the driveway in four minutes." My father's gigantic six-foot frame crunched down into my bottom bunk bed in our house in Winnetka. As I opened my eyes I could smell the shaving cream on his clean-shaven face. He'd been calling me Diz my whole life. That was my name out of his mouth, always. He pulled back the blue-and-white-striped bedspread and put his finger to his lips, reminding me, *Don't wake your sisters.*

I grinned and whispered to him, "I'll be down in three."

Over and over in my head I reminded myself, *Quiet as a mouse,* as I put on my red tights and my big gray sweater. It was Sunday morning. I never knew where we'd be going, exactly, and I never cared. Sunday morning was always my time with my dad. I ran to the back stairs and then remembered something. I dashed back to my room to feed Bonnie and Clyde; they were my turtles and I fed them every morning. I sprinkled some flakes into the tank and blew them a kiss. I grabbed my shoes and raced to the driveway. I stopped quickly, looked down at the dirt on my shoes, and took them off. No eating, no drinking, and no putting your feet up on the dashboard in dad's car. My father was a stickler for things being in their place and staying tidy. The smell of the deep, tan leather seats in his car reminded me that everything in the world was going to be okay. I eyed the pack of Beeman's gum sitting on the shelf beneath the radio, where it always was. My dad leaned over with a smile and offered me a piece.

We drove with the windows down, my curly hair swirling all around my face as the wind blew in and out. I loved the windy driving; it made me laugh for no reason. My dad turned on the radio and asked, "How about the bakery?"

"Yes, the bakery!" I shouted over the noisy wind. We drove until I saw the red-and-white awning over the French bakery in a nearby town. He grabbed the paper from the rack on the wall, and we sat on silver metal ice-cream chairs, me with a warm jelly Bismarck, my dad with his plain croissant.

"Let me show you something, Diz. You see this? What does it say?" He gestured for me to look at the paper.

"*The Wall Street Journal.*"

"Right, now this is an amazing paper. You know why?"

"Because it has news?"

"Yes, but also because it has a great way of covering all the different news. They take the biggest stories and condense each of them into little paragraphs and put them all on the front page, you see? So you can find out just enough information to know what's going on all over the world right here on the front page."

My dad was smart. He was the keeper of all the things I would need to know in order to make my life a place I'd want to be, and he had an incredible ability to make me feel that I was *something* in this world. Maybe because I fell in the middle of the millions of kids in our family, or maybe because he already knew how much I would need him. He was a man who didn't just believe his children would go out and tackle the world the right way; he *knew* they would. His standard for us was in place from the second we arrived on the planet, and his belief that we could meet that standard was so strong it worked. He didn't pressure, he simply expected—and we delivered. He was a composed, calculated kind of firm. Never lost it, just shot looks, lowered his voice, and commanded respect. The onus was on us to succeed. To disappoint our dad carried the kind of shame none of us ever wanted to feel.

He had the same name as his father and his grandfather: William Lee Pryor. He was William Lee Pryor III, but people called him Lee. We revered him, not just because he was our dad, but because it was clear how strongly he felt about the lessons he wanted to pass on to us. At our big nightly family dinners, Lee found his opportunity to hold court. Every night he checked in on our lives and shared the things he felt were so important in the world. None of us were overlooked. He made sure that every kid at the table would learn something. You had to be dressed, clean, and on your game before sitting down to eat in our dining room.

I remember being about ten years old, standing in our kitchen just before a family dinner, staring at the nine pork chops sizzling on our Viking range. I watched the juices ooze out of the fatty parts and run off to the side. The smell was making our dog Toby howl insanely. There was a gigantic bowl of mashed potatoes sitting next to the stove; I wanted to stick my finger in and sample it, but didn't dare. I waited for my mom to tell me to start carrying the food into the dining room. Finally she grabbed the big old cowbell with the round wooden handle and rang it, the sound echoing loudly through the house. I grabbed the mashed potatoes

and the bread and headed into the dining room. Everyone was filing in. I noticed my older brother John come in at the last second,
wearing a baseball hat. Then I saw "the look" on my father's face—
the look none of us ever wanted to be on the other end of. John
didn't flinch. He just sat down, rolled his eyes, and put his napkin
in his lap.

John was the bravest person I knew. He was the second child,
born about a year and a half after my older brother Bill, and he
happened to be the kid who was causing the most friction at the
moment. As in, he and my mother couldn't share the same air
without having an argument, and I'm not talking just a regular argument. She'd chase him through the house with frying pans; he'd
use the top-of-the-top worst swearwords right to her face. John
was consistently able to dissolve the small amount of glue that held
Dorothy together on a daily basis. But when our dad was around,
things were different. And he was home every night around six-
thirty unless he was traveling. As we settled at the table, my father
cleared his throat and addressed us.

"Who can tell me what is most obviously wrong with this
table?"

Several of us chimed in.

"John is wearing a hat."

"A baseball hat on John's head."

"Correct." My dad went on. "John, remove the hat, wash your
hands, and return with respect to this table. Apologize to your
mother for holding things up. And you will begin the discussion
when you return." No one ever wanted to begin the discussion.
My brother quickly removed his hat, got up from the table, and
responded with a quiet "Yes, sir." When he came back he gave a
tired apology to our mom, and my dad continued.

"Bill, remove your knife from the butter dish; it belongs on
your own plate. And, Kiley, do not begin without your mother
having taken her first bite. And now go ahead and share with the
family, John, something you learned today that you feel might be
of interest and could teach your sisters something."

John, with zero enthusiasm, offered: "I learned today that pigs are actually pretty clean animals. They have a bad rap for being dirty because they like to play in the mud and cover their coats with dirt because it cools them off. But really, they are one of the cleanest animals of all."

My dad paused for a moment and went on.

"Thank you, John. Jennifer, your napkin goes in your lap nicely, not crumpled, and, Diz, get your elbows off the table. Does anyone know what kind of meat comes from a pig?"

We all chimed in at the same time.

"Bacon."

"Ham."

"Pig's feet."

"Pickled pig's feet."

"Bologna."

"Headcheese."

"Sausage."

"Pig's tongue."

"Spam."

My dad quietly said to our mom, who was still fussing around the room, "Dorothy, can you please do us the favor of sitting down? These kids cannot eat until you've taken your first bite, for Christ's sake."

My mother quickly sat, put her napkin in her lap, and apologized. "Sorry, sorry, kids. Please eat." She always looked a little defeated, even before we started eating.

Bill was the oldest child, and our mother saw him as the Second Coming. My sisters and I followed suit and treated him like royalty. Bill was the fourth William Lee Pryor; he had a IV after his name. I thought it was pure fancy and wished I could have a number after my name. He hovered under the radar in the family, more reserved than the rest, and appeared humbly oblivious to the position he held as oldest. He was as tall as my dad and was the only other one in the family with curly hair like mine. What Bill did best was take unabashed advantage of having five little sisters;

he referred to us as his own personal servants. He snapped his fingers and we did whatever he asked.

But that night, Bill cleared *his* throat at the table and addressed our dad.

"Dad, why do you think it's so important for us to know all of these rules surrounding the dinner table and manners? Which forks to use, knives to save, soupspoon out of the bowl, serve from the left, take from the right—seriously, what does it really matter? Who the heck is going to even know all this stuff you pay so much attention to?"

The entire table went silent. I felt morbidly excited by Bill's confrontation. Really, what *was* the big deal about all of it?

After a long silence my dad responded. "You want to know, Bill. Do you all want to know?"

We looked at one another. Some of us shook our heads no, some whispered, but hell yes, we all wanted to know. It did seem so stupid, all of it. My dad continued.

"You don't just trust me that I am teaching you things you will value greatly when you're older? Then I'll tell you. What I'm teaching you, which you ignorantly claim to be so unnecessary, is the difference between knowing something and knowing nothing. It is my experience that knowledge is power, and it is my *job* to pass on to all of you the knowledge I have about how to make it in this world. Like it or not, we live in a society of rules, and etiquette and manners prominently exist. Manners are a sign of respect and being polite shows a person has thought and regard for others. This stuff you are questioning is the same stuff that delineates the men in this world from the gentlemen and the women from the ladies. What I am teaching you will enable you to eat dinner at the White House or marry royalty."

It probably wasn't the time to laugh, but a few of us couldn't help it. He ignored the laughter and carried on.

"Whether you end up dancing at the White House or dining with royalty is not the point. The point is if you're invited you'll know what to do. And knowing what to do gives you confidence, and confidence, kids, is the key to life."

My dad had an incredible influence on how I saw myself growing up. He was my dad, and in my eyes he knew *everything*. As far back as I can remember, he'd talked to me in a way that made me feel I already knew whatever it was he was saying, in a way that made me feel worthy and respected. He never doubted the person I was, and in turn I rarely doubted myself. It was like a language, and I learned it very early.

* * * *

It was the first time in my life that the dark felt good to me. I wanted to stay under my coat forever. But I thought I heard something at the door. I pushed the coat off my face and sat up. I did hear something. The light was shining through the window, and there was a soft tapping. I held my breath to keep quiet, but the tapping turned into knocking, so I tiptoed in my socks over to the door and listened for a minute.

"Yes?" I said softly.

Through the door I heard, "You awake? It's Alice; I work on the floor. If you're hungry you can go to breakfast, but if you don't go in the next half hour you'll have to wait for lunch." Alice was the resident supervisor, the lady who was there to help the girls, who Ms. Graham told me about yesterday. I put my hand on the door handle to make sure Alice didn't come in. There was no lock.

"Um, thank you. I'm not hungry." I was starving and feeling faint.

"Up to you," she said. And then I heard her footsteps walk back down the hall.

I looked around the sparse, empty room and felt the walls staring down at me, accusing me, as though they knew what a terrible, tarnished person I was. No one needed to remind me of how much I'd dishonored my parents, or what a disgrace I was to anyone who might have ever known me; I was breathing that shame every second. It was like a suffocating black cloak wrapping itself around my body.

I trusted my parents completely. I always had, and I knew they weren't cruel people; they were kind and sound, but they'd left me hundreds of miles away from home, alone and scared to death. I knew I was as bad as it could get, or else I wouldn't be here. I was living with all the other soiled, damaged stray girls because that was the kind of girl *I* was. It was slowly sinking in: I was completely alone. For the first time in my life, I had no one, and nowhere to turn.

The tears dripped one after another onto my coat. It was like they were the last pieces of good left inside me, trying to remind me they were still there. I couldn't stand the sight of myself in the bathroom mirror, so I turned the light off and waited in the dark for the shower to get warm. I stepped onto the cold tile as the hot water poured over me. I let the awful noise of the showerhead drown out the sounds of my sobbing. I wailed and wept a long time before I finally sat down on the tile and let the water beat me for as long as I could take it.

"Mom?"

"Hi, sweetheart. Lizzie, are you there? Is something wrong?"

Suddenly I couldn't talk. I'd made my way to the phone booth in the hall after finally venturing out of my room. But the second I heard my mom's voice, the ball in the back of my throat got the tears going. I shut the door of the phone booth as hard as I could. It was many minutes before I could get myself calm enough to speak.

"I'm here, Mom."

"Is everything okay, honey? What is it?"

"I just— I'm just— I can't do this, I'm so scared. . . ."

"It has only been one night, Liz. You *can* do this. Can you try to be brave, honey?"

"I don't know. Are Jennifer and Tory home? I, I want to talk to them."

"They are, but you sound so . . . not well. I don't want to scare them." My stomach dropped. I just wanted to try and feel normal for a moment. I just wanted to feel like me.

"I love you, Liz," my mom said. "Be brave. I have the number of the phone booth. I'll call you soon."

"Okay."

"Bye, sweetie."

The dial tone screamed in my ear. Brave . . . I had no idea how to be brave. I couldn't think of anything that felt even close to brave, here in this terrifying place. I tried to find the bright light, the hope that was such a part of me before, but it felt too far away.

I slunk back to my room, closed the door, and moved my suitcase in front of it, as though that would keep me safe. My guitar case was leaning up against the wall; it had a yellow ribbon tied on it from eighth grade when I took a trip with my friend Mary to visit her much older sister in Detroit. I had to check the guitar at the airport. I didn't feel like playing right now, I just felt like holding it. The sun was climbing up in the sky outside the window. I decided to put on my sneakers and my coat and head out the door. I retraced the path Ms. Graham and I had taken through the building the night before, when she first led me to my room. I hurried past the girls in the lounge and made my way to the main corridor, and to Ms. Graham's office. Her door was open, and she was sitting at the desk, reading, her glasses at the end of her nose. When she looked up, I tried to smile.

"Hi, Liz. How was your night?"

"Okay. Kind of bad." The tears were knocking at the back of my throat—of course they were—but I was learning that the more I fought them, the more they came. I swatted them away like little mosquitoes annoyingly landing on my cheeks.

"I was wondering, Ms. Graham, if I could get that pass you talked about. I'd like to go for a walk."

"Yes, of course, it's waiting for you at the guard desk." The same unfriendly black woman, with the same ignoring attitude as the day before, sat in her seat behind the fence at the front desk. Ms. Graham buzzed herself into the desk area through a door on the side. She came back around and handed me a red laminated card with a yellow string looped through, as though I was supposed to wear it around my neck. She handed it to me with both hands like it was important or fragile.

"Here you are; please keep ahold of it. And, Liz, you may not allow anyone else to use it."

"Okay, thanks."

"If I don't see you again, tomorrow is Tuesday. I'll see you at one o'clock, here at my office?"

The guard woman buzzed me outside. I let the heavy door slam behind me. I buttoned up my coat against the cold and headed toward the small parking lot, where my mother and I had parked the night before. The space was now empty. I stood in the middle of it for a while, making lines in the fresh snow with my sneaker. My ears and hands were beginning to feel numb from the cold; I wished to God everything could feel numb.

The grounds looked different in the daylight. It looked even more remote and vast than last night. And it was so very quiet. To the left of the facility building and down a bit was the hospital. There weren't a lot of cars or people, but there were some signs of life moving around it. To my right was a little cabin in the woods, like the house in the story of Hansel and Gretel might have looked. I peered around the trees to see if anyone was in the cabin, but I couldn't tell. Everywhere there were snow-covered trees; it reminded me of the forest preserve at home in Winnetka. I noticed a brick path beneath the snow running along the side of the facility building. I decided to follow it to the back of the building. It continued on past the building several hundred yards, and I kept following it until I came upon a small wooden chapel with a single cross on top. The path stopped at the chapel entrance.

There was snow piled high on the steps. I pushed the snow back with my shoe and opened the creaky door. There was a stained-glass window with the image of the Virgin Mary etched out in cobalt blue glass, the sun shining through it. The chapel was empty and warm as I stepped inside and shut the door behind me. I was sure God was mad at me. I was really sure my mother had told him everything, all about how horrible I was. There was a small basin of holy water on the wall by the door. I almost reached in with my hand, but changed my mind. I saw the neat rows of little red votive candles lined up along the side wall; they were the candles you light for someone you love, or someone who died. I made my way to a pew in the back and sat down. I realized I'd never been alone in a church before. I'd gone every Sunday since I could remember with my brothers and sisters and my mom, while our dad stayed home in the living room and read the Sunday paper. Lee was definitely not a man of faith. I wasn't sure if he even believed in God. I asked him once why he didn't go to church, and he told me that sailing was his religion and his boat was his church, but he didn't mention anything about God.

But Dorothy said that the least we kids could do was give one hour a week to God, one simple hour. We took up almost an entire pew, all of us shoving and pushing not to sit next to our mom. Dorothy would cross herself and kneel when she got to the seat. She'd whisper her prayers aloud, sighing, weeping loud enough for people to hear, while everyone else prayed in their heads. I mostly prayed for her to be quiet. My sisters and I spent a lot of time trying to figure out what the closing hymn would be. Would it be something our mom knew, or kind of knew? God forbid it was "Amazing Grace" or "Hallelujah" because there would be no stopping her from singing her lights out—I mean belting, as if she were auditioning for a role in a Broadway show. No matter how good she was, that wasn't the point. We were not in the kind of church where people spoke to Jesus through song. This was a Catholic church in Winnetka, Illinois. When the other parishioners strained and turned to see who in the world was singing so loudly, our mom remained completely oblivious, looking up at the stained-glass windows, singing her heart out. Nothing could break the moment when Dorothy was in it.

I looked up at the small altar in the sweet chapel and realized my tears had finally stopped. My mind felt quieter. I got up and walked over to the little votive candles. I reached in my pocket, found a quarter, and placed it in the slot. I didn't know if I was loved or dead, but I lit one candle in the middle, closed my eyes, and asked God to forgive me for having sex.

. . . .

I could hear *Wheel of Fortune* playing in the lounge when I returned from my walk. I would have liked to watch TV but didn't dare go in. I remembered the red-earring girl from the night before. I took the long way, all the way around three hallways, rather than walk through the lounge to get to my room. I held tight to the pass in my pocket. Just as I got to my door, someone called my name from down the hall. It was Alice, the woman who'd been knocking on my door earlier.

"Liz, hey, Liz, well there you are. Hello, hello!" She put her hands on her hips and smiled big. Alice was older, maybe in her fifties. There were deep lines all over her pale face, and her light blue eyes closed almost all the way when she smiled. She was small and wobbly in a funny-looking way, like a Weebles toy. Her midwestern accent was so thick that I had to pay particularly close attention to understand what she was saying. She didn't look like a supervisor, she looked more like a little grandmother, but she sounded like a supervisor. She shouted a bit when she spoke.

"Dinner is at five-thirty, and even if you're not hungry, Liz, that baby in your belly is." I wasn't used to acknowledging the baby in my stomach; it had only been a few days since I had even known the baby existed. It still made me uncomfortable. I didn't want to, but I followed her into the lounge. Everyone stopped talking when I walked in. I didn't have the energy to be scared; I just stood there.

Alice shouted, "Well, come on, girls, let's go. It's Salisbury steak night."

The girls slowly got up and filed out. We went down a hall, and then down a staircase, and into a basement hall with no windows. I smelled a funky, rank smell and hoped it wasn't the food. I held back in the line and watched as the girls filed into a small cafeteria-type room with two long tables. There were a few older women wearing hairnets standing over a cafeteria-type dish-the-food-out setup. I took a tray and a milk and waited. I was the last person in the line. An older-looking black lady dishing the food out said to me, "New girl?"

"Yes."

"What's your name?"

"Liz."

"How far along are you, Liz?"

"Four and a half months."

"You kidding me, child? You don't even look pregnant! You gotta feed that baby. Here, you don't have to say it, but I'm gonna give you double portions." She slopped two huge spoonfuls of what looked like dog food onto a plate, then passed the plate to the next lady. She added two spoonfuls of stewed, watery, green spinach-esque slop and some sort of mealy white thing. She handed the plate back to me, and I put it on the tray and tried not to look disgusted. That rank smell *was* the food. I sat a few feet away from the last girl on the bench and felt everyone's eyes on me. I almost thought I would be sick to my stomach. This was way beyond anything I'd smelled on an airplane, or in a hospital, or in our fridge at home when something went bad—this was gnarly bad. I drank a few sips of the milk, but there wasn't a chance I could eat the food. I waited to see what we were supposed to do with our dirty trays and followed the girls when they stood up to leave. The cafeteria woman watched me as I dumped the food into the garbage.

I was famished. I saw a vending machine with snacks and soda; maybe I could go back later to get something. I hadn't eaten since my Ritz crackers from the gas station the day before. On the way up the stairs, I started to feel dizzy. I stopped for a second to try to steady myself, but my knees gave out and I fell down a few steps to the landing. One of the really pregnant girls saw me; she screamed super loud, and the Alice lady came. Everything went dark. Next thing I knew, I was on a table in a small room. A doctor was looking in my eyes with a light.

"You okay, young lady?"

"Where am I?"

"You're in purgatory," he said with sort of a rude sneer. "You're dehydrated and malnourished is what you are, and more importantly you're pregnant. We're going to have to hook up an IV and get some fluids in you. You have a child in your stomach that needs sustenance."

I'd never met a doctor who didn't at least pretend to be nice; this man was cold, and clearly annoyed by me. He put a needle in my arm, hooked a bottle to a big stand, and left.

As I looked around the small and unfamiliar room, I thought about the doctor, and the girls, and the cafeteria, and the facility, and then it hit me, just how alone I really was in this strange and terrible place. Everything had happened so quickly. Only three days ago I was fighting in the kitchen with the twins, getting mad at them for wearing my clothes without asking. I missed home so much. I closed my eyes and took myself back.

* * * *

There was a night when my parents were having a party, downstairs in our living room. I was about five years old. I'd climbed into bed and was waiting for my mom to come up and tuck me in. I could hear Dorothy's laughter roaring above everyone else's, and it made me smile. I heard the swooshing of her party dress coming down the hall. She peeked in and smiled.

"You still up?"

"Yep."

"Good night, sweetheart. Don't forget to say your prayers." I could smell the hint of alcohol mixed with her Aqua Net hairspray as she leaned forward to push the hair off my face. Her string of pearls moved back and forth and touched my chin as she tucked me in.

"Can I have your dress when I get older, Mom?"

"*May* you have my dress? Of course you may, sweetie."

"I like the sparkles."

"Me too." She smiled and kissed my forehead.

"Good night, Mom. Sounds like fun down there." And then my dad appeared at the door. He poked his face in, smiled at my mom, and said, "You better go down, Dorth; they want you to sing."

My mom stood up, straightened her dress, and said, with a casual air, "I'm not going to sing."

My dad looked at her, then at me, and as she walked out we both rolled our eyes and together said, "She's gonna sing."

After my dad tucked me in and kissed me good night, we sat and listened to the amazing sound of my mother's voice from downstairs.

Blue moon
You saw me standing alone
Without a dream in my heart . . .

I opened my eyes to find Ms. Graham standing at the end of the bed.

"How you feeling, Liz?"

"Where am I?"

"You're in the medical room just two doors down from the cafeteria, in the basement of the facility."

"Okay. Can I go back to my room or no?"

"Yes, you can go back soon. I'll have to call your parents and let them know you've had an incident, but the doctor says the baby is just fine, healthy heartbeat and all. He just wants to monitor you a little bit longer."

The baby—right, I'd almost forgotten. The whole reason I was here. I was groggy as I made my way back to my room. I slept through the entire night. The next morning, I took a shower and let the warm water fall hard on my bruised arm from the IV. I had no towels, so I dried myself off with one of my T-shirts. I put on a new pair of underwear, threw a big sweater over my head, and slipped into my soft sweatpants with the name of my high school prominently displayed in big letters down the thigh. New Trier East. I'd waited my whole life to get to New Trier, to be an Indian, part of the great school that had been around since even before my mom was a little girl. Where Charlton Heston, Rock Hudson, Ann-Margret, and all sorts of famous people had gone. Where my older sisters and brothers drove off together every day. Where I could watch my sister Kiley, a tiny rubber band of a cheerleader who balanced herself each week at the top of the insanely high human pyramid on the football field at halftime. She was the star, and she never fell, not once. I rubbed my hand along the letters on my sweatpants and thought about chorus class, and my phenomenal English teacher, and the lunchroom the size of Texas where they blasted Bruce Springsteen's "Tenth Avenue Freeze-Out" every day. And then I heard a loud knock at the door. It was the Alice lady again.

"There will be no skipping meals for you anymore, Liz. Breakfast is in ten minutes and you need to get there."

On the way to breakfast I passed the big, big pregnant girl who screamed for help for me the night before, when I fainted.

She looked at me and asked, "Are you all right?"

Her entire face was covered in huge red pimples or boils. I'd never seen anything like it; it jolted me enough to have to turn away.

I looked at the ground and said, "Yes, thank you."

She walked past me and hollered, "That's okay. I'm a good screamer."

The cafeteria didn't smell as disgusting in the morning. There were toasters and bags of bread and little boxes of cereal next to small cartons of milk. I grabbed a box of Froot Loops, sat at the far end of the bench, away from the other girls, and ate slowly. On my way out, the girl with the red hoop earrings stuck her leg out in front of me. I stopped before I got to it. She smiled and said, "Don't trip, girl."

My heart was pounding; all I wanted to do was get the hell out. I showed the guard my pass and she buzzed me out. I walked as fast as I could without running. I got all the way to the main road thinking, hoping, I would find a sign of life besides the facility, of the normal world I'd left behind. But once I got to the road, all I could see for miles and miles were trees and snow. It was pure nothing. I could scream and shout and no one would hear me. I felt as small as I could ever remember feeling as I stared out at the trees.

It reminded me of summer camp, which was also in the middle of the same kind of nowhere, tree-filled Indiana. I went three years in a row. I stayed for four weeks each time, and I loved almost every second of it. It's where I learned how to canoe, shoot a gun, and whistle "Dixie" with crackers in my mouth. I jumped off swings into the lake, made lanyards, and sang ridiculously stupid songs. They blared the most amazing rendition of "Taps" every night for the whole camp, through loudspeakers hidden way up above the cabins in the forest, before we went to bed. "Taps" was the most beautiful piece of music I'd ever heard. In the mornings, the same speakers blared the suddenly not-so-beautiful "Reveille" to let us know it was time to get out of bed and begin another day.

The last year I'd gone to camp I was twelve years old. I got a letter from my mother about midway through the session, telling me that our family was thinking of moving to a new house. Enclosed in the letter was a picture she'd drawn on a small piece of paper of a bedroom with a bed, a desk, and a dressing table. At the top of the page she'd written:

This will be your room if we move. Love, Mom.

I couldn't believe it. I couldn't believe they would consider moving while I was *gone*. I didn't know what could be going on at home. Everything was fine when I left. My dad had been traveling a little more than usual, but otherwise things were normal. The idea that our family was actually going to move was unthinkable. I crumpled the letter up and tried to forget it ever arrived. As camp came to an end a few weeks later, I received another letter from my mother saying that she looked forward to seeing me when I returned. She said someone would be there at the Winnetka community house to meet the camp bus and drive me home when I got back.

After the long drive home on the crowded bus, we arrived at the Winnetka community house. All of the other parents were waiting for their children in the parking lot. I spotted a black car from my dad's company parked near the front, with a driver I'd never met. He walked up, grabbed my trunk, and told me I could get in the car. I climbed into the back of the black Town Car, wondering where the heck my parents were. There were two *Playboy* magazines stuck in the flap just in front of my knees behind the driver's seat. I was creeped out and wondered why they were there; were they my dad's? The driver headed the wrong way on Winnetka Avenue.

I spoke up. "Um . . . I think you're going the wrong way. Our house is the other way."

"You moved. You live in Northfield now; it's just at the other end of Winnetka." Seriously? Were they kidding—new house, new town even? I was stunned and didn't know what to think as the car drove past the lush suburban lawns. The fancy streetlights and the set-back houses were always a shock when you'd been gone for a while. Winnetka was, as it always was, beautiful. We pulled onto a street I'd never seen, called Sunset Ridge Road, and then into a driveway. The tires crunched over gravel as we pulled all the way in. Then it was quiet. The house was white, with two stories, and a big front yard. There were no lights on. Was this the right house?

There were no cars, no signs of life. The driver had carried my trunk to the door before I even got out of the car.

"Have a good night, Miss Pryor," he said. I looked up at the strange white house, which was completely different from our old house, where I'd lived most of my life. It was totally surreal. Like I was in a strange dream where you recognize things from your life, but they're totally out of context.

I walked up the stone pathway toward the door. Next to the path was a cement statue of a lion sitting on its hind legs with a ring in its mouth. It *was* our house; I knew that lion; that was our statue from the old house, except the ring in its mouth was now broken, and it was leaning lopsided up against a bush. The door was unlocked. Inside, first thing I saw was my little sister's green umbrella on the floor. There was our desk, and my dad's boat paintings, and our rug, the one my mom got in Mexico. My grandfather's medals in the glass frames were on the wall, and the yellow-and-white-striped couches now looked much bigger in what appeared to be the living room. The staircase had all sorts of half-folded laundry, toys, and schoolbooks strewn about. Yep, this was our house. I stepped down a small step to the kitchen. Dishes were piled up in the sink, and there was a lot of mud on the floor. I looked out the window over the sink, and through the dark I saw a sprawling backyard with a few tree swings. I did love swings. . . . I eventually made my way up the stairs in search of my room. Where were my mom, my dad, and my sisters and brothers? It was utterly quiet, and I was starting to worry. I found a small bedroom with bunk beds and saw that the floor was crammed with boxes. When I looked at the beds, I saw my little twin sisters, sleeping.

I shook Jennifer's shoulder. She turned and with a sleepy smile said, "Hi, Liz." Her face was a surprising comfort to me.

"Hi, Jen. Where's Mom?"

"She's gone. She's been gone for two days."

"Two days? Where's Dad?"

"Downtown, I think."

"Where did Mom go, Jen?"

"We don't know." She closed her eyes and then opened them again. "Your room's next to ours."

I peeked up at Tory sleeping soundly in the bunk above. They were nine years old. I looked into the room next door and knew it had to be mine. All my Laura Ingalls Wilder books were on the shelf, and my Madame Alexander dolls were in a box on the floor. I checked in the drawers and boxes for my things—it was all here— and found my locked diary at the bottom of a shoe box. I went to the box that had the beautiful dolls I'd been collecting since first grade. They were all historical female icons of some sort, with brilliant handmade dresses. I had Betsy Ross; Amy, Meg, and Jo from *Little Women;* and Cleopatra. But I was searching for Scarlett O'Hara specifically. I finally saw the green ribbon from her straw hat poking out of some tissue. I lifted up her green-and-white-flowered dress and the crinoline underneath and took off her tiny black velvet shoe with a real snap on it. I checked inside the fancy white lace sock and found what I was looking for: my diary key. Thank God! I couldn't stop wondering where my mother was; why hadn't someone picked me up at the bus? I had a bad feeling in my stomach that night. I woke up early the next morning and made my way down the strange stairs. I found Dorothy in the kitchen.

"*Mom,* hi, where have you been?"

"Hi, Liz. Welcome home, darling. I was walking."

"Walking? What do you mean walking?"

"I don't know, just walking, honey. I needed some air."

One of the twins, sitting eating cereal and reading the back of the box, chimed in.

"Yep, for a whole day and a night and another day." She rolled her eyes at me behind Dorothy's back.

"Mom, you left them here that long?"

She ignored me. "I'm sorry I couldn't be there to pick you up at the bus, but I'm glad you're home, Liz."

Everything was upside down that summer. My older sisters

were in high school, busy and preoccupied with their boyfriends and teenage stuff. I barely saw them. My brothers were working, and gone most of the time. And I hadn't seen my dad in weeks. I got the feeling most of my siblings knew that my parents' marriage was breaking up. No one told me anything, but I overheard my brothers talking once, late at night on the boat, about my dad moving away from the family. I hadn't actually heard the word *divorce*, but I wondered if that wasn't what was happening. The thought made me sick. I couldn't imagine my life without my dad there.

A couple weeks after my return from camp, on a wicked humid summer morning, I was awoken very early by a loud, grunting, shrieking noise. After sitting up in my bed, in my still-new bedroom, I listened again as it got louder. I made my way down the hall toward the sound, which was clearly coming from the master bedroom. I slowly opened the door. I saw my mother in her underwear and a button-down shirt, kneeling down on the carpet. The mattress from her bed was cockeyed on the floor. With all her strength, it appeared she was trying to fold the mattress or roll it up. She had a bunch of my dad's ties and belts on the floor beside her. The mattress was five times the size of her small frame. I shut the door and stood in the hallway for another few moments, terrified, and then decided to go in and see if I could help. When she saw me she screamed loudly, like a crazy woman: "GET OUT, GET OUT OF MY ROOM." I froze until she started again, and then I ran out of the room. I'd never ever seen her that way. A few minutes later my sisters woke up and came to see what was going on. When I told them, they decided to go in themselves, and sure enough Dorothy shouted again, loudly and with vengeance, "LEAVE ME ALONE AND GET OUT!"

We had no idea what we should do. I thought about calling our grandfather, but Dorothy might have become even crazier, so we stayed out of her room. She stayed in the room with the door shut the whole day and never came out. She spent hours rolling up the mattress from her bed; it was nothing short of miraculous. Finally she got the mattress rolled up and tied with my dad's ties and belts. With all her five feet and two inches of strength, she shoved that queen mattress out the small second-story window of her bedroom. Yes, she pushed and shoved and tweaked and pushed and tweaked until the mattress made its way through the opening and floated down from the second story of our new house onto the ground. I watched it fall from the kitchen window downstairs. When it hit the ground in the backyard, I ran upstairs and there she stood, short of breath, sweaty, and quiet, still in the button-down shirt and her underwear.

"Mom, what the heck? Why did you *do* that?"

She paused and then answered, "Why, sweetheart? Because I had *seven* children with your father on that mattress and I wanted it out of my room and out of my life, and now it is." My mom and dad got divorced at the end of that summer.

chapter 3

made my way down the path, back through the cold wintry trees. It was almost one o'clock and it was Tuesday, which meant I had to be back for my appointment with the social worker woman, Ms. Graham.

"Thank you for being on time, Liz. Have you ever been to a social worker before?"

"No." I looked around the office and saw the empty chair my mom had sat in a few days earlier, when she dropped me off, which felt like a lifetime ago. Ms. Graham kept talking.

"We're just going to talk. I'm here to help you along if you have anything on your mind."

"Okay."

"I spoke with your mother this morning and told her about your fainting spell. She was very concerned but I assured her you and the baby are doing fine now. How are you feeling?"

"Fine."

"She said she'd let your father know and keep him informed."

I looked out the little window in her office. "No, she won't."

"She said she would."

"But she won't."

"Why not?"

"They don't speak."

"I see. Why is that?"

I paused. "They hate each other."

"That's an awfully strong term."

"I know."

I didn't want to get into it with Ms. Graham, but the simple truth was that my father had asked my mother for a divorce the day before I got home from camp that summer, just after we moved to the new house. That was when she walked for two days. Some months later my parents divorced. And after that my dad married a woman who used to work for him. From then on, for the last five years, my parents hadn't spoken. It was a radically difficult time for all of us. I was waiting for things between my parents to calm down, for our lives to become easier, or find some new version of normal. But nothing ever really changed. Nothing between them, or around them, got easier. What I felt like was that I couldn't love my dad when I was around my mom, and I couldn't love my mom when I was around my dad. The two people who had been sitting in the same place in my heart my whole life were now forcing me to hold them in two different places.

"Are they divorced?"

"Yes."

"That's hard."

"Yeah, hard for my mom."

Our mom was completely shattered when our dad left—not the regular kind of shattered, *brutally* shattered from head to toe. Like someone-stuck-a-hand-down-her-throat-pulled-her-heart-out-and-threw-it-against-a-moving-train shattered. And that was only the beginning. I'd been slowly learning some truths about life over the past few years. I knew that one brief moment at any given time could destroy how a person exists in the world. Almost like the earth stops rotating just for a second, and the force of the stop pulls everything that's good away . . . and some people never find their way back. My brothers and sisters and I were right there watching when the earth stopped rotating for our mom. She loved our father; she loved him so much she waited for years for him to come back. She quit smoking—"gave it up to God," she said—so that he might bring our dad home, but Lee never came back. It's a rare anguish for a child to watch the person they love the most in the world suffer so profoundly, especially when there's no way to help. I listened to my mom's sadness through the walls of my bedroom almost every night before I went to sleep, for years after Lee left. Some nights it made me so sad I wept along with her from my own bed.

Ms. Graham looked at me a long time and then asked, "Was the divorce hard for you?"

"Kind of . . . Yes. I miss my dad."

"How often do you see him?"

"Not very much."

"Your parents don't speak at all?"

"No, they don't. But a few days ago they had to."

* * * *

Lee's classic wooden schooner, the *Malabar X*, built in 1930, moved our dad to a place I only saw when we were sailing. It was like a peek at the underbelly of his soul, where joy, and ease, and purpose all came together at the same time. Our time with our dad on the boat was unlike anything else.

Ten days before I arrived at the facility, my dad had taken some of us kids and his new wife on vacation to the British Virgin Islands. We cruised through the crystal-clear waters for ten incredible days. The Caribbean was an amazingly beautiful place. We took turns at the helm, trimmed the sails, dodged jellyfish, and caught starfish. We pretended to be pirates, counted stars, and shaved our legs in buckets of freshwater on the deck. We bought muffins and bread from little kids and their dads in old wooden dinghies motoring around the harbors in the mornings. Some of our greatest times together as a family were spent sailing, navigating small living quarters with too many siblings, and talking our heads off about things we might never have discussed under other circumstances. The confines of the boat were part of the beauty of sailing. And I was pretty sure that's what our dad had in mind.

Every day on the Caribbean, I found a different secret spot to sit, and be alone; in furled sails, out on the bowsprit, in the corners of the cockpit, and down below deck. It was on the water where I really learned how to be alone. That trip I spent a lot of time thinking about my life, how much I'd done and seen, and how quickly it was passing. I was seventeen years old, and I would be leaving for college soon. Everything was about to change and open up in a new way. It was the most exhilarating feeling I could remember ever having. Life was going to turn, and I was ready.

One particular day, partway through the vacation, we were all hanging around on the hot deck, sunburned and full to the brim with our lunch of delicious freshly caught yellow tuna. I noticed my dad's new wife staring at me. She smiled a couple times when I looked over, but I didn't think much about it. Later that afternoon, I was down below deck feeling terribly seasick, which was unusual for me. I was sitting alone in the main salon when I noticed the new wife making her way down the ladder in her yellow string bikini. She smiled and asked if she could join me. I could smell the rich Bain de Soleil oil she had slathered all over her tanned body.

She sat quietly with me for a bit before she very casually asked, "Is there any way you could be pregnant, Liz?"

The words clashed in my brain. Pregnant? I thought about it. I mean I couldn't actually be pregnant—with a baby in my body? No way. The thought had crossed my mind, but not exactly. Not in the real kind of way. I excused myself from the couch to get sick in the bathroom again. I pumped and flushed the little toilet, rinsed my mouth, and when I came out she was still sitting there, waiting, with her pretty hair.

"Do you remember when you last got your period, Lizzie?"

"No. I only got my first period like a year and a half ago, and it never really comes every month, so . . . I don't know. I haven't had it in a long time."

"Have you had sex with your boyfriend?"

"Yes." Holy crap, yes, but not in the we're-going-to-have-sex planned kind of way. More in the it-went-too-far kind of way. We'd never even talked about it. About what happened. Maybe if my boyfriend Daniel and I had talked about it, discussed it, or planned it, it wouldn't have gone so far. It would have made it more real than it felt in the moment.

"I think it would be a good idea to take you to a doctor. You're probably not pregnant but we should make sure, huh?" My whole body felt numb as the reality of what she was saying hit.

"What doctor?"

"I have a doctor you could see; we could go when we get back. We don't have to say anything to your dad just yet." She was so calm and nice, but I started to panic. I wanted to know right then that I wasn't pregnant; the idea of it was too big to process. How could I have ignored my growing stomach, and this new nausea? How could I have been so stupid? A new, overwhelming reality was sinking in. The wife said she wouldn't mention anything to my dad. She was such a nice lady, which made it hard to hate her, and I wanted to hate her . . . for my mom. She handed me some saltines, stroked my hair, and sauntered the French bikini back up the ladder. She was young, and really cool, and looked remarkably like Farrah Fawcett.

We left the Caribbean after ten days and arrived back in Chicago late at night. Dorothy was asleep when we returned. I was supposed to go to school the next day. I'd already missed two days because of our vacation. I could barely function, living with the notion that I might be pregnant. A hellish fury of fear was taking over. I got up early the next morning, dressed, and left the house so I wouldn't have to see my mom or anyone. I was sweating even though it was freezing cold that day. I drove downtown to meet the new wife at her doctor's office. They did a pregnancy test and then the doctor put an instrument on my stomach that sounded exactly like the ocean, like the crashing of the waves against the boat when we sailed. We heard a thump, swoosh, thump, swoosh, thump, swoosh. The doctor and Farrah Fawcett looked at each other, and then the doctor said to me: "That sound . . . is the heartbeat of a baby."

What? What the fuck? I pushed his hand away from my body and went into some sort of shock. I couldn't speak; I could barely breathe.

The wife called my dad and told him to meet us at their apartment in the city, right after the doctor's appointment. I was still in disbelief. How had I let it come to this? How did the wife figure this out before me? We sat down in the fancy living room with my dad and the wife, whose name was actually Kate, and she told him I was pregnant. My father looked at me a long time, and then out the window over the buildings at Lake Michigan, and then told me he was really sorry for me; he was sorry for the situation. He was sad—really sad. I'd never seen him like that, and it ripped hard at me. I didn't know Lee even had that kind of emotion inside. I knew what a massive disappointment this was. I knew that *I* had made him feel this unbearable unhappiness. It was unforgivable. My dad stood up and said he'd have to call my mother. He was going to ask her to come downtown to meet us at his and Kate's apartment, which threw me into a complete tailspin.

"No, Dad, please no. I will tell Mom myself. I'll drive home right now and tell her, and then call you." My mother and father hadn't really spoken since the divorce. And my mother had never met the Farrah Fawcett wife, and I didn't want her to have to endure all of that because of me.

"That will not do, Diz," my father said. "She needs to come here and we will all talk about it and figure out the plan."

"Dad, we can do that tomorrow at a restaurant or something, but please don't do this. Don't have her come here. I think that would be really hard for her. Please."

"Stop it, Liz, that's ridiculous. Your mother is a grown woman. I'm going in to call her." I kept begging, but he turned around sharply and told me to sit down, which I did. I always did what he asked; that's who I was.

My mom arrived an hour later. She was wearing her black pencil skirt, with black pumps, a navy blue wool coat with brass buttons, and a paisley silk scarf around her neck, composed like always. But the look on her face will remain fixed in my memory forever. I watched Dorothy take in the elegant apartment with its floor-to-ceiling windows. She looked at the walls, the carpet, the lush upholstered furniture, the life my dad was living without her, and then stopped at the astounding view of the city and Lake Michigan out the window. And finally she looked at me, and I wanted to disappear. She didn't know yet.

I remember the moments before he told her, thinking to myself, The second my mother knows it will all become real. My hell, my pain, the reality of my shame will begin. I don't know why that was true, but it was. She sat down in an overstuffed chair in the living room, keeping on her coat. Maybe she didn't think she'd need to stay long. I was on the couch and my dad was in another big chair, and we formed a triangle. Farrah Fawcett sashayed into the room wearing a short flowery dress and cowboy boots. Oh God, I thought, she's here in front of my mom. She smiled and offered us beverages. I could barely watch. My mother managed a soft Katharine Hepburn "Hellllloo." There was a framed picture of my dad, the wife, and the wife's four-year-old daughter on the table next to the couch. Dorothy noticed it and then looked back out the window. It was excruciating: to watch my mom seeing my dad together with his new wife, seeing their home, their contentment together.

Lee wasted no time. He wore his blue-and-white pin-striped Brooks Brothers button-down, khaki pants, and soft leather loafers, and had his vodka with a splash of soda next to him on the table. He looked at my mom—everything about him attractive—and began, "Dorothy, our daughter—the daughter *you* live with every single day of your life—is more than four months pregnant." There was a long pause. My mother didn't move. My dad continued, never raising his voice: "How in the world can that be? Do you see nothing? You don't know when or if your own daughter gets her period, or gains weight, or throws up? What the hell is going on in that house?"

My mom was staring past Farrah Fawcett, out the huge plate glass windows; her face was surrendered, her eyes blank. Kate was uncomfortably messing with the tray of drinks. I could not hold back the tears. The tears came for a million reasons: I was pregnant, it was now indisputably real, and my father was torturing my mother, stabbing her with a horrible knife of blame, turning it over and over again. I couldn't believe what was happening—and all because of me. I let out an audible cry. My mother turned to me with a look I'd never seen and a voice I'd rarely heard, strong and cold.

"Pull yourself together, Liz, and *stop* crying." Then, with what I'm sure was the last shred of dignity she could find, she politely asked Farrah Fawcett to leave the room.

Kate stood up and said, "Of course."

Lee went on. "It took *my* wife one day, Dorothy, *one* day of being around Liz to ask her if she might be pregnant. You've had seven children, for Christ's sake. What kind of a mother does this?"

I wanted to die. The room was still. I was choking back everything that wanted to come out. I wanted to say, But, Dad, I was in a bathing suit on the boat, she's been seeing me in winter coats. That's not fair . . . But then my mother, with seamless composure, answered, "Perhaps, Lee, if Liz had a father in her life, one who showed up more than one Sunday a month, who cared about her more than himself and hadn't deserted his family, she wouldn't feel the need to be *having sex*. As far as the kind of mother I am, I imagine the answer to that is not going to change the fact that she is pregnant. It would be wise for us to figure out what to do here, Lee, rather than cast stones."

Her eloquence floored me. But then my dad continued.

"The doctor has informed us that an abortion is out of the question," Lee said. "She is too far along; it would endanger her life, so that is off the table."

"What doctor, Lee?"

"My wife's doctor, who saw Liz this morning."

She responded, "I see."

Shit. Now Dorothy was going to think I'd confided in Farrah Fawcett. She was going to imagine I trusted Farrah Fawcett to take me to a doctor rather than her. She would know I ditched school that day, lied to her, and instead shared the truth with my dad, the man who left her. She'd think I liked the new wife better than her. When that wasn't at all how any of it happened. There were so many levels of awful to all of this.

My mother said softly, "We have to find a place for Liz to go to have this child. She cannot have it here. No one can find out about this, Lee."

My dad furrowed his forehead. "Obviously."

They discussed me for a long time, almost like I wasn't right there. I watched them like a game of Ping-Pong. My dad thought I could go to Europe. But my mom said that was too far; she wanted to be near me. Dad said they could rent an apartment for me, but my mom said I was too young to live alone. They were both clear that whatever I did, wherever I went, no one could find out. All I could think was what havoc and pain I'd wreaked on my parents, both of them. I wanted to curl up and disappear. My mother finally declared she needed a day or two to find a place for me. Then she said the words, mapping out my future in plain English for the first time.

"You will give this baby up for adoption, Liz."

My dad added, "That makes sense. Anyone would be lucky to

have her child." Lee stood up and paced the soft carpet in his loafers, and then turned to me. "Does Daniel know?"

Daniel was my boyfriend.

"Know what, Dad?"

"Know that you're pregnant?"

"No, Dad, I didn't know until today. No, he doesn't know."

"Well, you're going to have to tell him, and then you're going to have to explain to him that he will not be telling anyone else." Daniel and I had been together for more than two years, since the middle of my freshman year of high school. He was my first boyfriend, he was in the grade above me, and we were crazy about each other. I lived, drank, and breathed Daniel for a couple years. We began to fall in and fall out—it was complicated as high school relationships can be—but the road just kept leading back to each other. I think we both knew our lives were headed onto different tracks. We were back together, at the end of the summer, before Daniel left for college. I'd gone to visit him once in the last four months.

"Lizzie, go call him right now and tell him the situation, and be sure to let him know he is not to tell anyone about this. Is that clear?"

"Yes."

"And then get his parents' phone number for me." His parents' number? My dad pointed to the hallway and said, "Go in my bedroom."

I sat down on the bed and dialed Daniel's number. As I told Daniel what was happening, I felt a piercing pain in my chest. I hadn't had time to think or process what was happening. I'd been with my parents the whole time. I was crying hard and couldn't speak for a few moments, but Daniel's voice calmed me down and I got it out—I was pregnant. He was shocked and worried. I wondered if he also wished we'd talked about it, instead of letting things go too far. It was way too late now. I told him my parents were going to call his parents and that no one could find out. He was quiet and then said he would call his parents first. Daniel's parents lived a simpler life than ours. His family had been incredibly kind and gracious to me over the years, and I knew them a lot better than my family knew Daniel. And in all the time we'd been together, our parents' paths had never crossed. They didn't know Dorothy and Lee, what they were like, how they handled things. My dad knocked on the door and walked in.

"Is that him on the phone?"

"Yes."

"Did you get his parents' number?"

"Yes."

"Tell him goodbye." I told Daniel I had to go. I hung up the phone and felt my dad looking at me.

"This is *unbelievable*, Liz." It was unbelievable. Everything inside me stopped, and I felt myself go dark. Like a horrible, black reset button on my life had been hit. Disappointing my parents like this was a torture I could barely take. It was almost more frightening than the pregnancy itself. I saw the sadness, and love, and defeat on my dad's face. But it was too hard to look in the eyes of the man who had believed I could be something great in this world.

* * * *

Ms. Graham offered me a cup of water and some nuts toward the end of our Tuesday afternoon session. I figured I should eat them, since I wasn't going to be eating dinner. I was never going to be eating dinner there ever again.

"Thank you," I said.

"How did you end up deciding to come to the facility, Liz?" Ms. Graham asked.

"My mom found it. She told me it was a Catholic home for unwed mothers, which isn't exactly what this is, right?"

"Right, not exactly."

"She told my dad the same thing, so maybe he doesn't know this is a locked facility. I don't know."

"Liz, you're not locked in here. You are free to come and go as you please."

"Yeah, but the people who live here aren't, right?"

"Correct. They cannot come and go. But I can assure you, as I have assured your mother, that you'll be taken care of here, and you will adapt." Those words didn't mean anything to me. I wondered why adults always imagined they knew things about young people, when in truth they were clueless. Ms. Graham carried on. "If you don't mind, I'd like to talk about your health and the baby. I question if you know how important it is to make sure that you do what you need to do to keep yourself and your baby healthy."

"I know that fainting is not a good thing, and I don't want it to happen again."

"Good, that's what I mean."

"I can see that I have to pay more attention to eating, but I have a hard time feeling hungry when everything feels so sad. And no offense, the food—at dinnertime, anyway—well it's terrible, even for someone who is starving."

"Okay, perhaps we can figure out something beyond the cafeteria for you for dinner food. I know that it's not very good at all; the girls are used to it, I guess. Maybe you could get a hotplate for your room; you can warm up soup and things?"

"Yeah, okay." Anything to keep me out of the mainstream would be a good thing. I knew I would never feel comfortable here.

"And how are you feeling about the baby?"

"What do you mean?"

"I mean have you felt it kick? Do you think about it, do you wonder if it's a boy or a girl?" This baffled me. Did she not get that the baby in my stomach was the reason that my life was ruined? Did she not get that I'd never regretted anything more in my life than having sex and making this baby? That the baby was the reason I was separated from everyone I loved? That I was now tarnished, and bad? That my parents were going to have to suffer and lie because of me . . . and this baby?

"I don't . . . see it as a baby."

"What do you see it as?"

"I don't know . . . a thing . . . I guess?"

"But it's not a thing. It's a small life there in your stomach, and you are in charge of it until it comes out."

I thought about it for a moment. "I guess I'm not very good at that."

"Is there any way you could begin to see that the baby didn't do this to you, Liz?" Of course Ms. Graham was saying that I *did it*, the baby was an innocent and I was a perpetrator. She went on: "The baby is just a little life that didn't mean to cause you pain and doesn't know any of this. All it knows is the sound of your voice and the beat of your heart and the food and drinks that go down and feed it . . . when you eat." I sat quiet for a long time. Her words were hard to hear, all this talk about the innocent baby.

"Okay, I guess I should get a hotplate."

"Maybe your mom can bring one when she comes to visit. I also need to let you know that you are required to go to school here. The girls head over in the late morning and they stay until lunch. In order to meet the requirements for credit you must attend. Starting tomorrow, as you haven't been since you arrived."

"All right." The lump in my throat was coming back. I really didn't want to cry in front of this woman again.

"Is it the idea of school that is upsetting you?" Ms. Graham asked.

"No, not really, it's everything . . . sorry." It was that there was an actual person in my body. It was trapped, I was trapped, and there was nothing I could do to change it.

"I can see how difficult this is for you, and I wish I knew a way to make it easier."

But there was nothing anyone could do. Every minute that passed made that clearer to me. There was no way to erase this. I listened to the muffled buzzing in and out of the main door in the hallway. And then I asked Ms. Graham, "Are you a nun?"

She laughed a little. "No, no, I'm not a nun. I'm just a social worker. Do I seem like a nun?"

"You're calm and nice like one, I guess."

"That's sweet."

"Well, are there nuns here?"

"There were a long time ago, but the facility has taken on a new face since then. There are no nuns working here."

"Okay. Are we finished?"

"Do you want to be?"

"Kind of, if that's okay."

"That's fine. I'll see you here next Tuesday, same time. Wait, I want to give you something." She handed me a card. "You can call me anytime." There was a drawing of a silhouette of a girl with a pregnant stomach on the side of the card, and Ms. Graham's name and phone number.

* * * *

I took the long way to the phone booth on my wing.

"Mom?"

"Hi, Liz, I'm just running out to the new office." My mom had never had a job in her life until recently. She'd gone from her parents' house, to college, to marrying my dad and having seven children. When my parents got divorced, it wasn't just that she had to adjust to becoming a single mom with so many children—she was also trying to run the household financially, something she had never done. She told us all the time that the money she got from our dad just wasn't enough. And it was pretty clear as time went on that we were living a lifestyle she couldn't afford. Dorothy had been a devoted learner, a straight-A student her entire life, and a graduate of Northwestern. I imagine she could have done anything she wanted for work, but she was now forty-seven years old, and her only real experience was raising children and running a home. She made the decision, with the encouragement of my grandfather, to go to real estate school. To try and bring in the money she needed to keep up our life. She studied, got her license, and began selling houses. In a way it was perfect. I couldn't think of anyone who knew more about our community than Dorothy.

She was an almost obnoxious North Shore enthusiast. She knew every historical fact, hidden street, secret beach, beautiful home, forest preserve, government building, and grocery store in all the surrounding areas. But to me, the most impressive part was that she also knew exactly where, and what time, and for how long, the Good Humor man would be parked with his ice-cream truck on hot summer days.

"Are you okay, Lizzie? You fainted?"

"Yeah, I fainted. I'm fine, Mom."

"Ms. Graham said you're not eating. You understand you must eat?"

"I get it, Mom, but the food is not just bad, it's there's-no-way-I-can-eat-it bad. So do you think when you come this weekend you could bring me a hot plate and some food? And there are no towels. I need bath towels. And I don't have a clock or a watch so can you bring those things?"

"Oh, well yes, of course, honey. Listen, ends up I'm not going to be able to make it this weekend. I have several house showings that just came in for my new listing. Remember that big house on Sheridan Road? I am so sorry, honey, but I need to try to sell it. I *will* come up the following week, I promise."

I knew she had to work, but I could feel a black wall of terror rising as she spoke. She wasn't coming. . . .

"Mom, you said . . ."

"I know I did. But I am just getting this business going, I must stay here. Now promise me you will eat, Liz."

"Okay, I have to go, Mom."

"Bye, sweetie."

I took a deep breath and dialed the next number: the only other person who knew the truth and could maybe help.

• • • •

"Hi, Kate, it's Liz. Is my dad there?"

"Hi, Liz. No, he's on his way home. How is it?"

"It's . . . it's bad."

"I'm sorry, it must be really hard. Do you want me to have your dad call you?"

"I don't know, I guess."

"Well, do you need anything? Anything at all?"

I paused, fighting the tears, and then said, "No, that's okay." And then I changed my mind. "Actually . . . I do. Could you tell my dad I need a hotplate and some bath towels and a clock, and . . . I guess some food for the hotplate."

"Sure, and what about some clothes? Do you have stuff that fits you?"

"Not really."

"How about I get some stuff that'll fit you and the other things and I'll overnight them to you? Would that work?"

"Yeah, thank you, Kate."

"And when your dad gets in I'll have him give you a call. He has a number for you at a phone booth there, is that right?"

"Yes, that's right. Thanks again, Kate."

"Anytime. And don't forget to look for your stuff tomorrow afternoon wherever it is you get mail there; I'll get the address from your dad." Wow, Farrah Fawcett was such an incredibly nice person, which made everything so confusing.

As I hung up the phone I noticed a girl hanging around in the hall, watching. If I weren't in the facility, I would have thought she was homeless. I figured she needed to use the phone, so I quickly opened the door.

"Sorry, did you want to use the phone?"

"No, I'm just bored. I'm Tilly." She was the skinniest pregnant girl ever, like an-olive-on-two-toothpicks skinny. Not tall, not short, just regular. Her hair was shortish, straight, and floppy. She had a long nose and pale skin and was wearing what looked like an art smock, with grimy blue jeans and sneakers that were way too big for her.

"I'm Liz," I said.

"Yeah, I know."

After an awkward silence I said, "Well . . . see ya." I made my way down the hall and back toward my room. The other girls were all in the lounge, as usual; the TV wasn't on, but I could hear the chatter. Then from down the hall there was a shout. "See ya around, Liz!" Tilly was waving so I waved back. She reminded me of a Raggedy Ann doll.

I sat down on the bed and thought about my mom. Maybe she had to work, but maybe also she didn't want to see me. Maybe it would be too hard for her. I was a nightmare for her on top of her already broken life. Maybe she would never come, and I would be there alone forever. I remembered something my grandfather used to say when I'd tell him my mom had forgotten to pick me up somewhere, like that day at CCD when Father Joseph scolded her. He'd chuckle and say, "Out of sight, out of mind, sweetheart." I felt a pit in my stomach, remembering his words. It was like I was quietly disappearing and I didn't know where to reach to hang on to myself.

My guitar was leaning up against the bed. I reached for it and started picking. I started singing and playing one of the songs I'd played a thousand times for people,

I need you,
Like the winter needs the spring
You know I need you

As the music filled the room, something let up. The walls stopped staring at me; the sun stopped yelling at me; everything felt a little less horrible. I'd paused the war zone that had become my mind. The lyrics had nowhere to land—I had no one to need—but the music knew me, it reminded me who I was, no matter where I was, no matter what was happening. I played song after song, I couldn't stop; I wanted to stay inside the music forever. It took me away from the facility, and it felt like home. But while right in the middle of Kenny Loggins's "House at Pooh Corner," I heard a loud banging on my door. Louder than loud, with voices behind it. It startled me off the bed. I dropped the guitar on the floor and immediately looked for something to block the door, but the dressers and beds were attached to the walls. The window only opened a foot; there was no way out. I was trapped. What did those girls want? Like a caged animal, I ran around the room looking for something to help me escape. I thought about locking myself in the bathroom. The banging was relentless; I covered my ears and then tripped over my guitar and landed on the floor. I crawled my way into the bathroom.

"You in there? *Open the door.*"

I went up to the door and softly answered, "What do you want?"

"*Open* the *goddamned* door." That voice—it was for sure the voice of the girl with the big red earrings, the one who told me to stay the fuck away from her. I was certain she wanted to kill me. But the door was not locked, so if she was going to kill me, she probably would have come in and done it already. With my hand shaking like crazy, I opened the door a few inches. There were at least five or six girls standing at my door with the red-earring girl at the front.

Red-earring girl angrily asked, "You got a radio in there?"

"No."

"Yeah, you do, show me your fucking radio."

"I—I don't have a radio."

"We heard the music." The olive-on-two-toothpicks girl Tilly was standing in the back of the group. And the big pregnant screamer girl, the one with the boils on her face, was on the side looking at me.

I said, "Well, I really don't have a radio or a Walkman or anything. I guess that was me. I don't have a radio, I honestly don't." Red-earring girl scrunched her face up and leaned closer. Her eyes were filled with rage.

"Why you lie, why do *people* lie? What do you mean, it was you?"

"I have a guitar. I play the guitar and I—I . . . sing. So that was me I think you're talking about."

"No shit?"

"Um, no."

"Well, we want to hear it close up then." All the girls started talking, asking, "Yeah we do, can we?" Red-earring girl scoffed, still skeptical. "That wasn't her, she's full-a shit. That was a radio." She blew past me and into my room, looked all around in the closet, everywhere. And then she saw my guitar on the floor. She looked at me, and then sat down on the empty bed opposite mine. The other girls filed in after her. They sat on the bed and the floor. One of them handed me the guitar off the floor.

My hands were still shaking; I wasn't sure I could actually do it. I sat down on my bed, with Henry at the pillow. They were all looking at me, waiting. Red-earring girl grabbed Henry off the bed. "What the fuck? How old are you, you still got a stuffed dog?" They all laughed.

"Yeah, I know, too old. I've had it since I was like seven. I just can't get rid of it, I guess."

"I don't got nothing from when I was seven years old," red-earring girl barked. "That's a long time. Now go, radio girl, you go on and play us something." I was trying to calm down, calm my heart from racing and stop my hands from shaking. I'd played "There's a Place for Us" at my aunt's wedding a couple years earlier, in front of a hundred people. But I felt even more petrified in front of these girls—all of these strangers in a strange place. I closed my eyes, took a deep breath, and pretended they weren't all sitting two feet away. They were looking around the room now and talking, almost like they'd forgotten what they asked me to do, so I just started. I played the Eagles' "Peaceful Easy Feeling," and within a few seconds everyone was quiet. I played the whole song, sang all three verses, never looked up.

When I finished they were clapping and whistling. Something lifted inside me. Red-earring girl was biting her nails and watching me carefully. She threw Henry back up on the bed and said, "Well, no shit, you can fucking play. Play another one."

I played a few more. I'd gained some confidence and gradually began to feel stronger. When I finished, red-earring girl stood up and said, "Give the radio girl some space, man, get out of her room." Several girls left—clearly they listened when red-earring girl spoke. The really small young-looking girl with the horrid scar running all the way down her cheek walked up to me and whispered, "You sounded like an angel."

I smiled and asked, "How old are you?"

"Thirteen." *Thirteen?* She was thirteen? The big pregnant girl with the boil face, the screamer, was stuck on the floor. She looked up at me with a sweet smile that surprised me and said, "That's one of the only times I ever heard the little kid talk. I'm Nellie." She stuck her hand out for me to help her up. I grabbed it, and she grunted as we hoisted her up off the floor. Panting, she said, "This sucks, doesn't it? Fucking fat, tired, pregnant bullshit." I couldn't get over her face—it was so repulsive I could scarcely look at her—but then she smiled again and all I could see was her smile.

I answered, "Yeah, when is your baby going to come? You look really uncomfortable."

"I got twins in here. Not for a long time, can you believe that shit? I won't be able to fit through the door." I couldn't help thinking about my twin sisters. They were born almost three years after me, numbers six and seven, the end of the Pryor kid line. My mom referred to them, always, as her caboose.

Red-earring girl walked over to my dresser and picked up the jar of peanut butter. She turned to me and said, "I need some of this."

I looked at the peanut butter and answered, "Take it; take the crackers too."

"No shit?"

"No shit."

"Well I will, then. It ain't stealing if she told me to take it. You hear that, girls?" She walked out with the peanut butter and crackers. Nellie followed her. I felt myself exhale as the girls walked out of the room, and maybe I felt a pinhole of hope too. Maybe a small part of me could still feel okay about something. Tilly—Raggedy Ann—stayed in my room. She sat on the bed, smiling. Beyond the horrible clothes and floppy hair and shoes that were three sizes too big, there was something about her. Her eyes, I guess. They were sharp and bright. There was a kick to everything about her. These girls looked different when you got up close, really different. Tilly was as close to happy as anyone I'd seen in there, and it made me feel closer to safe. My mind and heart quieted, just for a moment, for the first time since I arrived.

"Who were you talking to on the phone before, Liz, your boyfriend?"

"No, my parents."

"You got a boyfriend?"

"Yeah, I do."

"So do I. His name is Rick. I can't wait to bring this baby home to him." Her eyes were twinkling and she was rubbing her stomach.

"How old are you, Tilly?"

"Fifteen. Deanna's fifteen too. Don't mind her, by the way. She's not all that bad and mean as she seems."

"Deanna, the girl with the big red earrings?"

"Yeah. Her foster dad raped her. Everyone says she tried to kill him after, but she didn't. She has to go back to juvie after this, but she can't bring her baby to juvie so the baby will have to go to foster care, and, well, you can guess how she feels now about foster care."

"What's juvie?"

"You *never heard* of juvie?"

"I don't think so."

"It's prison for kids. You don't know that? You can't go to prison till you're eighteen, so they have juvie. She's waiting to go to court on something but she's been in and out for a couple years."

"Why doesn't she give her baby up for adoption?"

"What?" Tilly looked at me like I was crazy—out-of-my-mind crazy. Like the idea of giving away a baby was completely nuts. The baby couldn't possibly come out and go live with someone else.

I was starting to understand just how truly different my life was from the other girls'. How polar opposite our experiences of the world were. Tilly looked at me, her face cocked like a confused little puppy, and said, "Are you kidding? Why would she do that? Why would anyone do that? She wants that baby; it's *her* very own. Who would give their own baby away?"

chapter 4

Later that day, I could hear the girls in the lounge getting ready to go to dinner. I hoped the Alice woman wasn't going to force me down to the cafeteria to eat that horrible food. I waited for the voices out in the hall to die down. When it was finally quiet, I headed out toward the vending machines I'd seen a few days earlier. They were down in the basement, buzzing a loud, unfriendly sound. I bought Fig Newtons, a Heath bar, pretzels, Fritos, cherry Life Savers, and a 7 Up and stuffed all the food in the pockets of my big coat. I was feeling slightly dizzy, walking back up the stairs, when I noticed a phone booth in the main hall. I sat down for a moment, holding the door open with my knee and trying to eat some Fritos. When I looked up at the shoddy black phone I thought of my best friend Laurie and how many hundreds of hours we'd spent on the phone. I wanted to call her badly, but I just couldn't. I couldn't tell her the truth. I hadn't spoken to her in weeks.

Laurie and I had been attached at the heart since fourth grade.

Nothing had happened to either of us that the other didn't know. We pondered most of our questions about life and the world in the dark, lying on twin beds in Laurie's bedroom on the edge of the lake in Winnetka. We spent dozens of summer nights down at Laurie's beach in front of the bonfire, laughing and talking until we fell asleep under the stars. Laurie was the one person in the world who knew the inside out and upside down of my heart and soul. She was a year older than me, and had gone off to college earlier that fall just like Daniel. What would happen when Laurie found out I was gone? When her calls weren't returned? When she came back from her freshman year at the University of Michigan in May, and I wasn't home? All my friends were a year older and off to college now. I had no contact with any of the girls in my own grade. People would no doubt begin making up stories about where I was and what I was doing—maybe Laurie would hear those through the grapevine. I hated the thought.

I unbuttoned my wool coat, put my head down, and tried to count how many days had gone by since I was sitting on my dad's wooden schooner in the crystal clear Caribbean waters, fighting with my sisters about whose sunburn was worse, happy, and unaware of what was happening to me. It was only *nine* days ago. And six days ago, I'd been dropped off and left here on the other side of the world.

I took a deep breath and stepped back out into the hall. As I threw the soda can in the trash, I passed a familiar man, the doctor from my fainting day yesterday. I smiled a little and got out a meek "Hi." He looked right at me but ignored me as he passed. *Geeeez.* And then I heard, farther down the hall, voices. A few of the girls were heading back from dinner in the cafeteria.

"Asshole Dr. Ratched." I turned around and saw Nellie, the boil-face girl. She caught my eye, smiled her big smile, and said, "Hey, Liz." Then she asked me really loudly, "Isn't *he* a fucker? That doctor? Isn't he such a fucker?"

She walked up next to me. I quietly answered, "Yes, he was rude to me when I fainted."

She shouted, "THAT'S 'CAUSE HE'S A FUCKER!" The doctor was still in sight and he heard Nellie. He turned around to look at us. It made me think of the times in my life when somewhere, way back in my mind, I would imagine but never, ever, *ever* say out loud something so terrible but true. It was almost impossible to wrap my mind around the idea that a kid could call a doctor a *fucker.* Nellie was unabashed in her shameless disrespect—but she was also right.

"We call him Dr. Ratched after the movie, you know, *One Flew Over the Cuckoo's Nest*? Nurse Ratched?"

"Yeah, that fits."

"He's such an asshole. He shouldn't work here if he hates all of us, ya know? And he does, let me tell ya. And, shit, if we have to go to him every week and spread our legs, God, I hate it more than anything."

What? Was *he* the doctor Ms. Graham said I would be seeing every week? What did she mean? Spread our legs? As my mind raced, I noticed Nellie gingerly holding her side, looking terribly uncomfortable. We slowed our walking to a stop. She leaned over her big stomach and pulled up the bottom of both her pant legs.

"Look." Her ankles were so swollen they looked disfigured. They were bulging out around her sneakers. It looked unbearably painful.

"Holy crap, what happened?"

"Pregnancy fucking happened. It's water swelling or some shit. Does that suck or what?"

"What can you do for that?"

"Nothing. Dr. *Ratched* says to stop eating salt . . . Whatever, I bet he's not even a real doctor. He doesn't know shit."

"Does everyone pregnant get that?"

"I don't know; I don't think so. Maybe it's 'cause I'm having twins." We walked a bit longer before she asked, "You having a party?"

"What?" I was distracted, wondering if my ankles were going to swell up. Being pregnant was such a weird thing.

"What are you doing with all that?" Nellie pointed to the candy and vending machine stuff sticking out of my coat pockets.

"Oh, I was trying not to faint again."

"Well, good thing you didn't eat the fish downstairs. Tilly almost threw up when she walked in and smelled the cafeteria. I guess I'm used to it."

I stuck out my hand. "Want some?" I offered, hoping she'd say no; I was pretty hungry. "No, that's okay, you better eat it," Nellie said, and then added, "unless you're not gonna; then I'll have some." She was looking at the Heath bar in my left pocket, so I handed it to her. A little later she asked me how old I was.

"Just turned seventeen; how about you?"

"Me too, a month ago. Lucky we're not eighteen. We couldn't be here; we'd have to be there." Nellie made a scary face and pointed to a door on the opposite side of our wing. "The people who live in there? Those are the over-eighteens, *high*-security fucking psycho crazy girls."

"What do you mean?"

"If you're eighteen you can live wherever the hell you want in the world; you're an adult. But the girls in there are crazy, with major problems, and they're pregnant, ya know? They *have* to be in there. We call it the real *Cuckoo's Nest.*" What? There was a wing full of eighteen-year-old pregnant psycho girls? *What?* How many were there?

"If you could be any character from *Cuckoo's Nest* who would you be, Liz?" Nellie was chomping on the Heath bar. I was still stuck on the psychos.

"What? You really like that movie, don't you?"

"You're catching on. I fucking love that movie; who doesn't love Jack Nicholson? Come on, it's soooo good. Who would you be? Tilly would be Billy; even though he dies, she likes him. I would be Mac, of course. What about you?" We were back in our wing by now, almost at the lounge. Alice spotted us and immediately came up to us.

"Nellie, you're behind, you know that, right?" she said, in her scolding tone.

Nellie put her hand on her hip. "I'm . . . what do you call it . . . damn, what's the word? I got it, I'm . . . *fatigued*, Alice. Yeah, I'm fatigued, and I got edema, and I got twins in my body. I don't know why you think I can get down on my hands and knees and do chores. I can't, and I ain't."

"You can and you will," Alice said. "And, Liz, you should start tonight, latest tomorrow morning."

"Okay, doing what?"

"What is wrong with you girls?" She seemed annoyed. I noticed the girls listened when Alice was not happy. They didn't always obey her, but she had the power. She was the mother hen in charge. She pointed to the big chore board in the lounge where it was clear as day: Liz P.—Sweep Lounge and Hall.

"Oh yeah, sorry, yes. How often do I do that?"

"Every day. Read the board!" Then she walked away with her weeble-wobble walk, shaking her head. Nellie's chores were toilets and phone booth. Nellie whispered, "Every day my ass. We do them maybe twice a week."

Tilly rounded the corner and tripped right into us. She smiled. I loved how happy Tilly always was. "Why is Liz out of her room?"

Nellie rolled her eyes. "She's not a dog, Tilly."

"I know, what I meant was that she's never out of her room. Hi, Liz, you're here in the lounge, that's great!"

Nellie pointed to the vending machine food in my pockets.

"Liz, show her your dinner." I pulled out a half a bag of Fritos, the whole roll of Life Savers, the pretzels, and the Fig Newtons. Tilly's eyes widened. I was still hungry, but I saw how badly Tilly wanted it.

"Want some?" I offered.

"Can I?"

"Take it." Tilly took the pretzels and opened the cherry Life Savers. I guess I could eat the Fig Newtons. There was a round table in the corner of the lounge with several chairs. Nellie sat down in the farthest corner chair.

"That's her spot," Tilly whispered. "Everyone has a spot. She plays solitaire there all day long, don't you, Nellie?"

"Well, if you morons could play anything, I wouldn't have to play solitaire so much."

"I know how to play cards," I said. My family loved cards.

"What do you play?" Nellie asked.

"Gin, crazy eights, spit, spoons, war, whatever."

"Thank fucking God. Maybe you can teach Tilly; I don't have the patience." The other girls began meandering into the lounge, on their way back from dinner. I sat in a chair at the round table next to Tilly. It had taken a little while, but maybe I'd found my spot. Deanna came in last, with her big red earrings. She told a girl to shut the fuck up when she walked in, and then plopped down in the empty La-Z-Boy chair. That must be her spot. I made a note never to sit there. The young girl with the scar walked in, with another strange-looking girl with long hair down to her butt, dyed black. Her skin was translucent white. She looked like Morticia from *The Addams Family.* They sat on separate sides of the couch, both of them staring blankly at the TV. There was another girl sitting cross-legged on the floor right in front of the TV. I felt as though I'd been plopped down in the land of the misfit toys. Tilly was smoking and ashing in the ashtray every five seconds. Everyone was smoking except for Nellie.

Nellie tapped my shoulder. "Let's see what you got. Gin?"

"Sure." Nellie and I went at gin. I liked Nellie. She made me laugh, but she also had something about her that made me feel . . . not scared.

I started teaching Tilly how to play spit. Then Nellie, Tilly, and I began a loud game of spit all together. We slapped the cards hard on the table with our palms, shrieking at one another. The other girls slowly gathered around, watching us play. The little girl with the scar was inching her way closer and closer. Suddenly, there were six of us at the table. After half a dozen games, Nellie told them all to clear out of her space. I lit up a cigarette and noticed Nellie staring at me.

"What? What are you looking at?" I said.

"Your coat. I like it; looks real warm."

"Thanks."

"Did you steal it?"

Tilly threw her head back, laughing. "Liz didn't *steal* it. She didn't even know what juvie was until I told her; she never stoled anything in her life."

Nellie thought about it. "I guess she doesn't need to steal, then."

"No, I didn't steal it; my mom gave it to me for my birthday."

Nellie smiled. "You got a good mom?"

"Yeah, she's good."

There was a long beat. Nellie lifted her head a little and said, "I'm gonna be a good mom." Her wire-framed glasses were taped on one side, and I could see she had some sort of medicine on the boils all over her face. I didn't really want to talk about being a mom. I didn't think of myself, or any of the other girls, that way. It's true that was the reason we were all here, but I still didn't want to think about it. I looked at Nellie's big belly and said, "I have little sisters that are twins."

Her jaw dropped. "You *do*?"

"Yeah."

"I don't know *any* twins, what are they like?"

"They're fine, good. It's cool to have a twin. I mean, they have the closest relationship of anyone I've ever known. They get to go through everything together. Kind of like having a friend who always has your back, you know?"

Tilly looked over at me. "What's the matter, Liz?"

I laughed a little as I wiped my face. "I don't know why I'm crying," I said.

Tilly looked at Nellie. "I think she misses her family?"

"Obviously. Don't be a dumbass, and quit talkin' about her like she's not here." They were quiet until Nellie shuffled the cards again and said, "You got a good family, don't you?"

"I guess."

"You seem like someone with a good family," Nellie said.

We were all silent until Tilly added, "You know what, Liz? They can come here and visit, your twin sisters can. You can have visitors here. That would make you happy, I bet."

Right. Like Dorothy was going to waltz into the misfit toy teenage pregnancy wing with the twins and take me out for a club sandwich.

"No, they can't come here," I said. "They won't be visiting."

"You're even hiding from your own family?" Tilly said. She immediately looked busted. "Sorry, we know you're hiding; they told us." The girls knew? I was strangely relieved that I wouldn't have to cover that up while I was there. I continued, "Yeah, my sisters don't know I'm here; only my parents know."

"Heavy shit, Liz. But don't worry, none of us have anyone who would visit," Nellie said.

"I do, I have Rick," Tilly said.

"Not *one* of us has had a fucking visitor since I been here, Tilly." Tilly put her head down and quietly said, "I know."

Nellie gathered up the cards. "Yeah, I been worried, what will it be like and all that shit to have twins." The thought of it blew my mind: Nellie was going to give birth to not one but two tiny babies.

The Morticia-looking girl came in from the hallway and told me I had a phone call. Before I got out the door, Tilly reminded me that her and Nellie's room was only two doors down from mine. I smiled.

"Hello?" I answered in the phone booth.

"Diz?"

"Hi, Dad. It's really good to hear your voice."

"How's it going?"

"Okay."

"That's good. Kate said you sounded pretty upset on the phone today. I feel terrible. I know it's not going to be easy, Diz. It's a tough situation all around, but you're a strong person."

"Yeah." I wasn't sure what he meant by that. I didn't feel strong at all. Maybe I used to be strong. But that felt long ago already.

"How you feeling? You still getting sick?" he asked.

"Sometimes. Dad, you think you could come visit?"

"Yes, of course."

"This place is really nothing like I thought, Dad . . . and it's, well, it's really hard here. Think you could come *this* weekend?"

"Your mom is coming this weekend."

"No, she's not anymore; she can't. So I was hoping maybe you could."

"I won't to be able to make it to you for a while. I thought you were at that place so your mother could easily come visit you." He paused. "I don't understand."

"She has to work, Dad, she's got a job." My mom was barely making ends meet.

"She made a commitment to come see you the first weekend. I'm sorry, I won't be able to make it up for several weeks. I have all this work I have to do."

The lump in the back of my throat was trying to suffocate me. It was hard to breathe.

"Okay, I guess I'll see you next month, then."

"Diz, stay strong. This will all be over soon; then everything will be back to normal." I didn't believe that. Nothing was ever going to be normal again. "Remember not to mention your last name, honey, or talk about yourself. You're a private person."

"I know, Dad."

"I'll talk to you soon. Take good care of yourself."

I hung the phone up and sat for a long time. I was out of hope. I was on my own, completely alone. I picked the phone back up, pulled the card out of my pocket, and dialed the number.

· · · ·

Ms. Graham's door was closed when I arrived, so I knocked.

"Come in," her voice said from inside.

"Hi. Sorry."

"No problem, of course. What's going on?"

"I don't know if I can do this, Ms. Graham. I'm trying really hard but five months is a long, long, long time. Every day, every night I—I know I have to, but I don't know how to . . . how to be here and feel okay."

"Are the girls giving you trouble?"

"I like some of them."

"Alice said there was a ruckus around your room this afternoon?"

I wasn't sure I should tell her how the girls scared the crap out of me, that I'd felt positive I was going to be killed, that red-earring Deanna was one scary-ass girl who got in my face and rampaged through my room. In fifth grade, back in Winnetka, there was a long stretch when the boys were mean to me every day. They bullied me, I told on them, and in the end it only made it worse. My brother John told me you should never ever rat. It always makes things worse. I remembered that now.

"No, there wasn't a ruckus, they just wanted to hear me play the guitar." And that was true, nothing bad happened. They'd only been curious.

"Oh, that's nice. I bet they enjoyed it." Ms. Graham got up and went over to a little refrigerator she kept in her office. She turned around and put a half a sandwich, a napkin, and a little carton of orange juice in front of me. "Go ahead. You didn't eat, I gather?"

"No, I didn't. Thank you." I took a bite of the fresh, normal turkey sandwich. I had so many thoughts spinning in my head, topped with the most recent: Neither my mother nor my father would be coming to visit this weekend, to bring me the piece of courage or hope or whatever it was I needed so badly. There was a long silence. Eventually it just came out. "I miss home, Ms. Graham. I want to go home, I really want to go home. I know I can't but I feel it so much." That's all, that was my truth in a sentence. I needed to be truthful to someone. The tears were pouring out, as usual.

"Thank you for telling me that. You are brave, Liz."

"I am?"

"Yes, you are. It takes courage to admit the truth and tell it to someone else." I felt a pang of relief for a second. Maybe it was only the turkey sandwich, but something felt better. Ms. Graham went on. "We can all do so much more than we think we can, Liz. Life has a strange way of showing us who we are. I do believe you can do this. You can find a way to be okay here. All we have to do is get you to believe you can."

I looked out the little window in her office at the dark landscape outside. The quiet and lonely fields and woods. I wanted to believe what she was saying, but didn't know if I could.

Ms. Graham looked at me. "You picked up the phone and called me . . . You're doing the best you can, right?"

"Yes." I waited a few moments. Then I stood up and slowly headed for the door. "My head feels a little less crowded. Thanks again."

"Liz?"

"Yeah, I mean, yes?"

"Yours was the first call I've gotten in almost all the years I've been here. I've given that card out I don't know how many times." Ms. Graham smiled, which she didn't do often.

As I walked back to my room, I felt like there was more space to breathe. Maybe I just needed to hear someone say it out loud: I was going to be okay. I'd messed up, but maybe it wouldn't be messed up forever . . . And doing the best I could was maybe enough for now.

chapter 5

The sun was blasting through the window again as I opened my eyes. There was an annoying tapping coming from my door.

"You going to school, Liz?" It was Tilly, from the other side of the door. I heard rustling and voices as I got my bearings. I was still there; it wasn't all a dream. I guess it was never going to be a dream. I leaned over my growing stomach to get up.

"Yeah. Come on in, Tilly." Tilly bounded in the door like a puppy.

"Hi, I got you some graham crackers and milk. You missed breakfast." She sat down on the opposite bed in the same art smock she'd been wearing since I arrived, almost a week ago. I grabbed my clothes off the dresser, tripped over my shoes, dropped the clothes, picked them back up, and stumbled my way to the bathroom.

"You're not a morning person, huh, Liz?" she said.

"Nope."

I turned on the faucet. The ice-cold water coming from the winter pipes slapped my face. I grabbed a dirty T-shirt to dry off and looked straight into my eyes in the mirror. I wondered if I would ever see who I used to be—the old me, before any of this happened. And then I heard, "Come on, bitches, let's move it." I looked again in the mirror and thought, Where the hell am I? Nellie was at the door, looking morning pregnant and miserable, with a weird winter hat and a men's oversized wool coat that was so big she looked like she was kidding. I threw my hair in a ponytail, reached for my coat, grabbed the graham crackers in the cup, and poured the milk in. Tilly pulled a plastic spoon out of her pocket and handed it to me.

"Gotta eat, girl. You don't want to faint again." She smiled and I ate as we walked toward the entrance. We stopped and stood in a line with the other girls at the guard gate entrance near Ms. Graham's office. Nellie grabbed me by the shoulder and walked me over to the guard woman, the same ignoring black woman I'd seen several times in the last few days. Nellie smiled at her, like they were good friends.

"Hey, Chief, this is Liz. Liz, meet Chief, you know, from *Cuckoo's Nest*?" The black lady smiled a big smile and high-fived Nellie through the gate.

"You don't mess with Chief, Liz," Nellie said. Chief smiled as Nellie shouted, "Hit it." She buzzed the steel door open for us. We headed outside, single file, and followed the path up the hill to the schoolhouse. It was the little Hansel and Gretel cabin I'd seen hiding in the trees during my walk around the grounds. It was the painful kind of freezing, snowy and windy, and Nellie was struggling with her massive stomach. She kept losing her balance and swearing like a trucker. I walked behind her and put my arm out a couple times to keep her from falling. She shouted through the wind to me, "Who are you from *Cuckoo's Nest*?"

I shouted back, "I have to think about it—there aren't too many characters left."

Finally we were there at the little schoolhouse. Nellie climbed up the two stairs and shook off the snow. There was a small room with several metal folding chairs and almost nothing else. There looked to be a couple of stairs in the back that led into another tiny room with some books. A nice-looking young woman with straight brown hair pulled back in a light blue ribbon was leaning against the window. Nellie struggled with her coat and then threw it on the floor. I picked it up and hung both our coats on a hook by the door. The girls all sat down in the chairs. There were about nine of them total. Tilly waved to me and pointed to the seat next to her. "Sit here. This will be the most boring fucking few hours of your life."

Red-earring Deanna had her coat wrapped around her like a blanket and a rancid look on her face. "What the fuck, is there no heat in here? You people trying to kill us?"

The woman with the ribbon in her hair looked up and spoke. "There is a problem with the heat. I apologize for that, but we're going to get the fireplace going. That should help until we can get the heat fixed."

"So now we're the little fucking house on the little fucking prairie?" Deanna said.

"We're waiting for maintenance to come light it," the ribbon woman said.

Nellie dragged a chair along the cold cement floor next to Tilly. The three of us sat quietly. The other girls were strangely resigned and lifeless, like there was nothing to be done about the cold and this boring situation, like this was just the way it was going to be forever.

After a while the ribbon lady walked up to my chair and said, "You must be Liz."

"Hi. Yes, I am."

"I'm Maryann. Nice to meet you, and welcome."

"Thank you."

"Do you have any questions for me?" I wondered who the heck

she was and what she did—did she work at the facility like Alice or Ms. Graham?—but I didn't want to ask. Deanna rolled her eyes and mockingly blurted out, "Do you have any questions? Thannnnk youuu, buuullllssshiiit, who cares?" She scoffed and flipped the finger to both of us. Maryann just ignored her and made her way to a seat near the big window. Nothing happened. This lady was a grown-up, and clearly the person in charge, but she didn't say or instruct anything, she just sat in her mittens reading a book. A good half hour passed. I was freezing. Nellie was miserable and looked sick. I finally stood up and approached the mitten-wearing Maryann.

"Um . . . do you think it would be okay for me to light a fire?"

"Well, I don't know. Do you know how?"

"Yes."

Nellie was listening. "If she knows how, she can . . . right, Maryann? Don't be a dumbfuck. We're freezing."

"Okay then, Liz, give it a go."

There were a couple of old logs in the fireplace. I went outside and found several dry twigs on the side of the schoolhouse and a pile of dry logs in the back. I grabbed everything I could carry and headed back in. There was notebook paper on a shelf in the little room. I scrunched several pieces into balls and then piled it all in under the logs, put a new log on, and asked Nellie if I could borrow her lighter. The girls watched me carefully. In a few seconds there was a pretty good fire going.

Tilly laughed. "Where did you learn to do that?"

"Girl Scouts. What? Has no one here ever been a Girl Scout?" As I turned around from fixing the fire, I could see no one was smiling. It was silent. Deanna finally said, "Yeah, that's why we're fucking here, 'cause we were all good little Girl Scouts. Fucking moron." I felt so foolish. I said a quiet "Sorry" under my breath. The girls all pulled their chairs closer to the fire. I walked around the chilly room, trying to figure out where we were and what we'd be doing. There were some old water-damaged Nancy Drew paperbacks on the floor, and several big picture books for toddlers. Tilly came over and stood next to me.

"Thanks for making the fire."

"Sure. What the heck is this place?"

"School."

School? This was the school? The place I'd be going so my credits could transfer and I could graduate from high school, and then go to college? What the heck?

I asked Tilly, "Do you do anything here? Read, write, work in workbooks, draw, anything?"

"Not really. Not much different from my real school actually. We used to read stuff here, but not anymore. Some of these girls don't know how to read anyway." They don't know how to *read*? I really was through the looking glass. I asked Tilly incredulously, "Is Maryann supposed to be the *teacher*?"

"She is the teacher."

"But she's just sitting there."

Tilly laughed. "Welcome to your new school." So that was it? The girls went to this room every day and *sat* for hours?

This was an entire world away from my high school, New Trier. I thought about my adviser, Ms. White. She was a teacher I was assigned to check in with every morning for the four years I would be there. She took attendance, discussed the rights and responsibilities we had as students, and chose topics to debate to get us to open up about our thoughts and lives. They looked out for us at New Trier, and no one slipped through the cracks. It was a school that was bursting with opportunity for overachieving students, whose sights were set on attending the best colleges in the country. It was ranked the third best public school in the United States, which my dad boasted about often. And until this moment, I'd never given any of it a thought. I was a casual student who had been somewhat uninterested in my studies, indifferent about my grades and participation. I got by reasonably well with little effort. Last time I saw my adviser, Ms. White, just before Christmas break, she'd sat me down and given me the old you-have-such-potential, why-don't-you-try-to-focus-on-your-studies lecture. I had taken all of it for granted: all of her respect and interest in me. I looked over at the ribbon lady, Maryann, and suddenly felt horrible. Mortified, actually.

The Morticia girl tapped my shoulder from behind. I was jolted back to the moment. She asked, "The fire's going out—can you fix it?" The girls were all warming their hands in front of their big bellies, fighting for a spot near the flames. I took Tilly outside and we filled a bucket with kindling and sticks and dry pinecones. We came back in with enough to keep a fire going for days. I put a new log on, and the girls moved closer. Nellie sat back quietly. I could feel her looking at me.

"Lighter."

"Oh yeah." I handed it back to her.

"She used to read stuff sometimes, but everyone got so rowdy Maryann stopped. I guess I can't blame her," Nellie said.

"What did she read?"

"I don't know, different stuff. There's a box of magazines and shit over there. I saved this one 'cause I want to read it." She pulled a worn copy of a *Reader's Digest* magazine out from her big coat pocket. I read the subtitles on the cover out loud.

"Complete guide to needlework, Your garden, your home, Parenting twins. Did you read the article on parenting twins?"

"Not yet." She handed me the magazine and said, "Here, you read it." I laughed, pushed it back, and said, "I'm not having twins, you read it." Then I realized: Holy crap, maybe Nellie couldn't read. I carefully reached back for the magazine and began to read the story about the twins out loud. It was written by a woman who had given birth to identical twins, a single mother who lived in northern California. Nellie was sitting so close she was almost in my lap. Tilly and a few of the other girls listened too. By the third page, everyone was listening.

Deanna interrupted. "Read fucking louder, radio girl, so we

can hear you." The story began by talking about the difficulties of carrying twins, and then moved into a slightly graphic description of the birth. The girls all screeched and groaned when the story got to the labor part. Then it moved on to meeting the babies and becoming a family. Nellie rubbed her big belly and said, "See? These babies are gonna make my life good."

Maryann, our non-teacher, walked toward me with a big box and placed it on the floor at my feet. It was filled with dozens of *Reader's Digest* magazines. I looked up at her, and she smiled a little and made her way back to the window. The girls swarmed the box. They talked about the pictures and some read the titles aloud. The young scar-faced girl sat down, opened one of the magazines to a story, and handed it to me.

I read seven stories from the magazines that morning. Most of the girls ended up lying on their coats on the floor in front of the fireplace. The snow outside never relented, and Deanna ended up tending the fire like an expert until it was time to leave a few hours later. The school day was over—a school day unlike any I'd had before.

When we got back to the facility, the guard lady—Chief—came out from around the gate and stood in front of me with two huge boxes. "You got some mail, girl."

Tilly took the boxes from her while I signed for them. We carried them back to my room.

"Who are they from?" Tilly asked.

"I think my dad and his wife."

She laughed. "Ha, not your stepmother? Your dad's wife?"

"Yeah. Well, yeah, I don't really see her as a stepmother."

Nellie handed me a key to open the box. I ran it down the side seam of the cardboard, reached in, and pulled out a brand-new hotplate, several cans of soup, four boxes of saltines, canned fruit, peanut butter, jelly, pretzels, raisins, Fruit Roll-Ups, a huge box of SweeTarts, and a few jars of peanuts. At the bottom was a wrapped box. I opened the box to find a windup alarm clock with Snoopy on the face and Woodstock on the top with a hammer to hit the bell. A note inside read: Hope this helps, we love you, Kate and Dad.

Nellie snickered. "Shit, sounds like a pretty fucking good step-mother to me. What's in the other one?" I opened the second box and pulled out three plush yellow bath towels, a few washcloths, and a pink terry-cloth robe.

"Man, come on, I've never had a robe. Can I try it on?" Tilly asked. I nodded and Tilly put the robe on over her smock. At the bottom of the box were two pairs of blue jeans. Nellie pulled them out and unfolded them.

"Look at this shit?" she said. The jeans had a sewn-in piece of black stretchy fabric; there was no button and zipper, just a big elastic panel. Nellie grabbed the black elastic part of the jeans and stretched it out about three feet; we all burst out laughing. Nellie was flabbergasted. "What the fuck? This is for your stomach . . . get it? It's for your big fat baby gut. That's fucking hilarious, pregnant jeans?"

Tilly grabbed the other pair and stretched the stomach part over her head. And then read the tag. "Look, it says Mama Jeans." I dug into the box again and pulled out a beautiful toasty fleece sweater and three maternity shirts.

I finally decided to unpack, to put the clothes and things from my suitcase in the drawers, along with the stuff Kate and my dad sent. It was all too real to ignore. *I surrender.* I was there, and I was going to be there a long, long time. I stuffed my suitcase in the back of the closet and put all the food in the other empty dresser. I pulled the fleece sweater over my head and felt the cozy soft warmth against my chest. Nellie and Tilly sat on the bed watching me put clothes away. They reminded me of the twins, just sitting there staring at me, the way Jennifer and Tory sometimes did. It comforted me—it made me feel like they might need me a little.

I asked them, "You guys want some food? Please take anything."

They both grabbed for the candy. Nellie talked while she chewed. "So what's the real story, Liz? Why are you hiding?"

"What do you mean?"

"I mean, so big deal, you got pregnant. Why hide?"

"Well . . . my parents think if people find out that I'm pregnant, it will ruin my life."

They thought this was funny. Tilly said, "Everyone I know knows I'm pregnant. Guess my life is ruined."

Nellie laughed, and then asked, "Why? Rich people don't get pregnant?"

"I don't know if we're rich people." I said.

Nellie almost spit her food out. "Oh no? Think again, Liz. You are soooo fucking rich people—it's not funny. Except most rich people suck, but you're a nice rich person."

Tilly smiled. "Yeah, you are. I mean, I don't know any rich people, I only see them on TV." She thought for a second. "What's it like to be rich, Liz?"

"I don't know, Tilly. What's it like to be . . . whatever you are?"

"Poor? That's easy; it sucks, makes everyone pissed off."

Nellie laughed. "Just so you know, Liz, poor, super poor, sucks cocks in hell. Not having enough makes people ugly and . . . tired."

Tilly laughed. "And pregnant."

They both cracked up—they'd moved on to the raisins by now. Nellie kept talking. "My mom is always mad about everything. I remember feeling so sorry for her, trying to help when I was little, but she was such a fuckup, got fired all the time and drank too much. . . . Why am I talking about this shit?" She went silent.

I looked at Nellie and then at Tilly and suddenly felt so stupid. I had never given an ounce of thought to people my age—kids—whose lives might be so different from mine, so insanely hard. Until that very moment, I truly imagined everyone knew their mom and dad, and had food, and a home, and love, and someone in the world who knew where they were, and paid attention to who they might become.

Nellie pulled a man's brown billfold out of her pocket. "I wish I could remember when I was a baby. Seems like my mom was so much happier. She looked happy, didn't she?" She pulled out of the billfold a worn picture of an adorable little baby in the arms of a young girl—a girl even younger than us.

"*That's* your mom?" I said. Holy crap.

"Yeah, why?"

"How old was she when she had you?"

"Just a little younger than me."

Tilly looked at the picture. "She's pretty, Nellie."

"Yeah. I must look like the asshole who fucked her."

What? What did she just say?

I asked her, "What do you mean, Nellie, you mean your dad?"

"Yeah. It was a one-night stand. My mom says she doesn't remember him; only thing she remembers is that he was an asshole. When she's super mad at me, she says I must be like the asshole who fucked her."

I was in shock. Nellie's words made me feel something way too deep and dark. It was so sad that Nellie could ever think or say those things about herself. My throat was tightening as I fought more tears back.

Tilly asked her, "So you never even met your dad?"

"I don't have a dad, Tilly. *No* dad, get it?"

We all sat there until Nellie said, "You got a picture of your mom or dad, Liz?"

"What? Um, no, but . . . I think I have a picture of my sisters and brothers when we were younger . . . I think." I went over to my journal, which I kept slightly hidden beneath the two books I'd brought, *Great Expectations* and *Terms of Endearment*. I opened the journal to the last page and pulled out a black-and-white family photo of the seven Pryor kids. At that moment, I almost didn't want to show it to them. I felt bad that I had a family . . . and a dad I knew, and food and love. It was as though I was seeing the real view of myself for the first time. What must the girls think? How could I never have known until now the luckiness of my life? The picture was a Christmas card photo taken by a professional photographer when I was younger, about six years old. My brothers were dressed in their Brooks Brothers button-downs, my older sisters and I in our knit dresses, and the twins were babies, sitting on my brothers' laps. We all dutifully stood in our places on and around the piano bench. Jennifer, one of the twins, was crying in the photo; I remember they couldn't get her to stop crying. In the dozens of pictures they took, she just kept crying. Dorothy, in her inimitable style, figured out a way to make it all work. On the Christmas card that year she had inscribed, "All the Pryors wish you a very merry Christmas . . . Well, almost all." I turned around and hesitantly handed the photo to Nellie. She was as shocked as I'd been a minute ago, for a different reason.

"Get the fuck outta here, no way. That's your family? Is that you? You're richer than rich. That looks like a picture in a god-damned magazine."

"Let me see." Tilly leaned down. "Holy cow, that's so cute. There are so many of you. And you all have the same father?"

What? "Yeah, we have the same dad," I said.

Nellie looked carefully. "Those are the twins?"

"Yeah."

Tilly softly said, "Liz has a real family."

"She sure fucking does." Nellie looked out the window and then said, "Play a song, will ya? And not those sad songs you like: fun ones." Tilly handed me the guitar. Nellie took off her cardigan and hollered, "Look out, 'cause I can sing." I jumped on the bed and started with "Sweet Home Alabama," while Nellie sang along. We laughed so hard Tilly almost peed her pants. We had missed lunch, so we fired up the new hotplate and ate Campbell's chicken soup with saltine crackers, a lot of saltine crackers. And a hundred SweeTarts for dessert. I looked over at Tilly and Nellie, and something felt different. Something let up inside, like a release. I had the feeling I get when I'm with my friends. Nellie and Tilly weren't strangers anymore, and I felt less like a stranger too.

Nellie stood up and stretched. She got so tired in the afternoons, she could barely keep her eyes open. Her ankles were even more swollen than the other day, and the boils on her face looked raw and painful. She took a handful of SweeTarts and left to take her afternoon nap. I looked over at Tilly and asked, "Can I ask you for a favor?"

She darted up. "Oh my God, yes. Fuck yes, please. What do you need?"

"Will you walk over there to the trash, take that damn art smock off, and throw it away?"

She looked at me, furrowed her brow, and asked, "What? Why?"

I walked over to the dresser, reached in the drawer, and pulled out one of the three new maternity shirts Kate sent: the one with the white Peter Pan collar and navy blue smocking over the green-and-blue-checkered flannel fabric. It was soft and warm and adorable. "Here, take this and keep it, please," I said, handing it to her.

"Don't fuck with me, Liz."

"I'm not. It's not my color and it's too small on me, so just take it and keep it, okay?" Tilly's round eyes filled with tears. She peeled her smock off, revealing her scraggly bra, huge belly, and thin little toothpick legs. She walked over, put the smock in my trash can, and laughed as she put the new shirt on. She stood in front of the mirror, wiped her eyes hard, and then ran her hands over the flannel and said, "I don't know what to say." She looked again in the mirror and then softly said, "It almost makes me kind of okay to look at." Holy hell, that was a sad, sad thing to hear her say.

"You look great, Tilly, you really do, you idiot. And here, give these to Nellie." I grabbed a pair of the maternity jeans out of the dresser—one pair was enough for me, I didn't need two.

"Oh God, Liz, she needs them. Her stomach kills her, even in sweatpants. She's gonna shit! Wow, I'm gonna walk around the lounge in my new designer maternity shirt." She was smiling. She looked happy, and I felt somewhere close to happy too.

I looked at her and said, "Yes, you fucking are; enjoy it." She jumped up, hugged me hard, and left the room. It was quiet for a moment, and I was alone again. Then I heard, loud as hell, "Nellie, wake the fuck up, Nellllllllieeeeeee, you won't believe it. . . ."

chapter 6

There was almost a foot of snow piled on the ledge outside the window when I woke up. It looked as though a white blanket had been placed over all of the trees, which were swaying back and forth in sync with the wind. For a second I forgot where I was . . . and then I looked down and saw the growing bump that was now my stomach. And it all came rushing back.

I got up, got dressed, and found the soft cream fisherman's sweater my dad had brought me, a long time ago, from one of his business trips, tucked away in the drawer. No matter where he traveled, we could count on our dad to bring back something, although he was clear that it was never just a *thing*. His gifts came with backstory: meaning, custom, teachings from some other life that was fundamentally different from ours. He'd gotten the fisherman's sweater in a little village in England, where he was traveling for work. He always delivered the information as though it were top secret and we, his kids, were the only ones given clearance to receive it. The village fishermen originally wore the sweaters, knit by their wives, to stay warm during the winter fishing season. Their catch was so plentiful the first time they wore the sweaters, they were declared lucky. Every man who ever fished any season during the year from then on wore the sweaters. I pulled the lucky sweater on and headed to the cafeteria. Miraculously, somehow, I had almost made it to the end of my first week. I rounded the corner in the basement and spotted Alice, fast approaching with her weeble-wobble walk.

"What are you doing, Liz?" she blasted in her loud midwestern voice.

"Ummm . . . getting breakfast?"

"It's Friday. You know what Friday is, right?" In her singsongy way, she said: "It's Dr. Lathem day. You need to go all the way down this hall and turn left, you have your first exam. Get goin', girl."

What? The spread-your-legs exam Nellie talked about? I froze for a second.

"Go on, git, girl," Alice said.

At the end of the hall, I saw Nellie standing in front of a big wooden door. She called me over: "Hey, Liz, look." She lifted up her shirt to show her huge pregnant stomach inside the stretchy panel of the maternity pants; she looked like the fat lady in the circus.

"Nice," I said, smiling.

She smiled back. "More than nice, I can breathe."

On the door next to Nellie, I saw a plaque that read Dr. Richard Lathem. Written over it in thick black marker, probably scrawled by one of the girls, was DR. DICK. My heart started to pound hard.

"Nellie, what exactly are we doing here?"

She straddled her legs wide on the floor and laughed. "What do you think we're doing? Spread 'em bitch. You gotta go in there, take your pants off, and spread your legs for that prick. And then he sticks his hand all the way up your cooch and says everything's okay. That's what we're doing here."

"I can't do that, Nellie." I took a few steps back from the door, "I'm *not* doing it."

"You gotta do it. No one wants to, unless you want to be like Deanna who got kicked out for a week when she wouldn't go in there." I started to feel light-headed and reached for the wall to steady myself. A woman with a weird beehive hairdo, wearing a nurse's outfit and white Earth shoes, opened the wooden door. She shouted "NEXT!" There were other girls lined up against the wall in the hallway, all of them with their eyes cast down, pretending like they couldn't hear the nurse.

Nellie rolled her eyes and said, "Fine, I'll just fucking go . . . whatever."

The door slammed behind her. I walked to the end of the line and stood behind the young girl with the scar on her face. She was scratching her hand so hard that a drop of blood rolled down her finger, but she just kept scratching. I watched as she mutilated her hand.

Without realizing it, I whispered, "You shouldn't do that."

She whispered back, "I know," but still didn't stop.

Beads of sweat were gathering on my forehead, and a wave of nausea swooped over me. I wanted to fall through the wall, or better, break my legs, or smash myself into something. I would have done anything to get out of that hall and away from whatever awaited in that doctor's office. There was a bathroom across the corridor. I went inside and steadied myself at one of the small sinks.

"I think I can, I think I can, I think I can," I said to myself in front of the mirror. Twenty times I said it, and then I leaned over and dunked my head under the faucet of cold water. I let it run for a long time, numbing the back of my neck, and finally I came up for air. I was unconvinced I was going to survive whatever was about to happen. I grabbed a paper towel, wet it, took a few more dry ones, and headed back out. Nellie was still in the office, behind that big wooden door. Why was it taking so long? I sat on the floor next to scar girl again and whispered, "I forgot your name." She was still scratching her hand; there were drops of blood all over the floor now.

"Wren," she said.

"Wren?"

"Yeah, Wren."

"Oh yeah, well here, give me your hand." I wiped the blood off her hand and fingers with the wet towel and wrapped the dry one around her scratched hand. Looking at the scar on her face made everything inside of me drop. None of these girls had had easy lives. The door flew open, and I finally heard Nellie's voice booming through.

"Thank you for nothing, *fucker*. Doesn't do shit about my ankles, treats us like animals!"

Wren looked up; she was four people from "NEXT!" She couldn't stop herself. She kept scratching through the paper towel.

A half hour passed. I sat in the hallway on the floor. I pulled a little on the linoleum tile that was peeling up at the corner. I thought about the sleek gray slate tile in the front entranceway of our old house in Winnetka. We played jacks on that tile for hours and hours, my sisters and I. I'd mastered the game all the way up from one-sies to ten-sies, and through to triples. I could place all ten jacks on the flat part of my fisted hand, throw them up, and turn and catch them in that same palm, to skip to the next level. I closed my eyes and pretended I was there, with Jennifer and Tory on the cool slate floor, the sun shining through the windows. The door flew open—I was next in line. Wren came out, waved the hand with the paper towel still wrapped around it, and turned down the hall. The nurse with the beehive barked at me to get moving.

It was a small room, with a table covered in dark orange plastic leather that had weird metal things at the bottom. There was a wooden stool, a sink, and a trash can. Everything looked miniature, except for the table.

"Take your pants and underwear off, wrap the gown around yourself, and wait on the table for the doctor," the scary nurse said. She slammed the door behind her, and I was alone.

My hands and legs were trembling as I took my clothes off. I covered up the bottom half of myself with the gown and climbed up on the orange table with the creepy metal things. I bit the front of my lucky sweater and waited and waited. The doctor finally came in.

He sat down on the stool at the end of the table, not looking at me, and said, "Lie down, please, and then scoot yourself as close to the end here as you can." I did what he said.

"Now put your feet in the stirrups."

I looked at him, confused, until he grabbed my left foot and put my heel in the cold metal thing. I slowly lifted my right foot and placed it in the other metal thing and tried to close my legs. The doctor blew air into a pair of rubber gloves and then rolled them onto his hand.

"Now hold still," he said.

I laid my head down, holding tightly to the cloth gown that was covering the front of me, and looked up at the cement ceiling.

"Let go of the gown and open your knees," he instructed.

I closed my eyes and stopped breathing while he pushed his hands inside me. The tears were spilling down my cheeks as he jabbed and nudged my insides. It was such a weird, alien feeling. What was happening? I tried to scooch back up the table away from him.

"Move back down, young lady, and lie still." The doctor then stood up, with one hand still in my body, took his other hand and pushed hard on the sides of my stomach. I gasped in pain.

"Relax, and for God sakes, breathe," he said. But I couldn't breathe. I'd forgotten how. Finally, he pulled his hand out of me, yanked the rubber gloves off, and threw them in the trash.

He started to walk out, and I asked, "Am I going to be all right?"

He grunted, "Probably."

And the door slammed behind him. Probably? What did that

mean? Was something wrong? I buried my face in my sweater and cried like a two-year-old. Everything was sore as I got dressed again. The nurse came in a few minutes later.

"I have to weigh you. Come with me." I followed her out of the room as the spontaneous sobs continued to erupt. I still couldn't catch my breath.

"Stop that . . . and get on the scale," she said. "The doctor needs to track your weight. You the one who fainted?"

"Yes."

I stepped on the scale; she rattled the little bar back and forth, and then scribbled on a chart.

"I'm trying to eat more," I said. "Am I going to be all right?"

Without looking at me, she answered, "Probably." She took her cat-eye reading glasses off and began cleaning them with her handkerchief. She looked up at me, aggravated, and said, "Go on, then, you're done. Jesus, Mary, and Joseph . . ."

I made my way down the empty hall, past the rank smell of the bad cafeteria food. The girls were gone. I'd missed breakfast. I dragged my fingers along the warm painted radiators in the hall, trying not to pay attention to the hollow feeling I had inside. Could a teenager die during pregnancy? Was I gonna die?

* * * *

Tilly was waiting for me when I got back, outside my room. "I didn't know where you were, so I thought I'd wait for you. You okay?" she asked.

"No," I said.

"Fridays suck. I go down early, get it out of the way. Dr. Dick told me I might have my baby sooner than the date."

"He did? How does he know that?"

"I don't know. I guess how big it is and stuff?"

"Well, when was it supposed to come?"

"Middle of May, but now he says maybe early May. Can I come in?"

She walked in, sat on the empty bed, and scrunched up her face as she looked at me. "You really don't look okay. . . . Are you?" It tipped me over the edge—Tilly's look of concern. Why did this always happen? The "you okay?" was like someone cutting the last tiny thread holding me together. I couldn't say I was okay, even if I wanted to. I just couldn't. Instead, the tears came, shoving the sadness out of me. Tilly's sympathy had opened the floodgates. Kind of like when I was homesick at camp the first year, I called my mom, and when I heard her voice it made me miss home even more. Like their care somehow makes it harder to fake it, and you lose it completely. Tilly watched me with a glum look on her face.

"You hate it here," she said. I nodded between sobs.

"I guess it's not like what you're used to, but you have a pass, you can go anytime you want."

"Go where?" I choked out. There was no escaping this.

"I don't know." She walked to the dresser and picked up my hairbrush, then put it back down. Then she picked up my necklace, the one Daniel gave me for Christmas. It had a sterling silver chain and little charms of my initials hanging on the end.

"'L.P.' Guess I can't borrow this." She laughed, and then turned to me. "You'll get used to Dr. Dick, he has to make sure the baby is okay and you're okay. He hates us. We think he got in trouble or something at a real hospital and had to come here 'cause nowhere else would take him."

Tilly picked up one of my headbands, pushed her short hair off her face, and looked at herself in the mirror. "You're gonna get used to it here, Liz, and you have me." She smiled a goofy smile and ran her hands over the flannel maternity shirt, which she hadn't taken off since I gave it to her. "You eat breakfast?"

"No, I guess I didn't," I said. I was beginning to calm down.

"You have to eat. Be right back." She left the room. Out the window, the snow hadn't let up. It was still falling fast, and the trees were swaying in the wind. It was mid-February, and we had many weeks of winter to go. Tilly came back in and handed me what looked like a Pop-Tart, in silver paper.

"What's this?"

"Strawberry, best you can get, eat it."

"Where'd you get it?"

"I take things from the cafeteria when I can. Just eat it." I opened the Pop-Tart, took a bite, and then heard the door squeak open. It was Nellie, and she was wearing her hair in two silly-looking tiny ponytails on top of her head.

"What's up? Liz recovered?" Nellie said.

"Not yet," Tilly answered.

"She will."

"Yeah, probably." They were talking like I wasn't there. I looked at Tilly, then Nellie, then Tilly again, like watching a tennis game.

"She has to get used to it, I guess."

"Gonna take some time. She hates it here."

I interrupted them. "There you go talking about me like I'm not here."

"Sorry, but you make it so easy," Nellie said. "Come on, *Bewitched* is on." I followed them into the lounge. *Bewitched* was their favorite TV show. Samantha the mom and her two-year-old daughter, Tabitha, were in Tabitha's nursery. Tabitha wanted her mother to hand her the doll that was on the shelf. Samantha told her she couldn't have her doll until after her nap. When Samantha left the room, little Tabitha stood up in her crib, reached her arms out, and tweaked her nose back and forth, which gave her magical powers. The doll floated from the shelf through the air, all on its own, into the little girl's arms. The girls in the lounge loved Tabitha. I listened to all of them laughing.

But the Morticia-looking girl, Elaine, the girl with the black hair almost to her butt, was leaning over the couch and cringing in pain. She grabbed her stomach and started crying. Wren got up off the couch and left the room, and so did a few others. Deanna just stared at her. Elaine was now doubled over. No one said anything, so I slowly walked over and asked what was wrong.

"My stomach, like really bad," she said.

I ran to get Alice, and when we came back to the lounge—Alice taking her time, walking slow—Elaine was now lying down on the floor. When Alice saw Elaine on the floor, her annoyance turned to concern.

"What's the problem, Elaine? Is it that bad you can't stand up?"

"I can't move," Elaine said. She was sweating badly and looked ashen. Alice called the paramedics from next door. A few minutes later, two guys came in with a gurney. They hoisted Elaine on and left.

I looked around and then asked, "How far along is she?"

A girl named Amy, who had a short blond pixie haircut, huge boobs, and a funky lazy eye, said, "Seven months, I think."

Deanna sat up from the recliner, sucking on a Tootsie Pop. "Maybe she did something stupid. She's got a baby in there; she better not be doing no drugs and shit."

"She doesn't do drugs, Deanna," Amy said.

Their bickering went on for a while, until Alice came back in and told us to be quiet. She said, "I think it would be a good idea to get your lazy rear ends outside. I am going to take anyone who wants to come on a walk."

"You shitting me? It's pouring snow." Deanna pointed to the window.

"I see that, Deanna," Alice said. "All the more reason to get out. The fresh air will do everyone some good."

"No fucking thank you." Deanna reclined back in her chair. Amy and Wren and Nellie and Tilly shook their heads too. But I got up and announced I was going.

They all looked at me. "What else am I going to do?" I said.

"Good, Liz, I'll take you. I can't get these girls out for the life of me." But then Tilly changed her mind. She was coming too. Then Nellie said she would as well. Amy too, and finally Wren. Deanna and the others stayed where they were.

We walked to the entrance of the facility past Ms. Graham's office, and Nellie hollered to the guard her usual refrain: "Yo, Chief, hit it!"

"You got it, Mac," the guard lady said, and buzzed the door open. We filed outside, behind Alice, who looked like the Michelin tire man from the TV commercials, with her puffy coat and round wobble. The grounds were wrapped in the new white snow. There was that just-after-a-big-snowfall thick silence outside, the kind that makes you want to whisper. For a second I felt something nice—peaceful almost—and then I felt a plop on the back of my head. The girls were throwing snowballs, kicking the loose snow up at one another, laughing and shouting. Alice stood and watched from afar with half a smile. I scooped up a load of snow and let it drop above Nellie's head. She tried to get me back but could barely move, she was so big and bulky. I lay down flat on my back in the soft snow and looked up at the sky. The sun was finally peeking through the dark clouds. Nellie came and nudged my side with her sneaker. "Get up, moron."

"Nope, gotta make snow angels," I said.

"What the fuck?"

"Come on, lie down."

"Not gonna happen, too cold."

"Wren, Tilly, come here . . . Amy. Who's made snow angels before?" I asked, but I was met with blank stares. Seriously? None of them knew about this? I decided to demonstrate.

"My God, okay, watch." The other girls stood around me in a circle as I began moving my arms and legs back and forth through the snow. Then carefully, I stood up and jumped to the side so as not to mess it up. A perfect lone imprint of what looked like an angel with wings glistened on the ground.

Tilly laughed. "Cool." She and Nellie lay down and started making angels. Wren and Amy watched for a second before they got on their backs too. We made more than twenty angels in a line, going almost all the way up the hill to the schoolhouse. Alice sat on the bench, watching. When we stepped back to view our masterpiece, we noticed that every fifth angel in the line looked twice as big as the others.

"I'm a fucking fat angel, all right?" Nellie said.

Alice looked over, and finally spoke. "You're a cherub, Nellie, a real cherub, especially with that mouth-a yours. Let's go. You guys are soaking wet."

We headed back inside and hung our wet coats on the radiators in the lounge. The snow and the walk were a tiny reminder that there was life beyond the lounge. Deanna was standing by the window. I wondered what she thought about in those moments. The TV was off, and a few other girls were scattered around the room. I'd barely ever seen Deanna out of her chair. I stood warming my hands at the radiator when Deanna finally spoke, addressing the room.

"Elaine's baby died in her stomach," she said. A long silence passed.

"What are you fucking talking about?" Nellie said.

"I'm fucking talking about that her stepmother came to get some of her things and told us that the baby died inside her."

Tilly stared at the ground. "I didn't know a baby *could* die in your stomach."

I thought, Me neither, and said, "How does that happen?"

"That's just the way, sometimes, is what the stepmom said." Deanna was back in the recliner. She curled herself in a ball. Everyone was quiet.

"She hates that stepmother," Amy said. "She told me she ran away for long enough so that lady wouldn't make her have an abortion. She lived on the streets waiting to get to four months. She really wanted the baby. She named it Angel. Are they coming back? Will we see her again?"

In my worst wildest imagination, I hadn't even considered a baby could die in someone's stomach. I made my way to the phone booth. The phone rang several times with no answer. I hung up, tried again, and let it ring more than ten times. Finally someone answered.

"Mom?" I said.

"Hi, sweetheart. How are you faring?"

"Do you know anything about babies dying inside people?"

"My gosh. Why are you asking me such a thing?"

"Because a girl here had a baby die inside of her, and it's freak-ing me out. Why, how does that happen?"

"I suppose there are a number of different reasons, but some-times it just happens. God makes decisions that are difficult to understand. In her poor case, he decided to take the baby before it was born. It's rare, honey."

"Well, I think that's terrible and mean of God."

"You never know why and how things happen, Liz."

"I want to come home."

"I know you do." We sat in phone silence a long time. I didn't want to make my mom feel bad—of course I couldn't come home. But I wanted to.

"I went to the doctor here today, it was horrible."

"Well, sweetie, people in your condition must go to the doctor often, it's not pleasant but it's part of it. Liz—you have to try to make it work there."

I knew that already. But I didn't like being reminded.

"Can I speak to one of the twins . . . please?"

"Yes, yes you *may*. Let me find them. Hold on a minute." My heart panged as I heard the yelling and recognizable chaos of home in the background. After what sounded like the phone dropping to the floor, I heard another familiar voice.

"Hello?"

"Jen?"

"Liz? Hi, oh my gosh, how are you?"

"I'm okay, how are you?"

"Well, we had two snow days in a row. How do you think we are? It's fantastic."

"I'm so jealous."

"We took the toboggan and went sledding down the driveway out onto the street. It was totally empty. You should have been here. Leann from next door got her dog to pull her sled. It was hilarious."

"Wow, sounds fun. How's Tory?"

"She's fine, she's soaking wet with snow right now. When are you coming home?"

"I . . . don't exactly know." The lump emerged in the back of my throat. I wasn't coming home for a long, long time, but I couldn't tell her that.

"You feeling okay? You feeling sick?"

"I'm okay."

"You sound different."

"I do?"

"Yeah, kind of."

"Well . . . I'm the same."

"Call us again, okay?" My mom came back on and said she'd see me next weekend—only a week away, but it felt like a lifetime.

I stayed a long time in the phone booth, thinking about what my sister Jennifer said. I sounded different . . . because I was different . . . and I didn't want to be. I could feel myself changing, and there was nothing I could do to stop it. I could visualize the happy, normal life I used to know in my mind, but I couldn't feel it. It was unreal now, fading away. So many things in life were bigger than me. I decided I hated change. It was like a frightening beast. The more I fought it, the harder it pushed its way in. All I wanted was to go back to the old, safe me. But the beast was winning. I was changing.

· · · ·

The girls were quiet when I returned to the lounge, still in shock from the news about Elaine. I sat down and looked at the clock on the wall. It was just like the clocks at school. Big, with black hands and numbers, and a red second hand. The quiet was killing me. I watched the red second hand and listened to the hard click of each second passing. "Time passes slowly here," I said.

"You want to see time *stop*, radio girl?" Deanna said. "Just take your lily-white ass over to juvie."

I thought about it and said, "I don't want to see it stop, no, thank you."

Deanna laughed a good, long laugh. "This is a fucking hotel compared to that shit."

Tilly was biting her nails, looking around the room. "I feel so bad for Elaine. Angel, that's a sweet name for a baby girl, isn't it, Liz? I know the name of this little guy in here, but I ain't telling till he comes out."

Nellie looked at her. "It's gonna be Rick Junior, duhhhh, right?"

"Maybe."

Deanna chimed in, pointing to her stomach. "If this thing's a guy, I'm naming it Rubin, and if it's a girl and it better be, I'm naming her Tracey. T-R-A-C-E-Y."

"You got a name for your baby, Liz?" Tilly asked.

"No."

"I have a baby name book if you want to use it."

"No, that's okay."

"Then you do have a name?"

"No . . . I'm not gonna need a name."

"You can't not name your baby."

"I'm not keeping my baby, Tilly," I said. Tilly stopped biting her nails and stared at me. I looked at the snow—it had started again—pouring outside through the window behind her.

"Why? Your parents won't let you?"

"No . . . I don't want to keep it."

"Listen to this shit, she don't even want her own baby," Deanna said.

Tilly put her arm on mine and asked, "What are you doing with it, then?"

"I'm giving it up for adoption. I'm too young to have a baby."

Deanna snickered. "Says fucking who? If you were too young to have a baby, you wouldn't be able to get pregnant." She was sitting up in her chair now, paying attention. Nellie took her taped glasses off her face and looked at me. They were all looking at me. Like I was some sort of freak. Someone who would actually choose to give up their baby? Deanna looked down at her belly and said,

"Yeah, well, I ain't going through all this shit to not have anything at the end. I ain't giving my baby to no one."

Nellie chimed in. "Yeah, you are, you got more time in juvie, girl, you'll be giving that baby to someone when it comes."

"I'm trying to get my sister to take the baby till I get out."

"Your sister ain't old enough, Deanna. You know that."

"Well I ain't giving it to some family I don't know and never seeing it again, not gonna happen."

Amy turned and asked me, "Will you get to meet the people that adopt your baby? I mean, can you choose them?"

"I don't know. I think I get to know about them. I mean, they get to know about me. But I'll be finding out more when I talk to Ms. Graham this week." Deanna scowled at the mention of her name.

"So you don't know who is adopting your baby, Liz?" Tilly asked.

"There's an adoption agency. They have all sorts of husbands and wives who can't have babies who might want my baby. My parents told me there are a whole lot of people in the world who really want to have kids and can't."

"Do *you* know anyone who's adopted?" Tilly asked.

"Yeah, my three cousins, and my sister's best friend Carrie."

"What are they like?" Nellie asked. Suddenly everyone had a lot of questions. "Are your cousins creepy? Do they seem like they don't belong there?"

"Why, because they're adopted? No, they're just my cousins. They're cool. I mean, I never even think about that they're adopted. My aunt and uncle got all of them when they were like two days old. So you know, they're family, just like the rest of us."

"I wouldn't want to be adopted." Deanna shook her head. "I'd want to know my people, see my mother, know where I fucking come from."

Nellie looked deep in thought—it seemed like she might be starting to get it, how someone could choose to do this—and then she turned to Deanna.

"Would you rather be adopted into some family who wants you real bad, where you know you'll live forever? Or go from one foster home to another, waiting for your mom to come get you, but she never makes it?" There was a long silence. Deanna didn't say anything.

"Were you in a foster home?" I asked Nellie.

"Yeah, a ton of 'em. It fucking sucked. I moved from bad place to bad place almost every year till I was nine."

"And then your mom came for you?"

"No, my grandparents came. Then my mom ended up there later. She was always in and out of trouble, couldn't keep her shit together."

Amy finally chimed in. "So if you're adopted, does the government give the people money? No, right? That would be better 'cause of all the shit-foster families who do it for the money. But I wouldn't have wanted to be adopted without my little sister. We were a team. We got separated once, into two foster families for more than a year, worst year of my life."

Amy got me thinking. So much of how I fit in the world came from how I fit in my family—my mom, my dad, my siblings. It was my place, my reliable constant. I'd always thought being with your family was the one thing that could never change. But I'd suddenly learned that wasn't true, not for everyone.

* * * *

After dinner that night, *The Wizard of Oz* came on TV. Most of the other girls hadn't seen it before. We brought our pillows and blankets to the lounge, and I brought out the rest of the SweeTarts and pretzels from my room. The girls were mesmerized, watching the scary flying monkeys tormenting Dorothy and the scarecrow. Just as the wicked witch was plotting her scheme, watching Dorothy and Toto in the little glass globe, we heard the door squeak open. Elaine walked in. Her long black hair was in a bun on the top of her head. She looked pale, and her big pregnant stomach from that morning was gone. Her stepmother trailed in behind her, yakking about Elaine moving too slowly. Elaine stopped in the middle of the room. "Bye, you guys," she said.

Amy and Wren got up and hugged her. Tilly walked over, took her hand, and said she was sorry about the baby. Elaine started crying, and then Tilly started crying too. And then Elaine said, "I guess God knew I'd make a shitty mother, so he took her from me."

The room went silent. The stepmother had gone to Elaine's room. She came back a while later, carrying Elaine's suitcase and stuffed bear.

"Come on, Elaine, let's go," she said. The woman reminded me of a carnival version of Cruella de Vil. She had on plastic red Barbie shoes and a fake leopard fur overcoat. She reeked of perfume. Elaine took the stuffed bear from under her stepmother's arm and walked over to Wren.

"Here, take him, and take care of yourself, Wren." Wren looked up, with her long scar running down her face and her big sad eyes. She held the bear by the paw and dangled it at her side, which made her look even younger than she was. She was only a kid—all of us were. Elaine patted Wren's pregnant stomach, one last time, and left. On the television, Dorothy had closed her eyes. She was clicking her heels and saying, "There's no place like home, there's no place like home."

chapter 7

"I appreciate you being so prompt, Liz, it's very considerate."
Ms. Graham was sitting at her desk, same look on her face,
same tweed suit, same tall glass of water halfway filled, sitting on
the wooden coaster in front of her legal pad. Since I was a little
girl, my father had been drilling the significance of being on time
into my young, malleable mind. To Lee, lateness was a crime of
disrespect—it was *robbing* people of their own time for you to be
late.

"You're welcome," I said.

"You look well. How are you doing?"

"Fine."

"You're adjusting?"

"I guess." I swallowed hard, twirling the pass in my pocket
round and round. Ms. Graham was writing something down on
the legal pad. I didn't really feel like talking. I felt like coiling up in a
ball and disappearing. Ever since it happened, a week ago, I'd been
imagining Elaine's baby drowning in the water in her stomach, or

getting its neck bent while Elaine slept in the wrong position, or getting the stomach flu and choking on its own throw up. There was so much that could go wrong, so much that overwhelmed me about the process. We sat for several minutes before it came out of my mouth. "How did Elaine's baby die?" I said.

Ms. Graham put her pencil down. "She had what they call a stillborn child. In her case they believe it had to do with an abnormality the baby had from the beginning. It is terribly unfortunate, a sad, sad situation." I looked down at my stomach, then up at Ms. Graham. She kept talking. "Elaine is the first to have this happen in all the years I've been here, Liz. It is extremely uncommon." I wondered why adults hide the truth, as though it will spare young people from some damaging reality. When the fact is that what we make up in our minds is a hundred times worse than the truth could ever be.

I took a deep breath. "I think someone should have told us what happened, a doctor, not the doctor here. But maybe a nurse or Alice, so we could know how it died instead of having to guess. Everyone is really upset."

"You have a good point," Ms. Graham said. "I'll make sure Alice explains to the girls what went on, so they know."

"Do they bury the baby and have a funeral for it?"

"Yes," Ms. Graham said. I'd also imagined receptacles at the hospital for babies who didn't make it, and rooms where the mothers of those babies go to wail and cry in the dark. I fought to get the picture of the dead baby out of my mind. It had haunted me all week.

"Elaine will be okay, Liz. She's young and healthy." Right, I thought. And hates her stepmother, and wanted the baby girl she named Angel so badly she ran away and lived on the streets so they wouldn't make her have an abortion. We both waited in the sad quiet before I asked, "When will you know who is going to adopt this baby?"

"Your baby?"

"Yeah."

"Well, we actually put some calls out and have found several couples who might be a good match. There is a lot of interest from people all over."

"Why?"

"Because you're healthy, and you come from a nice family, that kind of thing."

"Will I be meeting the people?"

"No, no, it will be a closed adoption. But I will be a part of the interviewing process and can share some things with you."

"Could some of these people adopt the other girls' babies too?"

"They could, I suppose. But none of the other girls are giving up their babies." Ms. Graham opened the desk drawer and pulled out a cream-colored folder. "Some of the folks have asked to know a few things about the father."

"Daniel," I said. I hadn't said his name aloud in weeks.

"Yes, Daniel. You don't talk about him much."

"He's in college. I mean we try to see each other as much as we can, but he's kind of far away. And after I go to college, we probably won't stay together. He feels really bad about all this, but he also doesn't get it. He's busy at school. I mean it's hard to explain what it's like here."

"I see," she said. "Tell me a little bit about Daniel."

I thought about Daniel, and the first time we met and how young I was, and how incredibly long ago it now felt.

I met Daniel in the cafeteria at school when I was almost fifteen years old. He was my first real boyfriend, and I adored him. Daniel was one of those people who had an extra skip in his step, all the time. He was a blast to be around, funny and sweet. He had a way of turning everything we did into something we would remember. That's just who he was. There was a day last summer, when I was sixteen, a boiling hot, boring day. We were driving around the neighborhood with nothing to do. Dan decided to pull a U-turn and parked the car on the side of the road near the lake. I'd never been to that section of Lake Michigan, and I was whining about it being so rocky. He took my hand, and we walked out onto these big rocks along the water. He told me to close my eyes for a minute. When I opened them he was standing on a huge lone flat rock at the very edge of the water with his hands up in the air. It looked like he was floating in the sky with the water behind him. We sat on the flat rock for hours, doing what we did best, talking and laughing. He kept looking out at the water and telling me he wanted to go to a million different places all over the world with me. And I remember thinking we didn't need to go anywhere. He took a hundred pictures of me that day. Most of them with my hands stretched out in front of my face trying to get him to stop.

"Daniel . . . He has a really great family," I said. "He likes to ski, he played football in high school, and he loves music." It felt impossible to describe who Dan was, and how well we got along. Ms. Graham probably thought I was some kind of have-sex-with-anyone slut girl. I wanted to tell her I wasn't. I wanted to tell her I regretted it, that I wished Daniel and I had talked about having sex. Had we planned some special time for it, maybe all this wouldn't have happened. But it wasn't like that, we didn't have sex routinely, and we didn't talk about it. Daniel hadn't asked me about my period, or the sex, or my body changing. We were clueless and stupid. I'd gone over it a thousand times in my head since that day in my dad's wife's doctor's office, when I heard the ocean-rolling heartbeat. My regret was enormous.

"Do you have any thoughts about what kind of people you'd like to adopt the baby?" Ms. Graham asked.

I had no idea what to say. "I guess I'd like them to be . . . nice." That was a stupid thing to say. I looked down at the floor and watched as it slowly blurred from my tears. I'd cried more in a couple weeks than I had in my entire lifetime.

"I am sorry, Liz, I know this is a lot for you."

"Whatever."

"No, not whatever, this is obviously upsetting. And I want to help if I can." But she couldn't—no one could. I wished I could put a roadblock up at the front entrance of my mind to stop all the new things coming in that were too hard. That I didn't want to know. Ms. Graham handed me the box of tissues.

"We can take this slowly, Liz, over the weeks. There's no reason you have to think about the adoptive parents right this second, all right?" There was a light knock at the door. I turned to see the guard, Chief, peeking her head in.

"Oh, sorry, didn't know you had a visitor." She looked over at me and smiled her nice smile. "Hey, girl, you all right? Ms. Graham treatin' you good?"

I looked down at my lap and squeezed out a "Yes." Ms. Graham stepped out of the room with Chief. I was frozen, my brain was screaming *stop*. It didn't want to think about dead babies or kids living on the streets with no one to care about them, or strangers taking home the baby in my stomach. I asked God or anything that might be listening to help me find a way to be brave. I closed my eyes and asked the tears to stop—I promised them I'd think about the bad stuff another time. I noticed the back of a picture frame sitting on Ms. Graham's desk. I turned it around to see a picture of a young girl with a man in a park. I sensed it wasn't a happy picture. I turned it back around and noticed a book sitting next to it. The jacket read *Sophie's Choice,* in black script writing. I'd seen this book before, at home in my mom's room, or maybe in her car.

"That's a great story," Ms. Graham said as she walked back in the room. "Would you like to borrow the book?"

"I don't know. Maybe."

"Do you like to read?"

"Yes." I shifted my aching body in the chair. I was constantly surprised by the size of my stomach and how it weighed on my back and legs. Then I remembered to ask her, "Why don't they have any books up at school?"

"Well, the facility doesn't have the money to put into the school, so we have to make do. Maryann works for little money, and some of the staff are kind enough to bring supplies and things from home." I wondered why they called it a school at all. Why didn't they just say the girls are going up the hill to nap in a cold room? How in the world my mom got the high school to accept "credits" transferring from that room was impossible to imagine. Ms. Graham was writing something down. She looked up and asked, "How *is* school?"

"It's pretty terrible. I mean, no offense, but it's not school, or anything even like school. Some of the girls don't know how to read. Did you know that? And most of them sleep the whole time we're there because we do nothing for hours."

"The school could use improvements, and, yes, I am aware there are a few girls under the literacy line." I looked at the diplomas in their shiny frames hanging on the wall behind Ms. Graham and then glanced over at her bookshelf. The girls really didn't like Ms. Graham. Maybe their worlds were just too far apart. Ms. Graham was an educated, reserved lady. To me, she seemed a person who wanted to do her job well and help the girls with their lives. But she couldn't seem to get that across in a way that worked. As I thought about it I realized adults are sort of the natural enemy for teenagers anyway, and Ms. Graham was an adult in a position of authority, which was even worse. And then I decided that Ms. Graham for sure didn't have children. She just didn't have that soft/hard I-have-kids-I-have-to-be-both thing about her.

"Is there a public library anywhere around here?" I asked.

"Yes, of course there is, why?"

"I don't know. You could check out books the girls would like, and that way they'd have something to read, or at least something to try to read. No one would have to pay for it."

She looked at me a long moment. "People have to want to learn, Liz."

"I think they want to learn."

"Maryann would disagree."

"They ask *me* to read to them. Nellie is smart. She knows a lot of things but I'm pretty sure she can't read."

"Many of these girls have not been to school regularly. And they aren't interested in learning. Nellie has yet to pass a literacy test. But the purpose of this facility is to offer a safe, comfortable setting for the girls as they wait to give birth. We can't take on their education. We're just not set up for that."

I was confused about everything. I thought I knew so much before all of this started.

"Some of the girls' lives here are unimaginable," Ms. Graham was saying. "I know it is very sad and, honestly, it must be very difficult for you, coming from where you do. But please remember that for some of them, most of them actually, this is a nice place to live. They are happy to be here." She'd said that before. And maybe it was true, but it didn't feel like an answer.

"I was just thinking if Nellie can't read, she could learn. She has nothing else to do," I said.

"You surprise me, Liz." Ms. Graham smiled.

"I don't mean to."

"I know you don't. I will see what I can do about getting more supplies to the school. And, Liz, I spoke to your mom today."

"What? Why?"

"She called to say she wants to come Thursday and keep you out overnight, which is fine. She'll be here when you get out of school that day."

"That's great, thank you," I said. My heart leaped. . . . Thank you, God!

"You miss home?"

"Yes."

"And there are seven children in your family, your mother was telling me?"

"Yep."

"That's a lot of children. Your mom took care of all the kids herself?"

"Yes. Well no, when we were little, we had a woman, an au pair, who lived with us and helped her." I thought back on those years with a new feeling of nostalgia. I was about eight years old when our au pair came to live with us. It felt like forever ago—that life was so unburdened, so simple and steadfast. Our dad took a trip to England in the summer in search of a person to help our mom with the house and the chaos of seven children. He came back with *Helen*. We stood, all of us wide-eyed, in the front entrance of our house, staring at her. She was tall and pretty, with long, light orange hair. She was an unusual combination of gentle and strong at the same time. Dorothy called Helen a saint, Lee deemed her competent, and we all adored her, especially me. Helen had grown up in Scotland and spoke with a thick accent that made us laugh.

My parents gave Helen every other Saturday off. The very first Saturday she was with us, she asked if I'd like to come downtown on the train with her to explore the city. I was so excited I could barely speak. I put on my patent leather party shoes, pulled my fancy coat out from the back of the closet, with the matching beret, and ran downstairs. Helen asked my mom if I could join her for the day and when Dorothy looked up from the newspaper, she was visibly aghast, "For Gooooooooooooood SAKES, Helen, why on earth would you want to bring an eight-year-old with you? Liz, let Helen go have fun with people of her own age, for crying out loud."

In the thick accent, Helen gently responded, "Oh, Mrs. Pryor, I very much would like to bring her. I would be grateful for her company." Imagine that, Helen wanted *me* to come. I put the knit beret on my head, smiled a sassy smile at my mom, and we set off for the Winnetka train station. Dorothy shouted as we left, "You're out of your *mind*, Helen!" The beautiful North Shore suburbs zoomed by as the train headed to downtown Chicago. There was a large crew of young sailors wearing crisp white sailor suits and hats in our train car. Several of them whistled loudly as Helen and I walked by. I looked over and one of them smiled at me.

"Why are they whistling, Helen?" I asked.

"Sailors whistle like that when they see beautiful little girls," she said. And I believed her. I looked down at my white tights and party shoes, smoothed my coat, and smiled to myself. We spent dozens of Saturdays together over the next few years, exploring different parts of the city around my home, places I didn't even know existed. Helen slowly took over a small corner of my heart that I knew would remain a part of me forever. I wondered what she'd think of me now.

* * * *

I jolted back to the present, in Ms. Graham's office.

"Large families are fascinating to me," she was saying. "I am an only child."

What? That was the first human-person thing I'd ever heard her say. I couldn't imagine Ms. Graham as a kid. She was one of those adults who had completely shed every trace of being young from every part of who she was.

"I bet you got to spend a lot of time with your mom," I said.

"What do you mean?"

"Well, you didn't have to share your mom with brothers and sisters. You got her all to yourself."

"I suppose you're right. I never thought of that." Something swooped over her face just for a moment—and then it was gone. I suddenly wanted to know more about Ms. Graham. Why did she wear such sad-looking suits every day? Why did the girls really dislike her so much? And why did she smile so rarely? I'd only seen two half smiles and maybe one full one in all the time I'd spent with her.

* * * *

It was killer, bitter, burning cold when I went outside after my session. The ground was still snowy from the blizzard a few days before. The wind was crushing. I could barely see a foot in front of me, but strangely, I liked the feeling. Only the cold could make everything disappear from my head, all the fears and worries. I walked and walked until my nose and fingers were numb. I'd taken a shower late that morning, and my hair hadn't completely dried. I could feel it freezing up into clumps, like it did once on a family ski trip to Colorado. I slowly made my way back around the building and toward the entranceway. I hadn't lasted very long. I leaned my whole body on the red button, hoping Chief would be right there to buzz me in, and she was. There was a loud suctioning sound when the air met the cold and then the door slammed hard behind me.

Chief was sitting in her usual spot at the desk behind the fence, glued to a soap opera playing on the small-screen TV.

"I told you, crazy girl, it's a cold one out there."

"Yeah, it's so cold it hurts." I leaned against the fence between us and shook the snow off my coat and shoes. My hair had clumped into frozen heavy chunks.

"Ever seen icicle hair, Chief?"

She looked carefully at my frozen hair. "I never seen that before, must be a white girl thing."

"I don't know. I think it's a go-out-in-the-cold-with-wet-hair thing." She was about to say something but then she put her hand flat up against the fence and shushed me. She reached over and turned up the TV, scooched her chair closer, and leaned in about five inches from the blaring screen. She loved her soap opera. When a commercial finally came on, she turned around toward me.

"Chrrriiiissssstttt Almighty, Luke just might cheat on Laura. You know Laura, these two been meant for each other since the beginning of time. She loves him. He's her man. But she's been gone now for a long time. Her nosy bitch aunt made her leave Port Charles, trying to keep them apart, kill their love, you believe that? But real love is too strong, yes it is. Luke is dying inside, thinks she doesn't care anymore, but she does. And now the nasty slut neighbor woman is goin' after him." Chief talked about them like real people she knew. The show came back on. The beautiful young woman on the tiny screen made her moves on the guy.

"Maybe he'll say no to the neighbor, Chief," I said.

"He's a *man*, Liz, and that neighbor-skank knows her business."
She was shaking her head and twisting her hands, worried and
nervous.

"Well, I'll see ya, Chief. You'll tell me what happens tomorrow."

I headed down the hallway and a few seconds later heard her
scream, "Don't do it, *Luke!*"

Time felt like something different to me. I could actually feel the
dragging of every minute, almost every second. Life had stopped
all sense of moving from point A to point B. There was nowhere
to go, nowhere to be. All there was to do was wait. My mom used
to say being bored was a sign of low intelligence. Clearly I had
very low intelligence. I was bored beyond reason. Bored out of my
mind. And flabbergasted that the other girls weren't *more* bored. A
day felt like two days, or even three. Five months would no doubt
feel like three years. The slow passing of time was becoming the
hardest part of all. That day I tried to nap some of the time away,
but Tilly barreled into my room. Amy and Nellie trailed behind
her.

"What the hell, where you been?" Tilly said.

"I went for a walk."

"Must be nice to come and go as you please," Tilly said. Amy
picked up my guitar. Nellie poked her finger into one of my wet
ringlets of hair and said, "There's a new girl in the lounge. . . . She's
taking Elaine's spot. Amy has to room with her."

"Poor Elaine," Tilly said. "I can't stop thinking about her baby."
They all went quiet for a second.

Nellie turned to me. "Liz, did you go to see graham cracker
lady?"

"Yeah, I did."

"Why the fuck do you even go there?"

"'Cause, I don't know, I kind of like her."

"You like people asking all about your shit?"

"Sometimes." They were all looking at me, so I changed the subject. "Does someone come get the laundry at some point? All my clothes are dirty."

Nellie burst out laughing so hard she had to sit down.

"What?" I said.

Nellie imitated me. "'Does anyone come and get the laundry?' Like fucking who? Cinderella?"

"Well, I don't know, how do our clothes get cleaned?"

"We clean 'em, dumbass, we put them in this thing called a *washing machine* and then in this other thing called a fucking dryer."

"Very funny, I know what a washing machine is."

"But you never actually used one!"

"Well, no," I admitted. Tilly offered to show me how. I started to gather my dirty clothes. Tilly took the sheets off my bed and systematically stuffed them into the pillowcase. She knew what she was doing. She threw the case over her shoulder, Santa Claus-style. I took change from the cup on the dresser—Tilly told me to—and I followed her out of the room. Nellie and Amy straggled behind. In the lounge, we saw the new girl. She was short and really pregnant, with big dark round eyes. She kind of looked like a creepy porcelain doll. Nellie slowed down and pointed to the new girl, saying, "That's Gina."

Tilly waved, and I said hi. Gina looked up and gave an uninterested nod, like a guy would give. We headed down to the basement and into a room with a few machines, a couple of folding chairs, and a table. Tilly took the coins out of my pocket and bought soap from a funky machine on the wall. She told me to separate the light clothes from the dark.

"Why?"

"'Cause you can't do them together."

"Right. Why?"

"'Cause your dark clothes'll run all over your light clothes and ruin them."

Nellie nodded. "She's a professional, listen to her."

I separated the clothes and then loaded the washers. Tilly showed me which dials to turn and then closed the lids. "That's it?" I asked.

"Yeah, now we wait."

Nellie stood up and circled the small room. "Attention people, Liz P. is doing her laundry. Yep, Liz P., from no one fucking knows where, is cleaning her goddamn clothes." She had her hands cupped around her mouth. They laughed, and I rolled my eyes. Amy and Nellie eventually went next door to the cafeteria for dinner, and Tilly and I sat down in the folding chairs, waiting for the load of laundry to finish.

"So, where *are* you from?" Tilly said. "I mean I know it's all secret and stuff, but I won't tell anyone. I swear to God I won't."

"Who told you I was hiding here?"

"Well, no one exactly. I mean Amy overheard Alice talking to graham cracker before you came, and then . . . well, they knew we knew, so they told us."

"Told you what?"

"They said you would be coming to live here because you didn't want anyone to know where you were. And that we weren't to ask you *any* questions about yourself. It was Nellie who figured out the rich girl part. So are you from somewhere like California?"

"No."

"Damn, I want to know what California is like. You ever been there?"

"No, I'm from Chicago."

"Oh, that's pretty far away."

"I guess."

"Do you live in one of those big city buildings?"

"No, no, I'm from a suburb, we live in a house. What about you?"

"Oh, I lived in a lot of places, never a house. Always around here somewhere, never been anywhere else. Tell me about your life, Liz. What's it like?" Her eyes got big.

"It's just a life," I said. I didn't know what to say, it was just normal to me.

"Come on, give me somethin'. What's your bedroom like?"

"A room with a bed."

"*Liz.*" Tilly was impatient. "What color is it? What does it have in it?"

"Okay. It's light blue and white, I guess, it has a brass bed, and a makeup table at the window. Eyelet curtains, the wallpaper has little flowers, there's a desk."

"Jesus shit—I wish I could see it."

"Yeah, it's nice."

"Do you have a backyard at your house?"

"Uh-huh, a big one. We used to have a horse in it, actually."

"What the hell, really? Do you live on a fucking farm?"

"No, just a regular house in a regular neighborhood, kinda weird that we had a horse. We moved into this house when my parents got divorced five years ago. My mom is the most *non-*animal person in the world, she can't even pet the dog. So she finds this great house with a big backyard, that has a pond, and swings and a barn and a *horse.* The house came with the horse."

"The house came with a goddamn horse?"

"Yeah, and no one in my family knew anything about horses, I mean nothing. None of us knew shit!"

"So why'd she get a house with a horse, then?"

I'd never thought about that before. I was suddenly noticing a bunch of things about my life that had never seemed strange or remarkable before, but I saw now that they clearly were. "I have no idea. Maybe because she liked the house?"

"Is it a nice house?"

"Yeah, really nice."

"What's the horse's name?"

"Scooter. He was brown with a long white line running down his nose. So we move in, and we're all excited about the barn and the horse but we have no idea what or how to do anything. So there's this neighbor girl we meet, Leann. She comes over one day and tells us she loves and knows everything about horses. I mean she knew *everything,* how to bridle and saddle him and clean and feed him and take care of the barn. She was so good with the horse. But when she wasn't there, Scooter was feisty. It's like the horse knew when Leann wasn't around and he behaved badly . . . and mean."

"It's because horses are smart and have to trust the people around them."

"Really?"

"I mean, yeah, I know that from this show I watched on TV. If you're scared of the horse, the horse knows it, so then it takes over like *it's* the boss. I can't believe you had a fucking horse at your house. Why'd you get rid of it? 'Cause it was mean?"

"Kind of. After a while Scooter's barn was like knee-high in horse poop and old hay. We'd grown tired of it all, and Leann stopped coming by so much. So one morning at like five A.M., Scooter got out of the gate that kept him in the field and barn area and was eating the leaves off the tree between our house and the neighbor's house, just chomping away, walking around the yard."

"Shit," Tilly said. Her eyes went so wide they looked like they might pop out of her face. She'd cozied up close to me on the chair and was looking at me like she was watching a scary movie. I continued the story.

"So the old lady neighbor calls on the phone. She asks my mom to get the horse off her tree. My mom wakes us up and asks us to get Scooter back in the barn, but none of us wanted to do it, we were too scared. We were arguing, shouting at each other back and forth until my mom got so mad she said she'd just do it herself. She went outside in her little blue nightgown. She's a small lady, much littler than me, like five foot two. She's never been around a horse. So she's standing kind of behind Scooter, making the come-here-horsey sound, trying to get him back in the field. Then the horse picks up its hind leg and kicks my mom so hard in the chest she flies a few feet back and then lands on the ground. I thought she was dead."

"HOLY SHIT."

"My sisters and I screamed, like really screamed. We go running down the stairs and outside to help her. We were so freaked. We called our grandfather and he came right over, put Scooter in the barn, and took our mom to the hospital."

"Was your mom okay?"

"Yeah, she broke a rib I think. She had bruises everywhere. The next day my grandfather came back over with a horse truck, walked Scooter up onto the ramp, didn't say anything to any of us, and we never saw Scooter again."

Tilly was looking at me in awe. Nellie peeked her head in the laundry room with a mouth full of food.

"What's going on?" Nellie asked. "What are you doing? Is Liz telling a story?"

Tilly turned to her. "You missed it."

"Fuck, was it a good one?"

"It was the best one I've heard."

"Fuck you both. You're telling me that fucking story later, you hear me, Liz?" Nellie left, and we switched the clothes from the washers to the dryers. Tilly and I headed to the nearly empty cafeteria. Dinner was almost over. Tilly grabbed a disgusting-looking sandwich, and then the woman behind the counter loaded her up with something that resembled macaroni and cheese with brown chunks in it. I took milk and spread peanut butter onto a piece of stale white bread—it was still the only thing I could stand. We sat at the end of one of the tables while the cafeteria lady swept the floor around us.

"Your life sounds exciting," Tilly said. The yellow mac and cheese thing smelled so bad I couldn't eat my peanut butter.

"It's not exciting. Maybe compared to here, but it's just normal."

"Come on, it's not fucking normal. Horses, ponds, tree swings. Get real, Liz. That's not normal."

"Well, I'll tell you what's not normal, Till, is the fucking food here."

"What, this? You never had mac and cheese with chunks of cat food in it?"

"*Tilly,* so gross, oh my God."

"Well *they* call it mac and cheese with tuna. We call it 9Lives mac-shit. You get used to it. Here, try a bite." She waved the chunk of cat food on her fork in my face and laughed at my reaction.

"What, it doesn't smell great to you? You just have to try it, Liz."

She got up and started chasing me around the room with the fork of smelly food. I ducked under a table. We were laughing our asses off. The cafeteria lady told us to be quiet and leave. Tilly stopped, put her hand on her hip, and said, "Simmer yourself, Jeanette . . . we're just havin' a laugh." Jeanette tried to shoo us out with the broom. "Just trying to get her to take a bite of your famous 9Lives mac and cheese," Tilly said.

Jeanette fired back, "That is some grade A tuna in there, young lady."

"Oh yeah, grade A? Did you hear that, Liz?" We ran out, still laughing. I started to head for the stairs. Tilly pulled on my sweater. "Did you forget something?"

"What?"

"First *fucking* rule of laundry—don't forget it!"

We went back to the laundry room and pulled the warm clothes out of the dryer. Tilly grabbed a shirt, made sure I was watching, and then laid it on the table and carefully flattened out the wrinkles with her forearm. Then, like a hotel chambermaid, she folded the sleeves in just so, folded the shirt in half, and then in half again. She did that several times at the speed of light, and in seconds all my clothes were folded. She placed them back in the clean pillowcase, handed it to me, and bowed.

"Impressive. Thanks, Till."

"My cousin used to work in a laundromat so it's one thing I know how to do. Problem is, I don't have enough clothes to have to do it for myself." She laughed. I thought about her one shirt, and laughed. Next thing I knew, we were stopped in the hall, doubled over laughing. It was like when my sisters and I would start giggling in church and couldn't stop. It went on for several minutes. I tried to get ahold of myself, but it was no use—we were having a full-on laughing attack. Every time we looked at each other we busted up. I finally made it back to my room, panting and exhausted. In all our laughing, for the first time in weeks, I'd forgotten about the bad stuff. I felt something I recognized from before—joy. And I wanted to hang on to it. I wanted to remember it, to hold it, to make sure it was real. But I just sat there for a moment, and felt it. Tilly had sparked something inside me. For the very first time, I began to believe that I might be okay at the end of all this.

I watched the snow pouring down outside the window and noticed the outline of the circle I'd made earlier on the glass. I drew with my finger two eyes and a slight smiling mouth. And then I felt something weird going on in my stomach—not a pain, but a nudge. I lifted up my sweater, looked down at my big belly, and noticed something pushing from the inside. My stomach stuck out in one little spot. I softly held my finger against the nudge. It went away and then it came back. I pushed it again, and it pushed back. There was a baby in there, moving around. And for the first time I realized, I really didn't want it to die.

chapter 8

A few days later, the girls were sleeping, but I was awake. It was late at night. I sat alone in the quiet phone booth. It felt like years of life had passed since I'd spoken to Daniel. There was screaming and music blaring through the other end of the phone. The music got louder as I waited for Daniel to come to the phone.

"Liz?" he said. "Hey, how you doing? How is it?" My throat tightened. Maybe it was the phone booth—the place I'd cried so many times before—or maybe it was the sound of real life happening far away, without me. I ignored the tears as they rolled down my cheeks.

"It's okay," I said.

"I can barely hear you."

"It's okay." I raised my voice.

"Where *is* the place?"

"I'm in Indiana somewhere."

"Shit, hang on." There were voices, and then I heard Daniel laugh. "Sorry, sorry, they're having this stupid party thing on the hall. Remember my friend Aaron? He's such a bonehead. He filled these trash cans with grain alcohol and Hawaiian Punch. Everyone is wasted."

The lightbulb was flickering on the ceiling of the phone booth. "Oh yeah, I remember him."

"Sorry. So what's it like? You okay? Shit, hang on, yeah I know, shithead. Wait, Liz, what did you say?"

"Nothing. You sound busy, Daniel. . . ."

"No, no, it's fine. We just finished midterms so everyone's crazy."

"I guess I just wanted to say hi." There was an awkward silence. I felt how starkly our lives had diverged.

"*Coming, man.* Sorry, I guess I should maybe call you tomorrow or something. I'm on the hall phone here, ya know?"

"It's okay, I get it."

"I'm sorry about all this, Liz."

"It's fine, I'll talk to you later."

I hung up the phone and looked down at the names and initials scratched into the wooden counter where the phone sat and wondered about all the girls who had come and gone.

I'd stopped counting exactly how many mornings had passed. Since I didn't know exactly when I was leaving, it was pointless. I rarely knew what day it was, because it didn't matter anymore. I had nowhere to go. I'd come to accept that this was my life, for now. It felt like the longest point A to point B I'd ever have to experience. There were a few unavoidable realities: I was going nowhere until the baby came. I would never feel like the person I used to be. And perhaps I *would* survive. I was beginning to understand that the experience of the facility would be a part of me forever. But my forever still felt like a pretty good thing. I had a lot waiting for me, and even more to look forward to. Most of the girls had no idea what their forever was even kind of going to look like. Many had to go back to juvie without their babies, a few had nowhere to go, and most of them didn't have people in their lives like I had—people who could help remind them that everything would eventually be okay.

· · · ·

My strange bulging body had gotten all tangled in my big T-shirt during the night. I kept my eyes shut as I struggled out of it and made my way to the dresser. I ignored the person in the bathroom mirror with the swollen boobs and sullen face. The lounge was dark and empty when I came through. The girls must have all gone to breakfast. The TV was blaring in the empty room. I walked over and flipped it off.

"Hey," a voice said. I turned around. Wren was sitting in the corner by the window.

"Oh, sorry, I didn't see you."

"It's fine, leave it off."

"You all right?"

"I don't feel so good," she said, making a face. Just then, weeble-wobble Alice hurried through the door with her loud ring of keys, carrying a big pile of newspapers and paper towels.

"Well, well, well. The two girls who shouldn't miss breakfast the most are sitting here in the dark. Perfect, juuuuust perfect." She turned on the bright lights, grabbed a chair, and moved it near the chore board. "I'm assigning new chores, and I mean it that you girls gotta do them before school. No one listens to me around here."

"Wren doesn't feel well," I said to Alice.

"Come here, Wren," Alice said. "Am I so bad you can't talk to me yourself?"

". . . Kind of," Wren said. I admired Wren's honesty. She, like most of the girls, said exactly what she thought. There was no guessing with them.

"Come on, that's not true. You can always come to me. What's the problem?"

"I'm bleeding."

"Bleeding bleeding?"

"Yeah."

"Okay, no problem. Liz, walk her down to the nurse for me, okay? And grab some food on your way. You girls have no idea how much better you'd feel if you ate your gosh-darned meals every day."

Wren and I headed out down to the basement. The nurse with the beehive told us to wait in the exam room for the doctor. It was the creepy room, with no windows. Wren's scar looked more purple against her pale face in the strangely dark room. She ran her finger over the scar. I tried not to notice, but she looked at me.

"You want to know how it happened?"

"Okay." I really did, actually.

"My mom fell asleep at the wheel, but I didn't die like some other people."

"Does it hurt?"

"No, it used to, it's just numb now. You ever been in a car accident?"

I flashed back in my mind.

I was about five years old and our whole family was getting ready to go ice-skating. My mom was flying around the house, trying to gather hats and coats and mittens, frantically piling ice skates at the front door. We kids walked circles around each other, searching for our things. Her friend was about to arrive in the big VW van with her own six kids to pick all of us up. We heard the loud familiar honk blasting from outside. Dorothy was crazed with so many of us—throwing coats, tying boots, wrapping scarves around necks, pushing us one after another out the door. I was the last one. She pulled me back by the hood of my puffy snowsuit and turned me around. In three seconds flat she tied the hood under my chin so hard I almost choked.

"Mom . . . ouch!"

"There," she said. "And keep it tied, a warm head makes a warm child." I waddled down the steps in my snowsuit and red snow boots and climbed into the van behind all the other kids. There were no seats left, so I sat on the floor with a few of the others. We were off, the van speeding down the street. The kids were bickering and pushing in the back—there were so many of us. I sat on the floor and tried to pull my too-tight hood off. Suddenly, we took a sharp right turn. A few kids fell off their seats, and out of nowhere the van door flew all the way open. I could see the street and houses outside buzzing by and then, like a Lincoln Log, I rolled out of the van and onto the street. Lying on my side, very still, all I could see were two headlights moving toward me. I closed my eyes so I didn't have to watch if I got squashed. But I guess the car stopped in time.

"Lizzie? Lizzie, can you hear me?" I opened my eyes and saw my mom kneeling over me on the road. She had a rare look of panic on her face.

"I think so," I said.

"Thank Goooooodddddd." Dorothy scooped me up and carried me with both arms out in front of her, like a sacrificial offering. She marched up to the nearest house, banged on the door with her boot, and asked the woman if we could come inside. She sat me down and checked my legs and arms and neck and back and feet, and then she looked at my face. I was holding my cheek in my hand. She untied the hood, pulled my hand off my cheek, and found a big scrape on the side of my face. She turned to the lady whose house we were in.

"May we please borrow a stick of butter?"

She unwrapped one end and then held it like a big fat crayon and began coloring my cheek with it.

"There," she said. "You're going to be just fine. You could have cracked your head open, Liz. Your snowsuit saved your life; thank you for keeping your hood on."

. . . .

I looked at Wren and the long scar on her face.

"I fell out of a car once. I mean, I guess that's an accident in a car. I rolled out of a van."

"You get hurt?"

"Not really."

"When I'm older I can have an operation to make this scar not so bad."

"I don't think it's too bad."

The doctor finally walked in. Wren grabbed my hand. I could tell she was scared.

"Which one of you is bleeding?" Wren raised her hand. He pointed to me and told me to wait outside. A few minutes later, Wren came out almost smiling.

"It's fine," she said. "It's normal, he said sometimes people have see-through, or breakthrough, something bleeding. . . ."

"So he didn't have to do anything?"

"Nope."

Thank God. One less thing to worry about.

· · · ·

Later that morning Tilly asked me, "What happened to Wren?" She was sitting in her usual spot, in the lounge.

"She's fine, she had some bleeding. Dr. Dick said it's normal."

Alice was marching around the room, trying to get the girls to do chores. Nellie put her hands on her hips in defiance.

"Alice, I ain't fuckin' changing lightbulbs. Go ask the doctor, see what he'd say, I'm not gettin' on no ladder."

"It's a step stool, Nellie, and watch your attitude." I was still floored at the way the girls spoke to the adults. Alice continued, "Now, all you guys, get on outta here and go to school. None of you keeps track of the time. You're like babies yourselves."

· · · ·

It was still cold, and snow still covered the grounds. Going up to school felt like entering a time-passing torture chamber. Maryann sat reading by herself, and most of the girls were nodding off as usual. Tilly handed me a piece of paper.

"Let's do that thing we did the other day, Liz. You put the letters in." She was talking about word searches; I'd made a few for the girls, just like the ones in the books my mom brought for us on long car rides. The waiting reminded me of how I'd hated waiting for anything else in life, times a thousand. After more doing nothing, three hours later, we were heading back down the hill. Tilly and I held Nellie's arms to make sure she didn't fall and roll down the hill. When we were back inside the facility building, Nellie hollered, as usual, "Yo, CHIEF, whattttt isssss up?"

Chief turned to us and flashed a big smile. "Well look who it is, the three pregnant stooges. Liz, you got a very white-lookin' visitor in Ms. Graham's office."

"Is her mom here?" Tilly asked.

"It's either her mom or the goddamn queen of England." My stomach dropped from excitement. I'd almost forgotten. The door to Ms. Graham's office opened.

"I want to meet her first," Nellie said.

"Fuck that, I'm meeting her first," Tilly said.

"Girls, language, *please*, you can both meet her." Ms. Graham stepped out in the hall, then my mom stepped out behind her. She had on her long red Ralph Lauren wool coat with the black velvet collar and a studded brooch pinned to the lapel. Her black patent leather boots shined under the fluorescent lights. She *did* look like a queen. She looked at me and smiled. I walked over and hugged her; she squeezed me hard.

"Hi, Liz," she said. I couldn't believe she was really here.

"Hi, Mom." She held my face with both hands and then hugged me again. Her eyes moved to Tilly, and then to Nellie. I turned to follow her gaze, and suddenly it was like I was seeing them for the first time too. I saw Nellie's boils again, the way they covered her whole face. Part of Tilly's naked belly was sticking out the bottom of her shirt, her big floppy shoes were untied, and you could barely see her eyes through her long, stringy bangs. Dorothy looked back at me; I smiled.

"Mom, I want you to meet these guys. This is Tilly, and this is Nellie."

Dorothy tried to hide her shock. I could tell what she was thinking. She took a deep breath and responded, long and slow, "Well, hellooo girls, it is veeeeerrrry nice to meet both of you."

"Holy shit, you look just like Liz but older, how you doin'?" Nellie blurted out.

"I'm verrrry wellll, thank you, and you?"

"Me? I guess I'm okay except for this big-ass stomach of mine." Nellie patted the top of her stomach, and then took the broken taped glasses off her face and started to clean them with her shirt. Dorothy looked away.

"Liz, dear, why don't we gather your things for tonight? We'll be staying at a hotel, you'll need some clothes. Ms. Graham has gotten me all caught up."

We all stood for an awkward moment, until Tilly grabbed Nellie's hand and said, "We gotta get back. You coming to the lounge, Liz?"

"Yeah, Till, we'll be there in a minute." Dorothy watched as Nellie and Tilly padded down the hall. A random "fuck" and then "shit" came out of Nellie's mouth as they walked away.

"What a *vulgar*-mouthed child," my mother finally said.

"Come on, Mom," I said. "I'll show you my room and stuff." While we walked through the halls, she was thinking so loudly, I could almost hear her. The click, click, click of her boots echoed through the corridors. The cement walls felt different with Dorothy here in them. Two worlds were colliding, and I was stuck somewhere between them. I was all jumbled up inside. We reached the open door of the lounge. The girls were sitting in their usual spots, most of them smoking. Wren was leaning against the wall. Dorothy recoiled at the sight of her scar, and then Wren almost smiled, which was rare.

"Mom, this is Wren," I said. Dorothy looked down at her with a sad smile, lifted her eyebrows, and said, "Helllloooo, Wren."

Wren got out a quiet "Hi."

Deanna was sitting on the La-Z-Boy in a tube top and sweats, her pregnant belly hanging out. She was holding a Dr Pepper and a cigarette. She didn't look over. Gina, the new porcelain doll girl, sat on the couch. Amy looked up from the TV. "Hey," she said.

"Mom, that's Amy."

"How do you do, Amy," Dorothy said.

Deanna glanced over at us with a rancid face. "What the fuck does *that* mean, 'how do you do'?" My heart dropped. I wasn't sure I could handle this.

Dorothy stayed still for a moment and then unbuttoned a few buttons on her coat and looked straight at Deanna. "That means . . . *nice to meet you.*" Dorothy stepped a few feet closer to the La-Z-Boy and pointedly asked Deanna, "And . . . *who* are *you*?"

Deanna rustled in the chair a bit and answered, "Deanna."

With a forced, perfect smile Dorothy said, "*How do you do, Deanna.*" Jesus Christ—were my mom and Deanna gonna go at it? Dorothy slipped her coat off and placed it over her arm. All eyes were on her. She straightened her shoulders to make herself taller than her five feet and almost two inches.

Deanna was quiet for once. I quickly veered my mom out of the lounge and into the hall.

In my room, Dorothy looked around. "Ahhh, well, it's quite nice really. It's clean and has some room. Did they supply all that?" She pointed to the burner and food piled on the dresser.

"No, no, Kate sent that. . . ." But the second I said it, I regretted it.

"Your father's *wife* sent you that?"

"Mom, it's no big deal."

"Did you *ask* her to send it to you?"

"Well, I asked you to bring me stuff, but you said you weren't coming to see me. So when I spoke to them, she asked if I needed anything and . . ."

"I see." Dorothy got the look, the pursed-lips-I'm-gonna-fucking-kill-someone, but-I'm-not-going-to-say-anything, I'm-just-going-to-keep-it-all-here-in-my-face look.

"Why don't you get your things together," she said. I took some clothes and shoved them into a tote. Dorothy peeked inside the bathroom. "That's right, you needed some towels, you said, so did *she* send those to you as well?" She pointed to the nice plush bath towels. God, why did I mention Kate? I should have just lied. Even in the middle of nowhere Indiana, I was caught between my mom and dad.

. . . .

Dorothy's blue Chevy Malibu was parked in the same spot she'd parked when she first brought me, several weeks ago. I took in the familiar smell of the car. There was a new pile of mess strewn across the dashboard, and I heard a few loud clanks from beneath our seats.

"I apologize for not coming sooner," Dorothy said in a soft voice. "I really do . . . I'm sorry."

"It's okay."

"Are you hungry?"

"*Yes*. I could eat a horse."

"Let's find a restaurant. How about a steak?"

"Anything would be good. Mom, the food here is uneatable."

"You mean *inedible*."

"I mean disgusting, horrible, soooooo gross."

We drove out of the parking lot. The car turned right and I rolled down the window. "Liz, it's *freezing*, roll it up," Dorothy said. I leaned my head all the way out into the open air and shouted.

"No wait." I took a huge breath. I just wanted to feel it. My mom shielded her hair with her hand while I let the cold wind whip my face. I felt the old me surfacing. I was alive and free. In a couple miles, we turned into the driveway of a small hotel with big flags out front. At the restaurant inside, we were seated at a table by a window. The room was swelteringly warm, with the heat turned up too high. Dorothy took her coat off and hung it over the extra chair. I started to take my coat off too.

"Lizzie, keep that on, please," she said.

"What? Why?"

She waited a moment, looked around, and then said in a quiet voice, "You need to keep your *stomach* covered."

"Oh, okay," I said. I was uncomfortably warm in my wool cape coat. We ordered steak, mashed potatoes, and vanilla milkshakes for both of us. Nobody loved vanilla milkshakes more than Dorothy. The waiter brought the shakes over. They had whipped cream on top and came with spoons and striped straws. Dorothy closed her eyes and took a long sip from the straw. In about four seconds she was sure to say something ridiculously melodramatic, and sure enough, she did.

"Now *that* is *pure unadulterated heaven,* is it not?"

I took a sip and nodded.

"I mean, *criminally divine,*" she went on. I kept sipping and smiled. She was wearing the same swirly gold clip-on earrings she always wore. Her hair had been recently done. She always had a beautiful patterned silk scarf somewhere close by; today it was wrapped around her shoulders over her thin black sweater, tied in a loose knot to the side.

"Mom," I said. "You know Nellie, the really big girl you met? She's pregnant with twins. That's why she's so big."

"I see."

"And she also has horrible water-something in her ankles, and she can barely walk sometimes. Did you have that when you were pregnant with the twins? Does that only happen to people who are having twins?"

"I don't know."

"I'm glad I don't have it. Oh, and, Mom, I wanted to tell you that the girl with the scar on her face? Wren, guess what? She's only thirteen years old, almost fourteen but still, she's the twins' age, can you believe that?"

"Tragic."

"She told me how she got the scar, she—"

But then Dorothy put both hands on her head. "Liz, *stop!*" she said. She covered her face with her hands.

"What? Mom?"

"My *God*, sweetheart, please *stop* talking about these girls. Honey, I don't want to know . . ."

"Okay, I'm sorry." She looked at me, and then up at the ceiling, as though she were inviting God into the conversation.

"This may not have been the right decision to bring you here—to live, day in and day out, with these degenerate unfortunate girls." I held my breath. Was Dorothy going to say I should come home?

"I am sorry, Liz, so very sorry. I had no idea it would be like this." She started to cry. I felt guilty and confused at the same time. Maybe I would get to go home and have snow days and a normal life again. She got up from her seat, came around the table, and sat in the chair next to me. She leaned over to hug me. I hugged her back.

"This is terrible," she said, "the whole thing . . . the girl in the lounge, what a frightening *ill-mannered creature*. I wanted to *slap* her right across the face."

"Everyone wants to slap her, Mom. But she was raped by her foster dad, that's how she's pregnant." There was a pause. Dorothy let out a quiet shriek and buried her face in her hands again.

I watched her carefully. I could feel the little beads of sweat falling down my forehead and nose; I was boiling up in my coat.

"You're perspiring, honey," Dorothy said.

"I'm super hot."

"Okay. Take off your coat."

"No, that's okay."

"Liz, take it off."

"You sure? I'll put it in my lap so you can't see my stomach."

Tears flooded her eyes. "No, it's okay, I'm sorry. I don't know why I said that. Please take it off." Dorothy helped me with the coat and threw it over the chair. I wiped the sweat off my face with a napkin.

"*You* are not like those girls, Liz. They are doomed people, and you are not."

Doomed? "Mom, but—"

"You have a beautiful life ahead of you, and I don't want this to mar that for you. You *must* not allow this to change you, to get inside of you. These people are hopeless and ignorant. Their stories are stories you shouldn't even know."

"But I do know them, Mom."

"I don't want you talking to the girls, bonding, sharing about *our* life and family, do you understand?" I nodded. She braced herself and said, "I wish we had another choice for you, but we just don't. We are going to have to be very strong and get through this the best we can."

"Okay." So there it was, I wasn't leaving. I was there for good.

"It's not so much longer that you have to be here."

"It's pretty long, Mom."

"Not in comparison to the rest of your life. It's a small bit of time."

Then she got the look on her face, the look I'd seen many times before. Her determined look. "You *can* get through this, Liz. You just have to find it inside yourself." Dorothy the cheerleader emerged. Her eyes lit up. "You are strong as an ox. You can do this, sweetheart. But you must not forget. You're here for *one* reason, to get this child out of you, *that's it*. Once it's over, you must try to forget about these times, move on, and put it behind you."

I was crying again. She stroked my hair, and I wondered if she knew what she was saying wasn't true. Did she actually believe that? I was never ever going to forget this place, these girls, and these stories. I could already feel it changing the person I was, and there was nothing I could do to stop it. Maybe my mom would never know the gravity of it, but this was something I was learning for myself—on my own.

Dorothy took a deep breath, fixed her scarf, and then took her lipstick out of her purse. Without a mirror, she flawlessly outlined her lips, then smudged them together and smiled at me. I tried to smile back.

"Gather yourself, honey. We're going to be fine, we have to be. Call upon your courage, Liz, and remember, you're only given what you can handle."

· · · ·

When we left the restaurant, my stomach was so full I could barely move. We decided to walk to the shopping center a few blocks away. The cold breeze felt good. I'd been aching for so long for the familiarity of my mother, for a little bit of home. Yet somehow this didn't feel as I'd imagined.

Dorothy was chattering while we walked, filling me in on everyone. My brother had just moved to San Diego, my older sister was now in a sorority, my other sister was thinking of staying and living in the South after college. And here I was: in a small town in Indiana, hiding my pregnant stomach, with Dorothy by my side. We passed a park with a small pond. Kids were ice-skating, and parents were standing on the side watching over them. I thought about our backyard at home and wondered if the pond was frozen over, if the twins were playing broom hockey on it. At the shopping center in town, Dorothy insisted on buying me a warm flannel nightgown like the ones I had at home, but bigger. There was a bookstore next door, and there was music playing behind the counter as we entered.

"You hear that, honey?" she said.

"Hear what, Mom?" Dorothy put her foot out a little, lifted her shoulder up, and started singing in her low full voice, "I hope that heeeee turns out to beeeeeee . . ." She turned, pointed to the speaker in the ceiling. "That's Ella Fitzgerald." The girl working behind the bookstore counter smiled. Dorothy got a little louder, "Someone to wattccch over meeeeeeeee."

"Hey you sound pretty good," the girl at the counter said.

Dorothy bowed a little and said out to the air, to no one in particular, "What a love song *that* is, boy, love is great isn't it?"

I meandered over to the paperback section while my mom

soft-shoed down a different aisle. I found a used-book shelf, grabbed several books, turned down another aisle, and grabbed some more. We bought the books, pens, and some stationery and then headed back to the hotel. It was my favorite time of day. The sun was setting and everything had that amber tint that makes you feel no matter where you are, life is reasonable, things are going to be okay. And then the dark comes.

I plopped down hard on the hotel bed. My mom walked over doing a little dance-walk thing, snapping her fingers.

"What, Mom, what is it?" I said.

"We'll order *room* service and find a good movie, shall we?" Dorothy grabbed the TV guide off the desk. She'd been an avid classic movie fanatic her entire life and had effectively converted all of us at very young ages. We were possibly the only children in the world who willingly watched black-and-white movies. "Oh, gosh, this is an arduous decision we have to make here, Liz. *Roman Holiday* or *Gaslight*. Which shall we watch?"

"*Roman Holiday.*"

"You sure? Don't you love *Gaslight*?"

"I do, but I'm feeling *Roman Holiday.*"

"You're absolutely right. One simply can't go wrong with Audrey Hepburn." I lay down next to my mom on the plush king-size bed. Dorothy was in her pink silk nightie as she drenched her face in Pond's cold cream. The smell reminded me of everything safe and easy. Audrey Hepburn, the princess, was standing in her bedroom wearing a nightgown that resembled a wedding dress. Dorothy's eyes were glued to the television.

"What an incredible room she has. Isn't it, sweetheart?" Audrey Hepburn's bed was the size of Texas, and the windows were floor to ceiling. My mom always talked during the movies. "Holy mackerel, Gregory Peck is handsome. My *God.*"

"Yeah, he is, Mom."

"Love is the key to life. You know that, right, honey?"

"I know."

"You'll find your Gregory Peck one day, Liz, and I'll let him know just how lucky he is to have found you."

My body felt tired and heavy. My mind was chasing thoughts in circles. I fell asleep to Dorothy's running commentary on the simple elegance of Audrey Hepburn's wardrobe.

⋆ ⋆ ⋆ ⋆

The next morning, I woke up to the sound of her voice.

"Good morning, honey, I let you sleep. There's a sweet roll and some orange juice for you."

I looked over and saw Dorothy sitting at the desk, reading *The New York Times*. She had on a red turtleneck sweater, her big gold chain necklace, and black-and-white checkered pants. I thought I was dreaming. She peered over her reading glasses at me.

"I have just a little time left. Is there anything you'd like to do?"

"I don't know." I hugged the soft blankets and felt the nice cool sheet on my face. She walked over, sat next to me, and put her hand on my back.

"I wish I could do something to make this easier."

"I'm fine, Mom." She started doing the whispering-to-herself thing, which I guess she did when *her* mind wouldn't shut off. "Mom, what are you saying?"

"I'm just thinking out loud, about Easter. Maybe I could get his royal highness to take the twins somewhere and you and I could have a few days together. Would you like that?"

"You mean Dad?"

"Yes."

"When is Easter?"

"In a couple of months."

"Yeah, that would be good."

"We'll work it out." She stood up and threw open the hotel drapes to let in the blaring sun.

"Rise and shine, my love. . . ."

"Mom, *don't*, I hate it when you do that." I buried my face in the blankets.

Her voice grew louder. "It's another gloooooooorrrriiiiious day. . . ."

"*Mom, stop!*" She laughed and spread her arms high in the air as I groggily made my way to the bathroom.

• • • •

We took a walk and puttered around, passing the morning. The thought of her leaving weighed heavily on both of us. It felt like an inside-out version of waiting for the time to pass in the facility.

"Will your father be coming to visit?" she asked at one point.

"I think so. Mom, I want you to know that I didn't confide in dad's wife about this whole pregnancy thing. It's not what you probably think."

"Liz, it's fine, I understand. It doesn't matter now. What matters is that you get through this. Your father and his *secrrrre-ttttaaarrrry* are of no concern to me."

It so sucked for Dorothy, all of it. She held her chin up high trying like hell to be fine. Fine with her pregnant teenager, and her ex-husband and his wife, fine with being a single working mother of seven kids.

"Life is hard, sweetheart, really hard. But what can we do? We just have to carry on. My husband left me with seven children. I still don't know why. Am I so bad, Lizzie? Am I so awful that he'd need to leave his entire family? God, I have no idea what I did to make him do this."

"Mom, you're not bad, you're great, really great. I'm sorry about it all, Mom."

"Guess your father wasn't my Gregory Peck." We both kind of laughed.

We finally drove down the long road back to the facility. She pulled into the same parking spot as before. We sat with the engine running, and I readied myself for walking out of one world and back into the other. Dorothy had the surrendered look on her face.

"Liz, I am just so sorry you have to be here, and I love you with all my heart."

"I love you too, Mom. Thanks for everything."

"Sweetheart, don't get attached to the child in your stomach, you know what we talked about."

"I know."

"There's a whole big world waiting for you out there." I stared out the windshield. The grounds looked oddly beautiful, like they did sometimes. I waited for the tears, but this time they didn't come. Dorothy's did, though. She wept into her hands as I gathered the bags.

"You coming in, Mom?"

"Can you make it in yourself?"

I reached under the seat and grabbed one of the clanking coffee mugs. "Here, now you won't have to listen to it the whole ride home."

"Oh, for God sakes, I don't hear it anyway." She took the mug and put it back on the floor. I kissed her forehead and climbed out of the car. I watched the dirty blue car pull off until I couldn't see it anymore.

I headed straight up the little hill to meet the girls at school. Most of them were sleeping when I arrived. I took my coat off, laid it on the floor, and sat on it. Tilly looked over, finally noticing me.

"You're *here*! I thought she might never let you come back."

"Your mom's a trip, Liz," Nellie said.

"Yeah, I know."

"I liked her, she's fancy." Tilly smiled. "Is she always like that?"

"Like what?"

"You know, swanky-talking, funny, dressed up?"

"Yeah, I guess."

"Did she tell you she hates us?" Nellie said, squinting.

"No, she just told me not to talk to you."

"Why? We might rub off on you?" Nellie laughed. Everyone cracked up, even Wren. Tilly scooched a bit closer.

"What'd you guys do?" Tilly asked.

"All sorts of stuff. Hung out, ate good food, shopped." I reached in the bag sitting next to me, the one from the bookstore, and pulled out a pile of word search books. I threw one to each of them, including Deanna.

"Look at that!" Nellie smiled. "A whole fucking book of 'em. We keepin' these?"

"Yeah."

"Fuckin' A."

I grabbed the paperbacks out of the bag too.

"What are those?" Tilly asked.

"Books. I'm supposed to be reading this one in school right now, it's good."

Tilly read the jacket out loud, "*Jane . . .* something."

"*Eyre.*"

"Looks old-fashioned. *Catcher I . . . the . . . Rye,* looks boring. I like this one with the pig. Look how cute that pig is. I remember that book, is it for kids?" Tilly asked.

"Yeah, kind of, but it's really good."

Nellie looked over and then hollered, "Read that one, Liz. I fucking love pigs."

Deanna perked up. "That's 'cause you fucking look like a pig."

"Fuck you, Deanna."

"No fucking thank you, Nellie."

I opened the book and started reading. The room went quiet. They all leaned in to listen to the first pages of *Charlotte's Web,* by E. B. White. For just a moment in the dreary little schoolhouse, it felt almost like a home.

chapter 9

Same stinking room, same girls, same TV shows, same card games. The lounge was growing smaller by the day, and time wasn't moving any faster. We'd had enough of each other. This was what Dorothy called cabin fever at home. Too many people in the same place for too long, *and* it was a Friday, which was never good, because Friday was Dr. Dick day.

"Shut up, Amy."

"You shut up, Deanna."

"You shut up."

I tried to tune them out as I looked at the snow falling outside the window in the midday dark sky. I was planning on going for a walk anyway, but just as I was about to get up, I heard a loud thumping noise coming from the hall, and then footsteps. We all turned in unison and looked at the door waiting to see who was coming. In walked a tall, pretty girl. She was wearing a sopping wet red windbreaker, flip-flops, and carrying a black trash bag. She shook the snow off her hair and stomped her wet flip-flops on the linoleum floor. She set the trash bag down and looked around until she locked eyes with Deanna. She gave her a guy-nod, no smile, no words. Deanna guy-nodded back.

"Who's Liz?" The new girl asked.

"Um, I am."

"Hey, I'm your new roommate."

Tilly laughed. "So they finally gave Liz a roommate." Just then, Alice whooshed through the door carrying a load of stuff in her arms.

"Hello, hello, girls that's Jill. Jill, did you meet them all? That's Liz there. Jill is new here, show her the ropes. I got a lotta work to do," Alice said, and then left. My heart was thumping. I didn't want a roommate, especially one who guy-nods with Deanna. Jill took off her wet windbreaker. She was wearing a black Led Zeppelin T-shirt and brown Levi's corduroys with holes in them. There was a little red heart tattoo on her hand. Leaning against the wall, she pulled a cigarette out of her bra and lit it with a Zippo lighter. She was less pregnant-looking than most of us girls, and she had something very cool about her.

"Don't worry, I don't take up too much room," she said.

"Oh no, it's fine," I said. I was uneasy, but curious.

She looked at Nellie, at the table with her cards. "You play poker?"

"Mostly solitaire and spit," Nellie said. She glanced out the window and asked, "What are the cops doing here?"

"They gave me a ride."

"Off the street?" Deanna asked.

"Yeah."

"Good thing you're fucking pregnant."

Jill smiled. "No shit!" Jill then looked over at Wren. Wren looked away, like she always did when people saw her scar for the first time. But Jill kept her eyes on Wren and said, "Cool shoes you got on." Wren was wearing black Converse. Wren looked up. Something was different about Jill, good different, but I couldn't put my finger on it.

"How do you know Deanna?" Nellie asked.

"Juvie, baby," Deanna said, laughing.

"Yeah, we lived together there for a little while," Jill said. She grabbed the trash bag and I led her to our room.

"Shit, nice," she said, walking in ahead of me. She threw the trash bag on the empty bed and looked around the room. I saw her notice the food on the dresser.

"Are you hungry?" I asked.

"Yeah, but that's your stuff, no problem."

"No, have it, I don't care. Want some soup? Crackers and stuff?"

"Yeah, wow. I haven't eaten in a while. I gotta take a shower though."

I pointed to the bathroom. "You can use the towels in there if you want." I nervously straightened up the room and made some soup while she was in the shower. Jill already kind of fascinated me. She was very comfortable with herself, and calm. I didn't think I'd want a roommate, but Jill wasn't like any roommate I thought I might have there. She stepped out of the bathroom in a T-shirt, with a towel on her head, and sat on the bed. I handed her a bowl of soup. Her eyes were deep sparkly blue bordered by long dark eyelashes.

"So what's your story?" she said.

"What do you mean? I'm pregnant, waiting to have my baby."

She shook her head. "Uh-uh, there's more."

But I didn't feel like talking about me, so I said, "Nope, that's it."

"Okay, whatever you say." She reached in her trash bag and pulled out a pair of sweatpants. I got up and hung her windbreaker on the radiator, so it would dry off. She looked out the window a long time and finally smiled.

"What?" I asked.

"It's good to be somewhere." She pointed to my guitar and asked, "You play?"

"Yeah."

"My old man's a guitar player."

"That's cool."

"Yeah, that's what your kid'll say about you."

"I guess." And then I remembered—no it won't. This kid would never know who I was.

Jill reached her hand deep into the trash bag, which I guess was her suitcase. "You like Battleship?" she asked.

"What? You mean the game?"

"Yeah." She pulled out a flimsy box held together with masking tape. "I've had this stupid game forever. I love it." We sat on the floor and started setting up the battleships. There was a knock on the door.

I shouted, without needing to ask who it was, "Come in, Tilly."

Tilly poked her head in. "How'd you know?"

"I guessed."

"What are you guys doing? Wait, is that . . . Battleship?"

"Yeah."

"Where'd you get it?"

I pointed to Jill's trash bag. Jill laughed. "I got my whole life in that bag."

"I play winner," Tilly said.

"That'll be me," Jill said.

"You got a boyfriend, Jill?" Tilly asked.

"Oh yeah, but he's no good, so it's gonna be just me and this baby. I really hope it's a girl. I want a girl bad."

"How far along are you?" Tilly asked.

"Four months. I was sick as shit until a few weeks ago, feeling better now."

"How old are you?"

"Just turned sixteen." Tilly's eyes got big.

"Wow, you seem older."

I elbowed her. "What?" Tilly said.

"Stop asking so many questions," I said.

"I don't mind," Jill said.

Tilly put her hand on the top of her stomach and smiled. "I

have a boyfriend, his name's Rick. He's the dad, we're gonna live in a nice place together when I get outta here. He's already buying stuff for this kid."

"Dads are key," Jill said. "You got a good dad?"

"No." Tilly laughed.

"Me neither."

"Liz does. Her dad's nice to her, sends her lots a shit, like all that food."

Jill grinned. "I knew there was more."

"Oh trust me, there's a whole lot to Liz's story, we're never gonna meet another Liz."

"Tilly, seriously, don't talk about me like I'm not here," I said. There was another knock on the door. Amy peeked her head in and asked if she could talk to me alone. Out in the hallway, she was wringing her hands and cracking her knuckles.

"What's the matter?" I said.

"I think I want to do the adoption thing. Maybe. I mean if you're sure it's like you said, and they'll keep the kid forever and stuff."

"Yeah, it's permanent. But you should talk to Ms. Graham. You want to see if she's around?"

"Yeah, but you'd have to come with me, I don't even know her." We headed through the lounge, down the hall, and out to the corridor, toward her office. Amy turned to me. "And she's not a bitch?"

"No, God no. Ms. Graham? She's not a bitch at all."

"What if she's pissed I never went to my sessions with her?"

"She'll be fine. None of you guys go to the sessions with her."

"You do."

"Yeah, I do."

"What if she says no one would want my kid?"

"Amy, shut up, she's not gonna say that." It was late in the afternoon and the hall lights were dim. We were just about to turn down the next hall when we saw a strange-looking girl walking toward us in what looked like pajamas. I couldn't see very well, and I didn't recognize her. Amy did a double take.

"What the *fuck*?" she said. As we got closer, we saw the girl was wearing a zip-up onesie pajama thing with feet attached. She was tall and pregnant, and we could hear her humming. Amy elbowed me. "Who *is* that?" As we got closer, the girl saw us and began crying, loudly. She had short, red, tangled hair and puffy eyes. The girl's crying turned to screaming. We stopped short and froze. Now she looked more like a woman, much older than us. She stood directly in front of us. She smelled bad and had big buckteeth. My heart was pounding out of my chest. "I'm fucking *outta here*," Amy said, and dodged around the girl and ran down the hall. "Come on Liz!" But I was paralyzed. The girl inched closer. I wanted to move, turn around, something, but I couldn't. She leaned in and screamed a piercing scream right in my face. I closed my eyes and covered my ears, and then she reached over to put her hand on my stomach.

"You have a *baby* in your *tummy*," she shouted. I tried to inch forward to get around her, but she kept cutting me off and laughing. I ducked under her arm, ran down the hall, and collided with a woman carrying a large ring of keys.

"Sorry," I said.

The woman moved around me to the girl and said, "There you are, Adelaide. Come on now, you know you can't wander the halls like this." The woman saw I was trembling. "Sorry, sweetheart, she's just a little short in the mind. She'd never hurt you." I was breathing heavily and sweat was pouring down my face. She looked at me more carefully. "Goodness, are you going to be all right?"

"Yeah, yes, I'm fine. I'll just head back now."

"You sure you're okay?"

"Oh yeah, I'm sure." She guided the girl down the hall toward the other wing in the facility—it must have been the crazy wing Nellie had told me about. I stopped at the drinking fountain and let the ice-cold water run all over my face. Then I sat on the floor next to the fountain and waited for my heart to calm down. I felt out-of-room-inside–at-capacity-full-up. Somehow the idea of the crazy wing and that girl put me over.

. . . .

Amy was sitting with Jill, Nellie, and Tilly in the lounge when I got back. Deanna was on her chair, and Wren was on the couch. Amy was telling the story when I walked in. She turned to me.

"I told them that fucking Looney Tune could have killed you. Why didn't you run when I did?"

"I don't know," I said.

"Are you crying?"

"No."

"Yeah, you are. Shit, did she hurt you?"

"No."

"Well, what happened?"

"Some lady came and got her."

Nellie looked over at me. "I bet you really want outta here now. Fuckin' cuckoo crazies."

"I think she was mentally retarded, not crazy."

"She was a total freakazoid, like in a scary movie," Amy said. "All she needed was a fucking ax in her hand."

"Radio girl, you look pretty shook-up," Deanna said.

"I'm fine."

"Hey, your dad called, and *I* talked to him," Tilly said.

"*My* dad called?"

"Anyone else here got a dad who calls?" Tilly said. Everyone laughed.

"What did he say?" I asked.

"He said he's coming to see you. He's coming a week from Wednesday, I'm supposed to tell you that." My dad was coming. The door to the lounge flew open, and we all looked over. Gina walked in with her bag and coat and a stuffed elephant under her arm. Nellie looked at her and said, *"Again?"*

"Yeah, they said it was false labor. I hate this."

"That's the second time *today*, Gina."

"Like I don't fucking know that, Nellie?" She put her stuff down and took a seat on the couch. Gina had gone to the hospital five times in the last two days, thinking she was going to have her baby. "The pains hurt pretty bad," Gina said.

"The real pains are gonna hurt like shit, Gina, not like . . . 'Oh yeah, that hurts a little,'" Deanna said.

"How do *you* know?"

"I just fucking know."

"I'm fucking tired of this." Gina hit the couch with her fist. "I just want my baby, I wanna see it, and I wanna get outta here."

"Try carrying around *two* kids inside you all fucking day," Nellie said. "Trust me, it sucks more."

"Just wait till you have to push those two kids out your snatch, Nellie," Deanna said. "*That's* what's gonna suck. My sister said it's like pushing a watermelon out a goddamn buttonhole, and you got two watermelons in there."

Nellie put her head down and covered her face with her hands. Tilly looked at Deanna. "What the *hell*, Deanna? Why'd you have to say that?"

None of us ever talked about giving birth. It was too terrifying. The closest we'd come was talking about the one thing all of us hated more than anything—having to go to Dr. Dick every Friday. Giving birth to our babies was the one thing we had in common, and it was also the one thing we never spoke about. All of us kept that fear tucked safely away in our own minds. I'd never ever seen Nellie upset, but she was crying now. Tears were falling down her face as she pretended to play solitaire.

"Nell, if my mom can do it seven times, we can do it once," I said.

"Six times. She had twins, dumbass."

"Oh yeah," I said.

"It's gonna hurt like shit, and I might suck as a mom. I mean, my mom sucks."

Gina raised her hand. "So does mine."

Wren raised her hand. "So does mine."

Nellie looked at me. "See? I'm gonna suck."

"Nellie, you have your shit together, you're not gonna suck," Tilly said. The girls all went quiet, even Deanna. We were all thinking about the stuff we didn't want to think about—the stuff we usually managed to ignore. Gina was fidgeting, trying to get comfortable with her big stomach on the couch.

"Is it true you're giving *your* baby away?" Gina said to me.

"I'm giving my baby up for adoption," I answered.

"Is that what people like you do? Give their kids away?"

"Shut the fuck up, Gina. Don't answer her, Liz," Nellie said.

"I don't know, Gina, that's just what I'm doing."

"So you're gonna go through all this shit, and walk away without your baby?"

"Yeah . . . I am."

"Stupidest thing I ever heard," Gina scoffed.

"It's not stupid, Gina," Tilly said. "She thinks it'll be better for the kid."

"Yeah, maybe it's even smart," Nellie said.

"Smart? What the *fuck*? How is that smart?" Gina said.

Then Amy chimed in—Amy who'd just been on her way to talk to Ms. Graham. She slammed her hand down and said, "Shut up, Gina, just *shut up*. You don't know shit, you don't even know what adoption *is*. It's not like throwing your baby away. They give the babies to families that can't have 'em, who have jobs and homes and shit. So *shut* up."

"So a *stranger* takes the kid and fucking *pretends* it's theirs? That's *fucked*-up," Gina lashed back.

"The kid won't think it's fucked-up when its life is all good, you moron!"

"What the fuck, Amy, like you're gonna give *your* baby up?"

"Maybe I will, Gina," Amy shouted back. "I don't have a job or a dad for it, or a fucking place to live. I don't have shit, and what is it to you, anyway?"

"It's *your kid*, you can't just give it to someone," Gina shouted.

"I can do what I want. It'll probably end up in foster care anyway, 'cause I'll fuck up. All these kids could get taken away from us, except for hers. Hers will be with a family that won't fuck up." Amy pointed at me.

Deanna glared over at me. "See the *shit* you started, radio girl?" She stood up and walked out of the room. Wren was biting her bloody cuticles. Nellie was staring out the window. Tilly looked uncomfortable. Amy, still on fire, turned to Gina.

"Get outta here, Gina, just get out, you're pissing me off. Go fake your fucking labor pains somewhere else." Gina flipped Amy off and left the room. Amy fell back onto Deanna's empty La-Z-Boy and sighed.

Nellie started slowly clapping, and said, "Thank you, Amy . . . that was good, I mean *really* good fighting, like no hits but still good." Nellie was back to her usual self, crying no more. I guess the fight had distracted her. Tilly started to laugh, so did I, and so did Wren. Amy put her feet up in the La-Z-Boy and smiled.

"You're welcome, Nell. I guess I *coulda* hit her, she's stupid enough."

"Talk about stupid, you better get outta that chair if you plan on living past today." No one had ever touched Deanna's La-Z-Boy, let alone sat in it. Wren walked over and pulled on Amy's arm. "Come on, get off a there." Wren and Amy wrestled until Amy got up out of the La-Z-Boy. Just then, Deanna returned. She cased the room and made her way to the chair. We were all quiet. Deanna looked over at me. "People don't need to hear that shit from you."

"What?" I said.

"You know what I'm talkin' about. You can keep your bullshit ideas to yourself, just confuses people."

"What people, Deanna?" Nellie said. "Don't fuckin' speak for us, did she confuse you? Anyone should think about giving a kid up for adoption it's you, I mean being *raped and all.*" As Nellie's words hit the air, I felt my body suddenly seize up, and almost forget to breathe. Everything stopped all at once. The only sound was the thumping hum of the ceiling fan, the fan above us that never turned off. It took several long spins as Deanna stared at the wall in front of her. Then, a tear rolled down her face, then one after another. Nellie put her head down. She knew immediately how badly she'd messed up.

"*I'm sorry. . . . I'm so sorry, Deanna. Fuck me,* I didn't mean that the way it sounded," Nellie said. Deanna was silent. I could not believe that inside that frighteningly angry, scary girl, there were these tears. My entire view of Deanna turned upside down in that one second. She was sitting still as a statue in the La-Z-Boy. Terrifying Deanna was just as sad as the rest of us.

I thought about what had happened to her. I mean I really thought about it, for the first time ever. To be raped by a man who was supposed to be taking care of you, and then find out you're pregnant with his child. Sometimes stories are just a bunch of words until you actually bring the words alive in your mind. Deanna's story was alive to me now, and it made me wonder about everything. I needed to get out of that lounge. But every time I felt the need to leave, or run, it wasn't until I got past the steel door and into the cold air that I remembered: There was nowhere to go. I would never be able to run from the truth of this part of my life. Outside, I stood and watched the sun set over the magnificent Indiana oak trees. I felt horrible and ashamed. I could feel the hope seeping in as I watched the sky. The faraway trees reminded me of the faraway life I had yet to live. The other girls might not be so lucky. I walked over to my mom's empty parking spot and sat down on the curb. There were so many different puzzle pieces floating around in my head. It felt like they were all waiting for me to fit them together, and I wasn't sure how. Life was not what I thought it was. People and things used to be what they seemed, and now they weren't.

. . . .

Later that night, according to Ms. Graham, we were having our first-ever movie night.

"It better be a good one," Nellie said, sipping on an Orange

Crush. Alice came in with four packages of Jiffy Pop. Wren offered to help pop them on the stove with her. Deanna was nowhere to be seen. Ms. Graham was waiting at the door of the upstairs lounge when we arrived. She looked different. She had on blue jeans and a button-down shirt.

"Hello, Liz, how are you?" Ms. Graham said.

"I'm okay."

"And you must be Jill, hello."

"Hey."

"Are you finding your way here?"

"Yeah, it's all good."

There was a movie projector and portable movie screen set up in the back of the room. Alice and Wren arrived with the popcorn and bowls. Deanna came in a few minutes later. She looked like herself again, aloof and angry.

Amy came over. "That's her, right?"

"Who? Oh yeah. Ms. Graham. Yes, come here." I grabbed Amy's arm, pulled her over, and told Ms. Graham Amy needed to talk to her. As I walked away, Amy seemed like she was getting along with her. I found a place on the couch and grabbed some popcorn.

Alice flicked the lights on and off to quiet us all down. Wren and Tilly were talking about what movie we might watch. Tilly whispered, "I hope it's *Alien*. Rick saw that movie and said it was trippy." Ms. Graham made her way to the front of the room.

"Girls, it is so nice to see your faces. Tonight we thought it would be a good idea to get you together to watch an educational movie that documents a real birth, because each of you has this experience coming up, and we thought it would . . ."

Tilly stood up, shouting, "Are you kidding? We don't want to see that." All the girls began moaning and complaining. Ms. Graham tried to continue, but no one would listen. Alice finally whistled a taxi whistle, and the girls quieted. Alice spoke loudly. She had more authority over us than Ms. Graham did.

"This is not optional. You have to grow up here, girls, and pay attention. This is what's going to go on when you have your babies. Ms. Graham here is trying to help, okay? So pipe down." Alice turned the lights off and started the movie projector. It reminded me of science or history class at school. The low, familiar whir-ring sound of the projector, and the weird beaming light shooting onto the screen. The movie opened with a sleepy-sounding nar-rator and a pregnant woman sitting in a hospital gown on a table in a doctor's office. This was our least favorite thing in the world. The lady opened the gown and we saw her big puffy boobs. The girls went crazy laughing; they hollered and whistled. The narra-tor in the movie was talking about the woman's breasts readying to become engorged with milk. The girls howled at almost every-thing that was said. Nellie covered her eyes with her hat, and Wren ducked under the coffee table. After a long, boring documentary-style what-happens-to-the-body-when-it's-pregnant half hour, we moved to the actual birth. The narrator was talking about the body readying for delivery, and the dilating cervix. The camera was close in on the unborn child's head, which looked like a hairy bowling ball pushing its way out of the woman's body. She was clearly in an enormous amount of pain.

It was too much. Nellie got up and left the room. Amy and Jill threw popcorn at the screen. The rest of the girls started yelling again. As the baby's head finally pushed through the vagina, all of us, including me, shrieked. Alice got up, turned the lights on, and stopped the movie. There was total chaos in the room. Wren was crying. Deanna was shouting at the screen, telling it it was full a shit. Ms. Graham turned the projector off. "My apologies, girls, you obviously are not ready for this."

Alice was fuming as she packed the projector into its case. She and Ms. Graham left the room together. The girls were clearing out, cursing the movie. After a while, after everyone left, someone flipped off the light. I stayed on the couch alone, in the dark. The big white portable movie screen was identical to the one we had at home in the front hall closet. My dad spent much of our young lives shooting movies of us, the seven kids, with his little black movie camera. He'd tell us to act casual when the camera was on: "Act like I'm not here." He filmed us sailing and skiing and opening Christmas presents and blowing out candles and watching fireworks and eating turkey at Thanksgiving. Occasionally, on a Friday or Saturday night, he'd announce we were having family movie night. We all loved family movie night. We'd gather in the living room to watch the soundless black-and-white film, our lives playing out on the big white screen. We'd *ohhh* and *ahhh* at our parents when they were younger and collapse with laughter watching ourselves as little kids. I closed my eyes on the couch in the facility lounge and watched my favorite family footage in my head.

It was Easter. We were dressed up, playing in the backyard before church. My older sisters and I were wearing our Easter hats, with our fancy dresses and white gloves. My older sister Alex was standing on the grass pushing Kiley and me on the swings. It was obvious in the movie that she was trying to be fair—she gave us each an equal number of pushes, because that is who Alex was. You could see Kiley and me loving the wind in our faces. At the same time, you could see that whenever Alex pushed a swing she would look down and check the palms of her gloves afterward. The faster the swings went, the faster she'd have to check her palms. Eventually we figured out she was making sure her white gloves hadn't gotten dirty. The film was a little faster than real life, and the image was hilarious. If you looked closely, you could see Dorothy in the background, in her fancy church suit with her caplet hat and white gloves, smoking a cigarette. You could see my brothers messing around on the lawn. I played the image over and over in my mind, trying to erase the horror of the swollen boobs and the birthing vagina from my mind.

* * * *

"Are you lost?" I looked up and saw Ms. Graham standing over me, in the dark.

"No. I was just sitting here, I guess." Ms. Graham walked over to the table, turned the lamp on, and plopped down in the chair next to me. She looked so different in her jeans and button-down shirt. She pulled a pack of cigarettes out of her pocket. *Holy crap,* I thought, *she smokes?*

"I don't know what I was thinking with that movie, what a bomb." I didn't say anything; I just looked at her puffing on the Kent cigarette, taking in the strange sight.

"I thought with the loss of Elaine's baby being so difficult for everyone, I might try to prepare you girls for what you will be experiencing." She ran her fingers through her short hair and laughed. "Boy, I mucked it up, huh?"

I thought about it. "Maybe it's better not to know things sometimes."

"That's probably true."

A moment later, the door to the room flew open. Tilly was panting. "Liz, you in here? Oh hey, well guess what? Gina's water broke in the hall, went everywhere, super gross. I guess she's *really* gonna have the baby."

Ms. Graham got up and rushed out to attend to Gina. Tilly came and sat next to me.

"What was she saying? That we suck?"

"No. That she shouldn't have shown the movie."

"Duh."

"So Gina has to have the baby now 'cause the water broke, right?"

"Yeah, they're taking her over now."

"Wow, so weird, isn't it?" She was looking at me funny. "What, Till?"

"Can I *pleeeaaasseee* meet your dad when he comes? I want to see what a real dad is like."

"What? Yeah, you want to come with us wherever we go, we'll probably go to lunch."

"Shit, yes. And Nellie can't come."

"Tilly, Nellie can come if she wants."

"No, just me." She jumped up off the couch and headed for the door. "See you back in the lounge."

I sat in the dark on the couch. I thought about Gina heading to the hospital to give birth to her baby. To go do what we were all there to do. Gina was the first since I'd arrived, and it felt strangely unexpected. Alice had told us many times, "You never know when the baby will come. When it does, your time is up." Gina would have the baby and leave immediately afterward. We all would. In a few days' time, it would be as if she were never there at all. New girls would arrive, and all traces of the others would vanish.

chapter 10

Gina looked like a completely different person. Her hair was washed and in two low pigtails. Her stomach was gone. She was wearing jeans and carrying her baby, swaddled in a big fuzzy pink blanket.

"Look at her, you guys, she's perfect, isn't she?" She was beaming. "Girls, this is Rosie. Rosie, these are the girls." The little baby was sleeping with one hand on top of the other. She was truly the cutest thing ever.

"Are they all that small?" Wren said.

"I think so."

Tilly was jumping up and down. "Can I please hold her just to see what it feels like, please, please?"

Gina handed the baby to Tilly and said, "Yeah, but don't fucking drop her."

Tilly held her in her arms. She smiled. "Look at her little nose, and her teensy-weensy fingers."

"How was it? I mean . . . the birth and stuff?" Nellie asked.

"It sucked, hurt so bad. I'm bleeding like a stuck pig but then look what you get? It's crazy. All that hell and then this." Gina leaned over and kissed the baby's head. We stood in a little circle around her, everyone talking at the same time in a giddy baby frenzy.

"Look, her hair is so silky."

"Oh my God, her ears . . ."

"Look at her tiny fingernails."

All of us were filled with the same thing—the thing that fills you up when you see a new baby. Even Deanna, who patiently waited to hold her, kissed and cooed and nestled the little bundle. We all felt it deeply: A brand-new life had just entered the lounge. Nothing could have quite prepared us for the significance of it, for the possibility it seemed to bring. Amy turned and tried handing me the baby.

"No, that's okay," I said. Something was going on inside of me, in my heart.

Nellie took Rosie instead and sat down in a chair. The baby moved her little angel lips around. We stared, entranced.

"So did you breast-feed and stuff?" Nellie asked Gina.

"No, fuck no. I tried but it hurts bad, like someone's pinching a clothespin onto your tit and turning it as hard as they can. I'm feeding her the formula milk stuff from a bottle, she likes it just fine."

"Gimme that sweet piece a sugar, will ya?" Alice said, wobbling in. Alice put the baby over her shoulder and walked to the window. She was a pro, you could tell. The little baby opened her eyes a bit. It looked like she saw the sky for the very first time. Alice rocked her and said to Gina, "I can give you two a ride to the bus station, sweetheart, but not until we get that phone call."

"Where you going?" Tilly asked.

"Michigan, to stay with my aunt," Gina said. She had a strange look on her face. "I called and left a message with her boyfriend to call here, so we're just waiting for her to call back."

"You can't stay here with the baby, Gina," Alice said. "You know that. Child services can watch her while you figure it out."

"She's gonna fucking call, Alice. Nobody's taking the baby." Gina took the baby back from Alice's arms.

"Gina, does your aunt know you had a kid?" Amy asked.

"I don't know, but I think she'll call me back."

"Where's your mom?"

"She's gone, she doesn't live in the same place as when I got here."

Alice looked over. "I think that little bundle of love needs a diaper change, mama Gina," she said. Gina rifled through the baby bag for a diaper. She laid a blanket down on the couch and then placed the baby on it. We all stood by, slightly grossed out, as Gina undid the Pamper. There was green slime all over the baby's legs and butt. Alice got a wet towel, came back, and cleaned the baby in two seconds flat.

"Gina, put the diaper on," Alice said.

"You do it."

"No, sweetheart. You gotta do it." Gina fumbled with the diaper but eventually got it on. The baby started crying as Gina tried to put her little outfit back on, and then the baby really started crying.

"You gotta pull the clothing," Alice said, "not the baby, when you dress her, Gina." We watched as Alice stretched the fabric of the pajama and gently placed the baby's arms and legs in.

Wren said, "That's scary, she's too little."

Alice rolled the baby up like a taco in the blanket and handed her to Gina. A few minutes later, Gina's aunt called and said she could take the bus to Michigan. When Gina stood in the doorway with Rosie, she suddenly looked as young as she really was. She had a brand-new baby in her arms, her mom was nowhere to be found, and she was getting on a bus alone to go somewhere she wasn't sure she could stay. My emotions were heavy and tangled. I knew with certainty how my life would look in the weeks and months and even years to come. Gina didn't. Standing in the lounge looking at Gina, I felt bad about that.

Gina smiled an awkward smile, and said, "Well . . . bye, you guys." We waited to hear the corridor door shut before we sat back down. Jill lit a cigarette, looked around the room, and said, "That's gonna be all of us. Who's next?"

"Shit, I think I am," Tilly said. "Then Nellie then Wren and Liz . . . right?" Tilly looked at Nellie. "Isn't Gina supposed to go back to juvie for something?"

"Yeah, she is, she gets a week after the kid is born, then she has to go back. She stole a car," Amy said. "She had it for like ten days."

"No kidding, that's pretty bad."

"She stole it to go pick up her mom somewhere. Her mom was sick, or strung out or something, the cops stopped her on the freeway. She didn't even have a license."

"So she knows how to hot-wire?" Jill asked.

"No. She followed some old lady into the grocery store from the parking lot, swiped the keys out of her purse, and then went back to the parking lot and drove off in her car."

"That's balls," Deanna said.

"I've stole some shit but never a car," Nellie said.

"Yeah, me too," Amy said.

"One of my sisters stole something once and got caught. She stole some makeup from the drugstore," I chimed in.

"And what happened?" Jill asked, laughing.

"She was in like sixth grade. The cops called. My mom had to go to the store. They didn't arrest her or anything. She gave the stuff back, and then my mom brought her home and made her write this long paper about what happened and why she did it. That's what my mom did when any of us ever got in big trouble. She kept a file in our basement. When we did a really bad thing, we had to write it down, say how sorry we were, tell every detail, and then my mom put it in the file. She said if we ever did it again, she'd show the papers to my dad."

"*That* is fucking funny," Nellie said. "Did you ever have to write anything? You *didn't,* did you?"

"Yes, I did." Maybe they would think what I had done wasn't so bad, but it was pretty bad and I was strangely relieved I'd done something to go in the file in our basement.

"What?"

"Well, when I was in eighth grade, I babysat for these people down the street and had a party at their house, and spilled beer in their fancy car in the garage. The people called my mom and said I was a disrespectful hoodlum. My mom was so mad that she sent my brother to pull me out of school. Then she made me go over to the house, apologize, clean the carpets and the car, and *then* I had to write it all down and she put it in the basement file."

"Did she ever show your fuckin' dad?" Deanna said.

"No, I don't think so."

"Smart lady. Got her kids afraid to do bad shit."

We all sat in silence for a second and then Nellie said, "Maybe I'll do that file thing with *my* kids, it's a fucking good idea."

· · · ·

Ms. Graham's office door was closed when I walked past a few days later. I knocked lightly and waited. I could hear her talking, so I peeked my head in.

"Hi, Liz, come in." I sat down and waited. "Sorry about that, I was actually talking to the adoption agency. How are things going?" Ms. Graham asked.

"Fine, I guess. Gina had her baby, and we all got to see it."

"Yes, a beautiful baby girl. Was that hard for you?"

"No." Actually, yes, it was, but in ways I didn't want to think or talk about.

Ms. Graham went on. "Oh, we got some books from the public library. Two dozen coming, to go up to the school. They range from fourth- to twelfth-grade levels."

She was writing something again on the legal pad. I noticed

on her desk a paper notepad calendar: Each day you rip it off to reveal the next. It read March 1. It was almost the twins' birthdays. My little sisters were born on two different days. Tory was born on the second of March, and Jennifer came just after midnight on the third. They were about to turn fourteen years old.

"Everything all right?" Ms. Graham asked.

"I guess."

"Anything you want to talk about?"

I thought about it for a while. "Is there any way a girl could have her baby and still finish high school while she takes care of it?"

"There are a few different programs set up to help teenage mothers. So yes. The answer is yes."

"Tilly wants to finish high school," I said.

"I'm glad to hear that," Ms. Graham said. "I can let her know about what is available to help make that happen."

She cleared her throat and pulled out a file from her top desk drawer. "I wanted to let you know, Liz, after a lot of interviewing and checking on things, we've narrowed down the adoptive parents for your baby to two different couples. Both have waited a long time for a child. If it's possible, they'd like to see a picture of you. Do you have one I could put in the file?"

I felt my brain pause, and my thoughts go slippery. I saw the image of Rosie, Gina's baby, slowly rise in my mind. I'd written a dozen versions of a letter to my own baby in my mind.

Dear little baby—
I'm going to ask your parents to give this letter to you when you are 16. That is the age I got pregnant with you. I wanted to ask you to make sure to keep music around you if you can. Play the guitar, or the piano, or the drums, anything you can, to get out that stuff that'll live inside you. That's what I do. I'm Liz, and you're the baby who grew in my stomach. My boyfriend, your dad I guess, is a nice, funny

guy, who had nothing to do with any of the decisions made about you. We're just kids. We've been together most of high school, but moving on and going to college, I doubt we'll stay together. I love sports, running is great if you're fast, I bet you will be, so be sure to run. What went on when I found out you were inside me is a long story, but I wanted to make sure you knew that even though I don't know you, I know you're probably a great person already. I hope you can understand about why I thought it was better for you to live with a real family rather than me, a kid. I hope your life is okay, I hope it's really good.

I looked up at Ms. Graham. "I can get some pictures of me to give you."

She was staring at me. She had a way of looking at me, like she could see straight through me. My tears were rolling, but I didn't care.

"Are you having reservations about giving up the baby?" Ms. Graham asked.

I looked up at the ceiling, which sometimes felt like it was caving in on me in that little office.

"No," I said.

"Well, it's understandable if you were."

"I'm not." But the reality was beginning to hit me. All our babies had just been thoughts or ideas until Gina's little girl came to the lounge. And we saw her. The baby was a real person. With a heart, and feet, and eyelashes, and a mind. My baby would soon be a real person too. Everything was shifting from thought to reality. I had stuff going on inside I'd never felt before. Almost as though I'd hit a layer I wasn't supposed to feel for a long, long time—something I wasn't ready for. Ready or not, it was here. Outside the small window in Ms. Graham's office, the clouds passed over the sun and made the sky dark and then light again. I hoped I could handle what lay ahead.

The next day, I headed into the lounge after a bad night of sleep. We didn't have to go to school that day. There was something going on with the plumbing in the schoolhouse. Nellie kept calling it a *shit* day instead of a *snow* day. The phone booth was cold; I held the receiver with one hand and shoved the other into my coat pocket.

"Hi, Mom, is Tory there?" I said when my mom picked up.

"Hi, sweetheart, she is. How very thoughtful of you to call." She sang Tory's name through the house, *"VICTORRRIIIAAAA . . ."* My heart dropped as always at the sound of life at home.

"Hello?"

"Happy birthday, Tory."

"Thanks, Liz. How you feeling?"

"Not bad." This would be the first of their birthdays I'd missed.

The Pryor birthday tradition was that the birthday boy or girl could pick any meal to be served that evening for dinner. Mine was always spareribs and artichokes. I heard the phone muffled again, and then Tory said, "I'm having hot dogs and potato chips."

"Of course you are."

"Hold on, Liz, she *won't* shut up."

I heard some muffle and then, "Liz, hi." Jennifer came on.

"Hi, Jen, happy birthday tomorrow."

"Thanks. You feeling good?"

"Yeah. I'm good." We chatted for a bit, and I got back on with Tory for a while. When I hung up the phone in the booth, my hands started to tremble. Life at home was moving farther and farther from my view, farther and farther away from who I felt I was. It terrified me. I began to wonder, as I straddled the two worlds, which world was the real one. I tried to tell myself what both my parents had told me: Once I got through this, life would go back to what it was. But I knew better now. I knew deep inside that having the baby and leaving the facility would never be behind me. None of it would ever be behind me. I looked up at the cracked dirty ceiling in the phone booth and thought about my favorite Saturday morning cartoon, *Underdog*. He was this goofy little dog, and when he stepped inside a phone booth, he could suddenly talk and fly. He'd zoom up in his cape, out of the top of the booth, and fly around his neighborhood helping people out of trouble. Too bad you have to grow up and find out that all the greatest things you learn as a kid aren't really true.

* * *

I made my way down the hall and back to my room. Jill was on the bed with her feet up on the wall. I lay down on my bed. She looked over at me.

"You good?" she asked.

"Yeah, you good?"

"Not really. I'm getting fat," Jill said.

"You're pregnant, not fat."

"Pregnant *is* fat. It's also fucking annoying, my back hurts, my ankles are swollen, and my boobs are killing me."

"Complain much?"

"All the time. Hey, you know any rock-and-roll songs on the guitar?"

"Not really, wait, 'Stairway to Heaven'?"

"Holy shit, I love that song, play it, will ya?" Jill scrunched up her face and started singing, "And she's buuuuying a stairrrway to heavvvven."

Just as I picked up the guitar, there was a knock at the door. Jill shouted, "Go away, Tilly!" The door opened and Alice stuck her head in.

"Liz, your dad is here. He's up at the guard gate." I'd almost forgotten he was visiting today. My stomach turned. I grabbed my coat and handed Jill the guitar.

"Here, practice the two chords I showed you, and when I get back you should be pretty good." Jill just laughed. In the lounge I found Tilly and Nellie in their coats. They'd been waiting to go to lunch with my dad a long time now. Nellie had a little makeup on and her hair was wet.

"You go first, Liz, and ask him. We'll wait here," Nellie said.

"Okay, I'll go first, but you guys come up in like five minutes, okay?"

"Okay."

At the entrance near the guard booth I saw my dad and Kate. He was wearing a navy blue sweater over a white button-down and holding his camel hair overcoat. After we hugged, my dad looked around, surveying the scene with his hands in his pockets.

"So we're going to take you out for lunch and find something to do and we'll have you back by dinner," he said. He sounded and looked exactly the same as he always did.

"Sounds good, Dad. I was wondering if I could bring a couple of the girls here with me, they don't get out much . . . and . . ." I stopped. He gave me a look I recognized. You don't tell Lee the plan; Lee tells you the plan.

"That's not a good idea. We're just going to be *us* today," he said.

"Okay, but I told the girls . . ." Lee just looked at me. I should have known better than to promise Nellie and Tilly. He started to put on his coat. "Let's go."

"Okay, I have to go tell them they can't come. I'll be right back." I headed down the long hall and saw Tilly and Nellie at the other end. When I saw Tilly's face, my heart dropped.

"You guys, God . . . I'm, I'm sorry. . . ."

Nellie rolled her eyes. She knew. "We can't come."

"Yeah, no, you can't. I guess he wants to be with me alone."

"Or he thinks we're juvie heads."

I looked at her. "No, Nellie, that's not it."

"It's okay," Tilly said. She shuffled her big shoes on the tiled floor and said, "We would have needed a pass anyway. . . ."

I didn't even think of that. It was so easy to forget that while we were living in the same place and were there for the same reason, they were locked in, and I wasn't.

We all three turned and looked as Lee and Kate made their way to the door. My dad glanced down the hall at us. Tilly gasped out loud.

"Jesus, he looks like a TV actor."

"And she really does look like Farrah Fawcett," Nellie said.

* * * *

My dad's hunter green Jaguar shined in the patches of sun that were sneaking through the trees. Spring was almost here; I could see the leaves finally filling in the branches. I climbed into the spotless backseat and smelled the familiar leather scent. Kate turned around and smiled.

"I brought you some more stuff," she said. "Food and all sorts of things." There were several shopping bags next to me in the backseat.

Lee pulled out of the driveway and grabbed a map from the glove compartment. He was a navigational professional, my dad. It was a gift. He could get anywhere with complete certainty. My mom told me once he was like a human compass; she said it was because he was born with Navy blood in him. His dad, his grandfather, and his great-uncle were captains, admirals, and other very important people in the Navy. Lee was obsessed with the blue-blooded Pryor lineage and keeping the history of his ancestors alive. My sisters and I were members of Daughters of the American Revolution. There were certificates to prove it. He was serious about his children having reverence for the notable line of Pryor history. In fact, as he told me, I was named after "Admiral Austin Knight, the commander in chief of the U.S. Asiatic fleet in 1854, who wrote a book on modern seamanship which was used for reference for eight decades." Yes, Elizabeth Knight Pryor the first. I'd say "the first" because I wanted that number after my name, like my older brother Bill had.

It was just like Lee to be able to find an incredible restaurant in the absolute middle of nowhere. He put the map down and said, "I know where we're going." We drove in the quiet, air-sealed car for a while, until we pulled up to a beautiful old building. It was covered in ivy, and there was a valet standing out front. Inside, we were seated at a big booth with black leather cushions and beautiful brass lanterns hanging above. Lee ordered fish, salad, and French fries for all of us. Then, he looked at me carefully. "So, Diz, how have you been?"

"Fine," I said.

He furrowed his brow. "I thought the place was supposed to be a Catholic home for unwed mothers."

"So did I."

"It's not, is it?"

"No."

"That is what your mother said it was."

"Well, I guess it *used* to be run by nuns."

Lee laughed a familiar, frustrated laugh. "That is sooooo Dorothy. *Used* to be."

I didn't say anything. Kate and Lee exchanged a glance.

"Has your mother been here yet?" he asked.

"She came a few weeks ago."

"So she's come once." He looked frustrated. And said in a loud whisper, "Unnnnnbelievable. The whole *goddamn* reason you're here in *this* specific place was so she could come see you all the time. Yet, she doesn't come. So typical."

"Lee, that doesn't help her," Kate said.

"Jesus Christ, help who?"

"It doesn't help Liz to talk about Dorothy. Let's focus on Liz and see how she's doing." Kate softly put her hand on my dad's.

My dad took a big breath, looked at me, and asked, "Okay, well how is it? Tell me what it's like. Are you okay here?"

He didn't know? He really didn't know, before this second, that it wasn't a Catholic home for unwed mothers? And all this time I thought he did. I wanted to tell him everything, all of it. I was sure if he knew the truth of what the facility was like, he would say it was unacceptable. I could already hear it in my head, Lee's voice declaring I couldn't stay there. But I also didn't want to tell him. If he took me out, where would I go? My mom's face appeared in my mind. The same face she had in Lee's apartment that day when he told her I was pregnant, when he said she was a terrible mother. I tried to blur the image, but it wouldn't move. Would Lee call her and tell her that she'd messed up once again? I couldn't imagine living with that. And I was closer now, closer to the end. The baby was going to come in just a couple of months. And what about the girls, who thought every time I left I was never coming back? My view of everything had already been permanently altered, and I knew it. No matter where I lived out the last weeks of the pregnancy, no matter who was with me and how it went down, nothing was ever going to change what I knew and where I'd been. It was too late for that.

"Yes, I'm okay here," I said to my dad.

"You sure? It's a pretty shady-looking place."

"Well, the hospital is right next door," I pointed out. Lee loves practicality.

"Yes, I saw that."

"So, when it's time I just go over there," I said. He looked pensive. Kate reached over and put her hand on my back. I don't know how she knew, but just as I felt her hand, the floodgates opened and the tears came rolling out.

"What is it?" my dad asked.

"I don't know."

"You're emotional. That's what happens with pregnancy," he said, like he knew.

"It really *didn't* look like a warm and fuzzy place, Lee," Kate said. "Liz, the girls, are they . . . well, are they all right?"

I wiped my face on my sleeve. "Yeah, most of them."

"Can you go in and out of there when you want?" Kate asked.

"Yeah, I have a pass. I take walks and stuff, but there's nowhere to go."

"Well, you're in the middle of nowhere here," Lee said. He

made a couple of low, frustrated sounds. "I'm sorry, Liz, this is an incredibly difficult situation, really tough stuff. I wish I could do more to help. Your mother seems to have made another questionable choice here."

I wanted to ask him a lot of things, but I didn't. Like why didn't he come up and see it before? And if Dorothy's so bad at everything, why did he let her make this decision? We sat quietly, all of us somewhere else. Kate smiled uncomfortably. Lee finally said, "You're going to be okay, Liz. Just got to get through this and put it behind you. This kind of thing will make you stronger, that's for sure."

We went on to talk about summer work, and my college opportunities. Lee had written the letters to have my applications sent and was taking care of everything to ensure I would be heading off to school in the fall. My dad did have an amazing ability to make you feel like things were going to be okay. However, my brain could hold only so much when it came to my parents and their dynamic. I decided to make sure Dorothy's name didn't come up again that day. Lee finally said, "We should try to make the best of the day, right? I mean we're here, and happy to see you. Think we can go peruse the area?"

I wanted to try to have a nice time. I wiped the tears from my face. "Okay, Dad, *peruse* the area?"

"You know, check it out after lunch, there's always *something* interesting."

We ate the fish and salad and French fries. Lee and Kate didn't ask anything else about the facility and I didn't offer. I looked at Kate and thought how lucky my dad was to be with such a nice person. I remembered one of the first times I ever met her, about four and a half years earlier. It was on the boat, in the summer, at the Chicago Yacht Club. My sisters and some friends and I showed up to go sailing. It was a really hot day, and all we wanted to do was get out on the lake and anchor the boat so we could jump off and swim. I noticed, when I got on the boat that day, there was a huge thick rope I'd never seen before, tied off on a cleat and hanging off the stern. We sailed out, anchored, and all of us kids jumped in. I looked over and screamed for Kate to watch, but I couldn't see her. When I climbed back up the ladder, I saw she had on a life jacket and was hanging on to the big rope off the back of the boat. That's when I realized she didn't know how to swim. When I asked her why, she said she had never learned, no one had ever taught her, and I remember thinking that was sad.

Lee took the last bite of his fish and moved his knife and fork to the proper position at twenty past four. He then looked over at my plate, where fork and knife were already in the proper position. He got up to see if he could find out where to go and what to do in the area. Kate and I sat quietly, just the two of us. She smiled her thousand-watt smile.

"It's good to see you, Liz," she said. "I think about you a lot, hoping you're okay. You are okay, right?"

"Yeah. Thanks, Kate."

"Do they know when your baby will come?"

"They're guessing the last week in May."

"You know, I had my daughter when I was very young, and the good news is that it will go quickly, because you're young and strong. Don't worry about that part."

"I am worried about that part. . . . I'll try not to."

"Is your mom going to come when you go into labor?"

"I think so, I hope so."

"That's a good idea. And they're talking to you about the adoption?"

"I talk to this one woman, Ms. Graham. She's the one who tells me all the stuff. She's a social worker."

"Oh, well, that's really good."

"Yeah, she's a nice lady."

Lee came back to the table, rubbing his hands together the way he always did. "Let's take a drive, there are a few interesting historical points." He was the same Lee, no matter how in the middle of nowhere we were.

* * * *

We had a good day. Kate fell asleep on the car ride back. I watched the sun lowering in the sky as the pit in my stomach dug deeper. I hated this part, leaving my old world and saying goodbye. It never got easier, the leaving. Lee pulled up to the front of the facility and turned to me.

"I should just head out, Diz. She's asleep. I don't know when I'll be able to make it back. I'll let you know."

"Okay, thanks for everything, Dad, especially the history lesson."

"Smart aleck," he said, smiling. "You're going to be okay, you know that, right? Let's just get this over with."

"Okay."

"Don't forget the bags there. Kate said you asked for some pictures of yourself, and she also got the art supplies."

I leaned over and kissed him on the cheek and petted Kate's sleeping shoulder.

He watched me walk to the door and waited till it buzzed me in. I waved and watched the car take off toward home, miles and miles away.

chapter 11

The trek up to school felt easier without the snow, although Nellie, who was growing bigger by the second, didn't seem to feel the difference in mid-March. A couple of weeks after I saw my dad, we walked in the schoolhouse door and saw the books from the library sitting on a steel shelf in the front of the schoolroom.

"Well, shit," Deanna said. "They finally thought it would be a good idea to put some books in this fucking school." She walked over and grabbed one. Amy followed, then Wren and Jill. Nellie was standing in front of the shelves, taking it all in.

"Nell, you should read this," I said. I took *Little House in the Big Woods* off the shelf and held it out to her. "I love these books, they're all about this family living out in the wilderness."

"They're for little kids."

"No, they're not, everyone likes them. *Your* kids might like them one day, Nell. Why don't you just try, and the words you can't understand, mark them with a pencil and I'll help you with them."

She took the book out of my hand and looked at it. "I fucking guess I should. Where's a pencil?"

Maryann—the teacher who never said anything—stood up from her chair at the other end of the room. She cleared her throat and addressed us.

"Girls, as you can see, we got some books. I want to let you know that they are on loan from the public library. So if you want to take them with you, out of this room, you have to sign them out with me. I need to know so we can bring them back or renew them, or they'll charge us." She waited for what I guess she thought would be an argument, but no one said anything. She continued, "Okay. Also, tomorrow, there will be two long tables brought up from the basement so you have a surface to write on. You can just pull the chairs up to the tables." Again, she looked ready for heckling.

"Well, it's about time you did fucking something," Deanna said.

I raised my hand. Maryann looked at it, like she'd never seen a raised hand before. "Ahhhhh, yes . . . Liz?"

"I just wanted to say thanks for getting the books."

Tilly laughed and raised her hand. Maryann said, "Yes, Tilly?"

"Yeah, thanks," added Tilly. Nellie smiled and raised her hand too.

Maryann said, "Yes . . . Nellie?"

"What, are we in a *classroom* now?" Nellie said.

. . . .

Most of the girls wanted to take the books back to their rooms when school was over for the day. They lined up and signed them out, and we all headed back down the hill. The bitter chill in the air was gone. The trees were beginning to look like trees instead of dark, tangled spears. Nellie was holding on to Tilly and me, complaining about her swollen ankles. Tilly was also huge and was having trouble holding her huge belly up with her tiny toothpick legs, but she never ever complained.

"This is what it's gonna be like when we're fucking old, you know that?" Nellie groaned. "I feel like my great-grandmother."

"Is she really fat?" Tilly asked.

"No, fuck off. I meant she has a hard time movin' around."

Inside, I tapped on Ms. Graham's door, stepped in, pulled two pictures out of my pocket, and put them on her desk. In the pictures I was standing with my head kind of bent to the side, smiling big at the camera. I was in front of the Christmas tree at my dad's apartment. Ms. Graham picked them up and smiled. "When was this?" she asked.

"This past Christmas," I said. I realized I didn't know in that picture, just a few months earlier, that I was pregnant. I didn't know any of what I knew now. I wondered if I'd ever look quite like that girl again.

"They're perfect, Liz, thank you."

When I came out of the office, Nellie and Tilly were waiting for me. They bickered, which they did a lot, the whole walk back. They reminded me of my sisters sometimes. They stayed in the lounge, and I headed for my room. Jill was already there, on her bed, with my guitar in her lap. She could play one song now, "Skip to My Lou." She played it *incessantly.*

"I got to teach you a different song," I said. She placed the guitar against the wall, leaned over, and dug for something in her trash bag. "You know you can put that stuff in the drawers, Jill," I said. She kept everything in the big trash bag, even her toothbrush.

"No, I'm used to it."

I decided to finally ask her, "So . . . what did you do to be in juvie with Deanna?"

"What crime did I commit?"

"I guess."

"I'm a runaway. I ran away one too many times, couldn't stand listening to my mom fight with her boyfriend. He's an asshole."

"That's not really a crime."

"It is if you're a minor." She smiled. "It is what it is, you just gotta roll with it." Jill was different from any of the other girls at the facility. She obviously had had a hard life, like the rest of them, but it seemed to sit differently inside her. She was at ease with herself. She was lying back on her bed, rubbing her growing stomach.

"What are you going to do after you have your baby?" I asked.

"My mom doesn't know about this kid. I don't want to bring it back there. And the father, well, he wouldn't be a good dad. But I got a friend. She used to be my neighbor. She's twenty-two, she has a kid and a place, so I'm gonna go there, and get a job I guess."

I grabbed two apples off my dresser and threw her one. She caught it.

"Well thanks, Liz P. Girl in hiding, guitar player, not keeping her baby, rich family, with a mom *and* a dad . . . that's what I've learned about you without asking a thing." She chomped on the apple.

"You can ask me anything you want."

"Really? Okay. You ever gonna see or talk to any of these girls after this?"

"I don't know. Probably not."

"That's honest. How many songs you think I can learn on the guitar before you have your baby and leave?"

"Maybe three. My turn. Are you afraid of *anything*?" I asked.

She thought about it for a while. "Yeah."

"What?"

"Fucking up with my kid. My turn. Where's the dad to your baby?" There was a knock on the door. Jill and I both looked over and yelled in unison, "Come in, Tilly."

Tilly peeked her head in, smiling. "Is Liz telling a story or something? Why aren't you out in the lounge?"

Jill sat up from the bed and shoved her socked feet into her flip-flops on the floor. She pushed and pushed until she got the socks to bend for the thong part between her toes. She looked at me and said, "We're not finished."

We all headed to the lounge. *The Love Boat* was just ending. Alice came in to check the chore chart.

"Alice," I asked. "How long do you think you'll keep the Christmas decorations up in here? Isn't it almost Easter?" There was a plastic green garland, drooping along the far two walls in the lounge. Alice squinted.

"Thanks, Liz. I'll just add that to the chore chart for you and Jill this week."

The phone rang loudly from the booth out in the hall. Tilly jumped up and ran like a bat out of hell, just like she always did, hoping it was Rick calling for her. We all waited for her to run back in and pout about it being for someone else, but she didn't return. Amy looked up from the card game and said, "Thank you, Rick!" Then she looked over at Jill, who was playing cards against Wren. "Jesus, Jill, you need to go play cards as your job. You've never lost one game to any of us."

"My mom is a master at cards," Jill said. "Only thing she really knows how to do. She played every day. I'd come home from grade school, couldn't see through the smoke in our front room to get to the kitchen. Poker, all day every day. Maybe it's in my blood."

"You could use that shit, Jill. Go play in some of those street games, make some money," Deanna said.

"What do you think I been doing?"

"No shit? You play in the alley?"

"That's where they found me before I came here."

Deanna laughed. I looked over at Nellie, to see if she knew what the alley was, but she was bent over her chair and breathing heavy. I jumped up.

"Nellie, you okay? What's the matter?" I asked.

"I don't know, something's wrong."

"SHIT, where's Alice? Nellie, you don't look good. Shit you guys, somebody go find Alice right now. Nellie, is it labor? Your stomach?"

"Yeah . . . hold my hand."

She squeezed it so tight I yelped. "Is this the first time you've felt a pain?"

"No."

"Nellie, you're supposed to tell us, remember?"

"I didn't want to be a faker like fuckin' Gina. Shit, fuck, fuck, it hurts."

Wren came back with Alice. Alice rushed over, bent down, and asked, "Think it's time, Nell?"

"Yeah, I think." I didn't know what was going on inside of me, but I was petrified for Nellie. My heart was pounding. And then it dawned on me. I really, really didn't want Nellie to leave. And having the babies meant she was leaving. Alice called the hospital from the lounge phone.

"They're sending a wheelchair," she said. "Nellie, just relax, and try to breathe normally."

"Alice, these babies aren't fucking due yet." Nellie looked terrified.

"Twins come early sometimes. It's fine." Alice stroked her hair. "They're going to take good care of you at the hospital."

"Liz," Nellie said.

"Yeah?"

"You know, if these babies come and I leave, or fucking die, you have to be Mac."

"*What?*"

"From *Cuckoo's Nest*. You never picked a person. So you're Mac, you're really Mac anyway."

"Okay, I'll be Mac, Nell. You're going to be fine."

"You're not dying, Nellie," Alice said. "You're having a couple babies, it's very different."

Nellie glared at Alice. "Well, it feels like I'm fuckin' dyin'."

Tilly came skipping into the room from the phone booth, smiling from her call with Rick until she saw what was happening. "What the fuck? What's happening? Nellie, what's the matter?"

"I'm fine, you moron, I'm fine." And then she roared in pain.

Tilly covered her eyes. "Is she . . . is she in labor?"

"Yes, dear. Please, Tilly, calm yourself," Alice said.

"But, but, Nell, I'm supposed to have mine first, you can't be going."

The wheelchair and two paramedics came through the door with a bag and an oxygen tank. Nellie howled in pain. Tilly and I let go of her hands as they lifted her to the chair and wheeled her out. Tilly stood frozen, her eyes on the door for several minutes. The girls were silent. Alice turned around to face us.

"Girls, my gosh, such dramatics. Nellie is *pregnant*. When you're pregnant, there is labor at the end. She is healthy and strong and will be fine. So stop acting like people are sick and dyin', okay? And, listen, we've told you all *dozens* of times, when you feel pains, you are to tell one another and time them. Remember? Once they get to ten minutes apart or so then you are to tell us. Does anyone *not* know this?" We all chimed in that we knew.

It felt easy sometimes to forget the reason we were all there together, passing the long hours and endless days. But today, the reason was shouting at us.

* * * *

It was three o'clock in the morning. I was awoken by a light tapping on the door. The door quietly opened.

"Who is it?" I whispered.

"It's me, I can't sleep alone. I miss her." It was Tilly.

Jill was snoring loudly. I got up and took one of my pillows and put it at the end of the bed and then undid the blanket at the bottom, like I'd done with my little sisters many times. "Come here, Till, get in and sleep with me on that end, and I'll sleep on this side."

"Thanks, Liz," she said, crawling into the bed.

"She's going to be all right, Tilly. She's just having her babies." I turned over and went back to sleep.

* * * *

When I opened my eyes, Jill was standing over me.

"Look at the pregnant lezbos," she said.

Tilly's foot was an inch from my face. She was still sound asleep. I rolled out of bed and sat on the floor.

"Very funny. She couldn't sleep."

"I already asked Alice early this morning. There's no news about Nellie yet."

I made my way to the bathroom. The shower had become what seemed like the only true luxury left in my life. The warm soothing water could make me forget everything, just for a few seconds. There were no clean towels, so I grabbed my robe, wrapped it around myself, and wrung the water out of my hair into the sink. When I walked out of the bathroom, Tilly was awake. She was sitting up in my bed with matted bed hair, wearing what looked like a T-shirt for a giant and one sock. She scrunched up her face.

"Sorry. Thanks for letting me sleep here."

"It's fine, I gotta do laundry." I got dressed and started trying to pile the sheets the way Tilly showed me. Tilly jumped out of bed.

"I'll help you. Jill, you got anything in that bag needs washing?"

"You offering?"

"Yeah."

Jill threw some clothes at her. Tilly grabbed change from my dresser and looked at Jill, proudly.

"I taught Liz how to do laundry."

"I hope she does it better than she plays gin," Jill said, smiling. I threw a quarter at Jill's head and we left. We passed through the lounge where Deanna was asleep on the La-Z-Boy. It looked like she might have slept out there all night. When we were heading down the stairs to the laundry room, I turned to Tilly.

"Does Deanna *sleep* all night in the lounge, Till?"

"I think she does sometimes. Has something to do with small rooms and beds and what happened to her. I don't know."

The laundry room was empty this early in the morning. Tilly made me do it myself this time. She sat leaning back in the folding chair watching to make sure I did it right, tipping far on the back legs.

"Don't do that with the chair, you're going to fall," I said.

"Don't put so much soap. You don't need all that." She put the chair legs back on the floor. "You think she's all right?"

"Yeah, she's just having her kids. When she's done she'll be so happy."

"I don't know, that's the part she was the most scared about—after. Hey, did I tell you Rick said on the phone that he gave the money for our place? And he's going to garage sales for baby stuff?"

"No, that's great. What else did he say?"

"He ran into this girlfriend of mine at the store. She said everyone's excited to meet my baby."

"Sounds good, Till. I talked to Ms. Graham. She said she can help you figure out a way you can go to school while you take care of the baby. There's some program or something. You got to go talk to her, okay?"

"Really?"

"Yeah."

She seemed excited by the idea, and I suddenly felt sure that Tilly would figure things out for herself, that things would maybe be okay for her too. I switched and folded and piled the laundry. After, we headed to the cafeteria for breakfast. The smell was eternally disgusting, no matter what they were serving. It was scrambled eggs with some sort of sausage that day. Tilly ate both hers and mine. I tried to stomach some milk and bread.

. . . .

"Hand me the damn hammer, will ya?" Jill was on the ladder with her arms stretched up to the ceiling. We were trying to get the Christmas decorations down in the lounge. I handed her a hammer. She pulled, and the garland finally came down. When we were done, Jill got off the ladder and sat down at the table in Nellie's usual spot. Tilly and I looked at each other. Then Amy looked at Jill.

"Too soon, Jill, sit over here," Amy said.

"Oh, shit, sorry I forgot about the everybody-has-a-seat thing. Where's my seat gonna be?"

Tilly pointed to Nellie's chair. "Probably there, I guess, but not till we hear, okay?"

Jill sat down in a different spot at the table and called to me, "Liz, get over here. Lemme teach *you* a little something, huh? You never know, even in that swanky life of yours, poker could come in handy."

She shuffled the deck like a magician. The only other person I'd seen handle cards like that was my grandfather Papa, who could count a deck of cards at his ear holding them in one hand. He'd put his thumb on the deck, let them rip, and in three seconds he could tell us how many cards were there. Jill looked at me with a serious expression. "I've changed my mind, let's start with black-jack. I'm gonna teach you about the deck, and odds, and busting, double downing, stiffing, standing, sitting, holding, all that good stuff, and then we'll move on."

"Fuckin' A, Jill, you sound like a Vegas dealer," Amy said. Jill smiled. She spent the next two hours trying to teach me cards. I couldn't remember anything, couldn't add fast enough, couldn't sit still. But the thing that really put Jill over the top was that I couldn't seem to hold a poker face. She claimed I gave away every hand with my face. I tried and tried again, but I couldn't hide it, and she just kept knowing what I had. She was so frustrated. She banned me from playing poker or blackjack at our table ever again. Amy and Tilly laughed the entire time.

Amy smiled big at the end and said, "We finally found something Liz really *sucks* at."

Wren read out loud from the TV guide that *Carrie* was on TV. We got our pillows, I brought out snacks, and we turned the lights off and sat transfixed by the movie. Just as the kids were about to dump the bucket of blood on Sissy Spacek's head, Alice came in. She turned on the lights and said, "I have news."

Tilly jumped up and turned off the TV. "What? What is it? Did she have them? Is she okay?"

"She had them and she's okay. The babies are healthy, and Nellie has a bit of a recovery now, but everyone is fine." The girls all clapped and started chatting and asking questions. Alice whistled to quiet us.

"Tilly, I need you to pack up all Nellie's things from your room. Liz, you can help her. They will be brought over to the hospital tomorrow."

"Why *all* her things? Isn't she coming back?" Tilly asked.

"No, sweetheart, her time is up. She's going to go home with her grandma when she's well. She's starting her life with her babies."

"What did she have?"

"She had a boy and a girl."

"Can we see her?"

"Tilly, I want to talk to you." Alice pulled her out in the hall, where the rest of us couldn't hear them. I could see Tilly looking down at the floor, and then she came back in.

"What did she say, Till?" I asked.

"She just lectured me about why we're here, that we're here to have these babies so we can go home. I just wanted to say bye to Nellie. It's not like I don't get that when we have the babies, we leave. Duh." Tilly seemed upset, more upset than I'd ever seen her.

Tilly and I headed to her and Nellie's room. I had never been inside before. The room looked like a waste pit. There was stuff everywhere, clothes everywhere, beds unmade, curtains closed, the room filled with crap all over.

"Geez, Tilly, this is a mess," I said.

"I know, we're pretty bad, but we're both bad so it doesn't matter."

"How do we tell whose stuff is whose? You don't even use the dressers?"

Tilly got Nellie's suitcase out and started throwing things in it. There was so much trash. We weeded through and finally got Nellie's stuff together in the suitcase. I checked under the bed and in the bathroom and all the drawers to make sure we didn't forget anything. When I picked up her pillow, I saw the book *Little House in the Big Woods* underneath. I flipped to the first page, and then turned to the next, and the next and the next. Every other word, for twenty pages, was circled in pencil.

"What is it?" Tilly said.

"Nothing, just her book."

"We gotta give it back so they can take it to the library."

"Yeah, okay, I'll bring it back to Maryann. You going to be okay sleeping in here?"

"Yeah, now I know she's okay, I'll be fine." I wondered if Tilly was nervous, realizing she was next.

. . . .

Jill was lying in bed, reading, when I got back to our room.

"You pack all her stuff up?"

"Yeah."

"Good for her, right? It's over."

"Yeah," I said. Or was it just beginning? Nellie's leaving felt so startling. I *knew* we were *all* going to have our babies and leave. Of course I knew. It was all I wanted since the day I arrived—to leave. But watching Nellie go hit me deeply. Like we were soldiers. People who'd grown to know and depend on each other, who'd built a shelter for existence together. And now part of the shelter would be gone. It felt like the war of survival was ending, person by person, until eventually all of us would be gone.

. . . .

The next morning I opened my eyes and saw on the Snoopy clock that it was 5:50 A.M. I tiptoed to the dresser and got dressed. As I stumbled my way through the hall, I tripped and dropped my boots loudly on the floor. As I was crouching down to pick them up, the door next to me opened. Tilly was standing in her bra, her stomach hanging out over her sweatpants. I dropped the boots again. She scratched her head.

"What are you doing? I thought maybe Nellie was back."

"Oh no, I'm . . . Well, shit, I'm going over there to see her." Tilly disappeared and came back in a second with her shirt on and a coat in her hand. "I'm coming," she said.

We made our way down the dark hall to the front gate, where the guard stopped us. "Whoa, whoa, whoa, where you two think you're going?"

"Shit," Tilly said. It was the all-night guard. Chief wasn't in for the day yet.

"Um, here, I have a pass." I pulled it out and showed it to her.

"Ah, yeah, I know *you* have a pass, but she don't have a pass."

Tilly looked at me like, *Do something.*

So I turned to the guard and said, "She always comes with me on my morning walk. I haven't been feeling well. Chief lets her come."

"You gotta work on your lying, girl. I know these kids can't leave, that's why I have a job. The rules are the rules. You can go but she can't."

Tilly turned to me. "You go, tell her I said hi and I miss her and I hope everything's okay, and I . . . I'm gonna wait right here till you get back."

I headed out the door into the brisk morning air. I buttoned up my coat and watched the auburn sun rising behind the trees. There were a few people standing around the entrance to the hospital, which was to the left and down about half a block from the facility entrance. Inside the hospital lobby, I found a sign with the names of departments on it. I followed the green arrows up an elevator, through a hall, and to a big desk that read Maternity. There was a chalkboard behind the desk, with patients' names written in pink and blue chalk. Nellie's name was written in both pink and blue with an asterisk next to it. As I walked down the too-bright hallway, I peeked into a few rooms. Balloons and baskets and flowers were scattered everywhere. People were whispering and laughing softly. Everyone on the floor seemed happy. I got to Nellie's door at the end of the hall and pushed it open. It was pitch-dark, the curtains were drawn, and the lights were off. Nellie had an IV in her arm and medical tape all over the back of her hands, and on her chest going up her neck. Her big stomach was gone. She was sound asleep. There were two empty cribs, side by side near the bed.

I opened the curtains a little. Dorothy always said sunlight makes people feel better. I could see the shiny roof of the facility nestled amid the trees. Then I walked back to the bed and stood over Nellie, asleep. Her hair was matted to her head, and her boils looked painful and swollen, but she'd done it. She'd given birth to a little boy and a little girl. I saw a notepad and pen on the table. I tried to write as simply and neatly as possible.

Nellie, you will be a great mom!
   Love, Liz

I pulled the *Little House in the Big Woods* book out of my coat, stuck the note in it, and set it on the table next to her bed. The smell of the hospital was making me queasy, or maybe it was just life. I stepped out of the room and leaned against the cold wall in the hallway. Sometimes I had to remind myself to breathe, and this was one of those times. I took a deep breath as I watched the world around me. There was a woman gingerly walking toward me, holding a new baby. People who looked like relatives and friends were bustling in and out of rooms. The hall was lively, with an impossible-to-miss joy. Across the way, I spotted a family in a sitting room. The mom sat in a hospital gown in a chair, as the dad paced the floor with the new baby. There were two little kids playing on the floor. One of the boys toddled up to his mom and kissed her on the cheek. The other one stood up and handed her a picture from a coloring book. The dad put the baby in the mom's arms, and the two boys leaned in to pet it, like a baby kitten. Something inside me dropped. I turned and took a last look at Nellie and the darkness, and then quietly closed the door to her room. I made my way back through the hall, down the elevator, and out of the hospital. The amber sky had turned into bright morning light. I found a bench near the side of the road. I sat for a long time before I looked down at the big round bump under my coat. I slowly unbuttoned the coat and looked more closely at my stomach. There was a person in there, attached to me, with fingers and toes and a heart. For the first time, I truly felt it. The truth was suddenly bigger than me, and I knew it could never be changed. No matter how far away I was, no matter what I said or how hard I tried to forget, the truth is unchangeable. Maybe that's why it's so powerful.

chapter 12

Nellie had been gone three weeks, four days, and a few hours. Jill had taken over her spot in the lounge. Tilly had to move to the couch—she was so big, she couldn't sit comfortably in the chair anymore. Amy took Tilly's spot. I sat in my chair and watched Jill methodically flipping cards for solitaire. I stared at the cards as they dropped flawlessly one on top of the other. I was lost in thought, thinking about the day *after* my mom found out I was pregnant.

Dorothy had left my dad's apartment in the city by herself that afternoon. I had driven down to the city in my own car and drove home separately, the long way. We didn't see each other again until the next morning. I woke up and I heard the sound of the twins chatting in the room next door before school. I looked up at the origami swan mobile, hanging above my head, and watched the weightless birds bump into one another. And then a cold haze of doom rushed through me. I was pregnant. This was real. The thing living in my stomach, the going away, the lie, the ruin of my life, it was all really going to happen. Downstairs, Dorothy was at the kitchen table, looking at the yellow pages. I glanced down and saw an advertisement with a picture of Jesus on a cross and the words Teenage Pregnancy/Catholic Services. Dorothy looked up at me— it was the same look she had when we all returned on Christmas Eve from my dad's house, to show her the piles of gifts that Kate had picked out for us. The look was there again when we left for the British Virgin Islands during the first week of January. It was stoic and silent, until you got up close and saw the crushing, palpable sadness behind it. It couldn't be missed or ignored. Every time I saw that look, I shivered. She forced a closed-mouth smile.

"Good morning, Liz."

"Hi, Mom . . . What are you doing?"

There was a long pause. "Looking for a place for you to *live*." I tried not to look at her. I couldn't take it. Her words came out in a sharp staccato rhythm. "You have an appointment today in Wilmette at the photo studio for graduation."

My brain froze. I couldn't think straight. "I can't do that, Mom. I can't have my senior picture taken *today*. . . ."

"You *can* and you *will*."

"No, Mom. Not after knowing what I know. Please, I can't."

But Dorothy stood up and stepped toward me, pointing her finger. "You will do this," she said. I backed up out of the kitchen, stumbling. She kept pointing her finger nearer, and finally *on* my chest, until I'd backed all the way up the stairs to the hallway. She pointed toward my room. I backed in the door, she silently pointed to the bed. I sat down. She stepped in, shut the door behind her, and looked at me with a frightening resolve.

"You will do *whatever* you have to do to *gradddduuuaaatteee* from high school, Liz Pryor. Taking this photograph is a part of *that*." She walked out the door and came back a few seconds later with a light blue oxford cloth button-down and placed it on my bed.

"You can wear this, it's clean and ironed. Brush your hair and come down to the car." I cried like a baby as I changed into the shirt. I looked at my puffy self in the mirror. I didn't want to have a picture of me, at the lowest point in my life, that would live in a yearbook until the end of time. I wanted to run and hide and bury myself somewhere, leaving behind no evidence. The entire car ride to the studio, I tried to convince Dorothy we should turn around. She wouldn't budge. We sat in the parking lot in front of the photography studio while I pleaded with her.

"Mom, please. Look at me. I don't look like myself. I don't want to see people now that I know. *Please*, I can't do it." She turned and said, "Get *out* of the car, and *pretend* that you can."

I slowly walked into the studio, wiped my tears, and *pretended* I was a normal girl. I said hi to a few kids I recognized. I waited my turn and walked into a little room with a brown cloth backdrop and a chair. The photographer put some cover-up under my eyes and told me to smile, and I did.

◆ ◆ ◆ ◆

Alice sauntered into the lounge. In her annoying singsongy voice, she announced she had some news. The priests from the church next door had invited all the girls in the facility to join them for Easter brunch at the rectory. Alice went on about bacon and sausage and pastries and chocolate Easter eggs, and the girls hooted with excitement.

"I imagine everyone will be able to make it? But we will need a head count," Alice said.

"I won't be there," I said. "My mom's coming to visit."

Tilly looked over at me. "So you're leaving for the only good meal we will ever have in this place? The only meal you could actually eat?"

"Sorry . . ." I said, smiling. I couldn't wait for Easter.

"Well, I hope this baby doesn't fall out of me while you're gone," Tilly said. She looked up at the ceiling with a pout.

"You may not have that kid while I'm gone, Tilly," I said. "I'm not kidding. I want to be here when you go."

"Well, she better cross her fucking legs, then. Look at her, she's about to burst," Amy said.

Jill cleared her throat and shuffled her deck loudly at the table. She expertly swooshed all fifty-two cards onto the table facedown and said to me and Tilly, "Both of you, pick a card." I reached over and picked the card on the end. Tilly picked one from the middle of the fan line.

"Show 'em to me," Jill said. I turned over the king of hearts; Tilly showed us the four of clubs. Jill smiled. "She's not gonna have that baby while you're gone."

. . . .

I couldn't wait for my mom to visit. I loved Easter as a kid, I mean I *loved* it. Waking up in the morning to our baskets at the end of our beds, filled with silly toys and jelly beans . . . We'd all get out of bed and line up at the top of the big staircase, gripping our baskets, waiting for the okay from our parents. When my mom gave the sign, we'd fly down the stairs like maniacs and into the giant open living room, where you could see hundreds of candy eggs hidden on top of pictures, inside lampshades, in the corners of couches and chairs, in the pleats of curtains, in plants, under the piano. And then we'd eat chocolate eggs till we were sick to our stomachs.

My memories of the holidays throughout the years lived very specifically inside me, glowing and permanent. My mom had a passion for tradition that went beyond the norm. She loved holidays and customs with every morsel of her being. I mean she *poured* her joy into those days like nothing else. Her contagious enthusiasm brought the magic, and surprisingly, year after year, it never failed to meet the expectation. This year, despite everything, it would be a scrap of normalcy—of happiness—for me to hang on to.

. . . .

Later, back in my room, Wren knocked on the door and shouted that I had a phone call.

I picked up and heard the familiar voice.

"Helllllooooo, Liz, dear."

"Hiiiiiii, Mom, how are you?"

"I'm well, honey. How is it going?"

"Okay, I guess. I mean I'm getting pretty tired of it here. I can't wait to see you. Where are we going for Easter? Wait, actually, I don't care. I just want to see you."

There was a long pause. I detected the slightest trace of the Katharine Hepburn voice as she began to answer.

"Liz, I . . . well, I couldn't exactly work it out with your father and the twins for Easter."

"What do you mean?" I asked.

"Your dad apparently has plans and couldn't accommodate taking the twins, so it doesn't look as though I can make it to you for Easter. It's just too difficult to work out. I can't bring the twins to you, and I can't leave them here for Easter, you see?" I felt everything inside me drop a notch.

"Well . . ."

"Of course, I can come after at some point. But probably not until the following week. The thing is, Rosemary and her family have invited us *all* down to Sea Island, Georgia. We haven't been anywhere in a long time. I thought I'd take the twins at least, and we can have a nice time. It won't be very Easter-like, but . . . I feel terrible, sweetheart. I know how much you would love it. Liz, are you there?"

"Yeah."

"I *am* sorry, honey, so sorry. I will be sure to get up to see you as soon as we return."

"How long will you and the twins be gone?"

"Just a week."

"Okay . . . I have to go."

"Lizzie, I love you. Happy Easter, sweet . . ." But I slammed the phone down before she finished. In fact I slammed it several times. I picked the receiver up again and again and again, slamming it back down harder and harder each time. I sat on the cold wooden seat in the phone booth and waited as my brain and my heart caught up with each other. I swallowed the rising ball in the back of my throat, the one that usually meant I was about to cry. But I pushed it back down and felt something different making its way through me. I shoved the phone booth door behind me and headed back to my room. Jill said something as I stormed in, but I didn't hear her. I lay down on my bed, crossed my arms, and stared up at the ceiling.

A few minutes later Tilly was standing over my bed, looking down at me. "What happened? Liz? *Liz!*" She turned to Jill. "What happened? What's wrong with her?"

"I don't know. She took the phone call and she's been lying there like that ever since. I think she's pissed about something." Tilly was pacing the room like a lawyer on a TV show. I lay as still as a corpse on my bed, staring up at the ceiling, feeling the rage brew inside me. I couldn't say anything. After trying to get me to talk for a few minutes, they gave up. Jill asked Tilly if she thought I would think it was okay if she borrowed one of the sketch pads that Kate and Lee brought for me. Tilly answered that she was sure I wouldn't mind. Jill pulled out a new sketch pad for both of them. Tilly talked about Rick while she drew Easter eggs. Jill sat on her bed with a pencil and pad and sketched quietly. I remained still as a statue. My mind tried to push the sadness of the Easter letdown to the front, but I rejected it. I turned it off. I closed it. I told it I was tired of being sad, in fact I was fucking *out* of sadness. I wasn't interested in going there—not anymore. I remained still for a long time, listening to Jill's pencil sketching, ignoring the pain trying to break me. I wasn't going to let that happen, not anymore. Tilly eventually went to bed, and I finally fell asleep.

. . . .

The next morning I woke up feeling something different. I couldn't quite put my finger on it. Jill was still sleeping, snoring like she always did. Her sketch pad was open at the end of my bed. I picked it up to see an incredible drawing. It was me, sitting on the bed. My hand was on my forehead, and I was smiling and holding my guitar in my lap. It had strange, bold, sharp lines—but the eyes looked just like mine. At the bottom Jill had written in perfect cursive, *Sunny Girl with Guitar, April 1979.*

I gazed over at Jill as she slept and wondered how on earth she was the way she was. I leaned the drawing up against the mirror on my dresser. After a long, hot shower, I put on clean clothes and walked down the hall to Alice's office. She was sitting at her desk.

"Well, look at the early riser, this is a first."

"I guess it's the new me," I said. "I wanted to let you know that I kept Nellie's book she got from the school. Actually I gave it to Nellie to keep."

"Oh yeah, Maryann mentioned that book. We couldn't find it in the room and Tilly hadn't seen it. So, what? It's gone?"

"I'll give you money for it."

"It doesn't make us look good, you know, to the library. Might have to give you a consequence for breaking the rules."

"What kind of consequence?"

"Well, I guess I'll assign you double chores for the week."

"All right. Also, I *am* going to be here for Easter now."

"Oh?" She looked up at me. "What happened?"

"My mom can't come," I said. And I didn't cry or get upset. It was just what it was. There was nothing I could do about it.

· · · ·

I headed down early for my Dr. Dick appointment that morning. I was the first one there. The freaky nurse lifted one eyebrow when she saw me. The doctor came in where I was waiting on the table in the creepy room. As usual, he didn't look at me.

"You know the drill, feet up in the stirrups." But I stayed sitting up, looking at him. My anger seemed to be stirring something different inside me.

"I have a couple questions," I said.

"What is it?" He seemed annoyed. But I could feel just a hint of something; I thought it might be strength. I looked him square in the eye.

"Can you please tell me when you think this baby will be ready to come out?"

"I guess I can try," he said.

"Okay. And can you tell me if there's anything I can do to make that part easier?"

"You mean the labor?"

"Yeah."

"Relaxing helps, but nothing's going to make it easy, young lady."

"Okay, and how long will it take?"

"I have no idea. It could take one hour, forty hours . . ." Forty hours? "Most of these girls, it's at least fourteen, maybe twenty hours." I sat back and put my feet up in the stirrups. I gritted my teeth as he poked and prodded. I felt the back of my throat swelling again, but I pushed it down when he told me to sit up.

"Looks like this baby will be ready in a few weeks. There is a note in your chart about being out by a certain date. Looks to me like that's going to happen. If it doesn't, we can use a drug to bring the labor on, speed up the process."

I had another question. I couldn't look at him when I asked, but I wanted to know. And I finally felt the courage to say it out loud.

"One more question. Um, there's this weird liquid or something coming out of my boob."

He rolled his eyes. "That's fine, you're getting ready to lactate. That happens in the last month or so. Some leaking from the nipples. You're planning to nurse this baby?"

"No, I'm giving this baby up for adoption."

He actually *chuckled,* which shocked me. "Well, that's the most practical thing I've heard all year. Good for you, young lady. I'll write in your chart here that we'll also be giving you a medication after delivery to help stop lactation, dry you up, all right?"

He threw his gloves in the trash and left. I stayed on the table a long time, thinking to myself. What if my mom doesn't come when I'm ready to have the baby? What if it was just me and Dr. Dick? What if the baby doesn't come out? What if there's something wrong with it? What if there's something wrong with it, and the people don't want to adopt it? What if something happens to me, and Dr. Dick doesn't give a shit? What if my parents never come back for me? What would I do? The weirdo nurse came to the doorway.

"Doctor wants me to weigh you again." I went along and followed her to the scale. She glanced at me as I got off the scale and said, "You're barely where you should be. You need to eat more."

• • • •

We did a whole lot of nothing for two straight days, waiting for the big Easter brunch. I did double chores because of the stolen library book—triple actually, 'cause Tilly was so big, she could barely move. The day before Easter, the phone in the hall rang. Amy ran for it and told me I had a call.

"Who is it?" I asked.

"It sure sounds like your fancy mom."

"Tell her I'm not available," I said. The room went silent.

"What the fuck, Liz, I'm not saying that," Amy said.

"Okay, then just hang the phone up."

"You really don't want to talk to her?" Tilly said.

"Nope."

Tilly got a determined look on her face, stood up, and said she'd do it herself. When she came back she announced, "Your mom wants you to *callllllllllll* her." Everyone laughed.

But I didn't. I didn't want to think about Sea Island, Georgia, the beach, their trip, any of it. Instead, I thought about my older brothers and sisters. I wondered where they were, what they were doing, and where they thought *I* was. What about my grandparents and my friends? I'd been gone for months. I'd vanished completely and until that moment, I hadn't realized that no one—not a single person—had reached out to hear my voice. No one had written a letter or demanded some kind of contact. It was as though I was fading into a mere speck of existence, in my own world, cut off from everything that came before. The realization almost choked me. Did no one miss me?

My mind wandered back to when I was a little girl. To all the nights I'd lain alone, on my back, on the deck of my dad's schooner. I liked to look up at the brilliantly lit night sky and the thousands of stars and planets. While everyone was sleeping down below, I'd play a game. I'd silently search and search and search for the tee-niest star. I'd squint and scan the enormous sky. When I thought I'd finally found it, the smallest fading speck of a star, I'd say out loud, "I found you and I see you, smallest star of them all." *I* was becoming smaller and smaller, and I was afraid I might fade and disappear.

* * *

The next morning I woke to the sound of church bells chiming. The sound was beautiful and familiar. For a moment I forgot where I was, I forgot *who* I was. I looked out at the flawless blue sky, and saw the sun resting at the top of the trees, waiting to warm the day. And then I remembered. It was Easter Sunday. I closed my eyes and listened carefully to the chime of each beautiful bell and decided I wanted to matter. I didn't care how small I felt, how much I'd faded. I needed to matter, at least to myself. I let the bells fill me up. They got louder and louder until I could actually feel the sound inside me. The more I listened, the stronger I felt. I finally opened my eyes and looked over at Jill. She wrapped her pillow around her head to cover her ears, and then she shouted out to the window, "*Fucking* bells."

I laughed and threw my pillow at her.

"*Motherfucking* bells, so loud."

"Happy Easter, Jill."

"Happy Easter, bitch," she said. We got out of bed and dressed.

Jill smoked a cigarette out the window in the room. Of course she'd figured out a way to nudge it open just so, so the smoke would go out of the room and not come in. Smoking was forbidden in the bedrooms. She finished the cigarette, closed the window, and tucked her white gauze Mexican shirt with the red-and-yellow smocking into her tan corduroy pants.

"Easter-y enough?" she asked me.

"Perfectly Easter-y," I said. We made our way to the lounge, where the girls were gathered, looking a lot more civilized than usual. Alice appeared at the door, wearing a puffy pink flowered dress and straw hat. The girls whistled and hooted. She twirled once around and then got to business.

"Okay, okay, that's enough. Happy Easter! Listen up. There's something I forgot to make clear to you girls about today—no church, no brunch! Got that? You all gotta go to mass." Amy and Deanna moaned the loudest, but we all went along. We weren't going to miss brunch, not for anything.

We followed Alice, navigating the dirt path around to the back of the facility in our nicer-than-usual shoes. Tilly had her hair in a tiny ponytail in the back of her head, with a sad green ribbon tied around it. The maternity shirt I'd given her barely covered her stomach now. She turned to me and smiled. "We're going somewhere, who cares if it's church, right? We're out and about!" She looked up at the sky and laughed. None of the girls had been anywhere in a long, long time. We followed the path past the chapel and down a hill. There were a few small buildings and a nice church at the end of the small road where the hospital was. As the wooden doors opened, I felt everything in my body pause. There was the extraordinary sound of the organ, and the familiar smell of Easter lilies. The girls fought about where to sit, and who would go in first, and if they should kneel or sit. Finally, I knelt down, last in the pew, and crossed myself. I craned my neck around to watch the organ player up in the balcony. The music soothed what felt so cracked inside me.

There was a little girl, sitting in the row in front of me, with her parents and baby brother. She was wearing an Easter bonnet and white tights. She kicked her party shoes against the back of the pew in front of her, and each time her mom told her to stop, she'd do it again. The church was filled with *life*. The kind of life none of us had seen in a long time. In the aisle, next to me, I saw an enormous white statue of the Virgin Mary holding baby Jesus. It looked almost suspended in air. The look on Mary's sweet face made me think of my older sister, who once asked my mom if she could pray to Mary instead of God because she was a girl. My mom said we could pray to any of them—to Jesus, to God, to Mary, and to all the saints. In that moment, I prayed to Mary. I asked her if she could help me give birth to the baby inside me. And then I talked to God. I told him I was sorry for all the things I had done wrong, for the mistakes I'd made, for being so careless about sex. I told him I would always be sorry for them, and then I asked him if he could help me be okay in the world, after all of this was over. If he could help make me feel like I mattered again. I hadn't cried in a while, in fact I was pretty sure I'd finally run out of tears, but as I asked God one last thing—to help me not be so upset with my mom for leaving me there at Easter—I felt the wet drops pouring out of my eyes.

· · · ·

Afterward, Alice led us into the rectory dining area. It was a handsome room, covered in shiny dark wood, with light coming through the stained-glass windows. Tulips sat on each of the tables, and dozens of crepe paper Easter eggs hung from the ceiling. The girls found the candy egg table, and several of them began shoving chocolates into their pockets. Jill ducked out for a smoke. At that moment, a very strange-looking group of pregnant girls walked through the door. They were older than us, and I'd never seen them before. Amy came up and whispered, "*That's* the fucking weird-ass red-haired girl. Look, look at her!" Sure enough, the girl with the red hair from the hall that day was in the group of girls. These must have been *all* of the over-eighteens from the other wing.

Deanna couldn't contain herself. She said out loud, for everyone to hear, "Holy shit. They let the crazy pregnant chicks out."

Wren covered her eyes. "I can't even look at that one girl. I know something is wrong with her but she scares me." There was a loopy-looking girl with wild frizzy hair who couldn't seem to walk straight. She moved her hands all over the place. She had a very low-hanging pregnant stomach and was making loud screeching noises.

"Nellie woulda eaten this shit up, sitting here with the whole crowd-a *Cuckoo's Nest* bitches," Deanna said. The older girls apparently had their own table, but a few of them decided to sit with us. One of them was playing with a wooden toy paddle that had a rubber ball attached by a rubber band. She was trying to paddle the ball, but kept hitting things on the table instead. A saltshaker and then a glass of water toppled over. Deanna got up, walked over, took the paddle out of the girl's hand, and slammed it down on the table. The girl started crying, and then she started screaming. The resident supervisor from the other wing came over and tried to calm the girl. I took a long sip of water and felt my stomach go weak as an elderly priest approached the front of the room and tried to get our attention.

He cleared his throat and began in a raspy, tired voice: "It is our great pleasure today to share with you girls this grand breakfast feast in honor of our Lord Jesus Christ. Remember that Jesus forgives all. To repent is how we free ourselves from wrongdoing." He told us that we should all experience the glory of confession. He talked about the Resurrection. I liked the idea of a second life, or Second Coming or whatever it was. At the end, he asked us again to take advantage of the confessionals that would remain open for two hours after brunch.

We were served warm croissants, bacon, sausage, pancakes,

fresh orange juice, and hot tea. I sat and watched the crazy girls, and my friends, and Alice, and the priests. The food was delicious, but for some reason I couldn't eat. I felt like standing up and screaming as loud as I possibly could. So instead, I walked over to Jill and asked her for a cigarette. She handed me her Zippo and a Marlboro. With a mouth full of food she said, "You don't give me that lighter back, I know where you live." I made my way outside, lit the cigarette with the Zippo, and puffed on the smoke. I thought about the confession booths inside of the church with the dutiful priests sitting in the dark. I'd always believed in God and tried to follow the rules of the church I'd been raised in, but I wasn't sure I believed I had to go to confession for God to forgive me. Or for me to forgive myself. I was having conflicting feelings about the things the priests so often said, and the things *I* believed about God. The only thing I knew for sure was that God was there somewhere. I could feel it. Maybe that was all that mattered.

I made my way back to the dining room. Everyone was gathered around our table, looking at something. I nudged my way through and saw Tilly on the floor.

Wren and Amy helped her sit up in a chair at the table. "Those pains are enough for me to send you over, Tilly, get you checked. You might be ready," Alice said.

"Okay," Tilly said.

Alice turned to me. "You know the way, you want to walk her to the hospital?" I nodded. Alice said she'd let them know we were on our way. Tilly and I walked out of the rectory, arm in arm, and headed down the road to the hospital.

"Does it hurt?" I asked.

"Yeah, but not that bad." I smiled. "*Yet*," she added.

We got to the entrance of the hospital and decided to sit down on the bench outside for a second. We were quiet for a while, and then I said: "Till, you think you can remember this? What I'm going to tell you?"

"Yeah, I don't think you lose your memory when you have a kid. What?"

"The name of my dad's company is *Pryor Corporation*. It's listed in the phone book in Chicago. You can always know where I am or get me by calling there, okay?"

"Got it."

I looked at her carefully. "Are you scared?"

"Yeah, shitless, but, like you said, if everyone else can do it, I can do it, right?"

We walked into the hospital and made our way to labor and delivery. They were expecting Tilly. We waited in a small room until a nurse came and handed Tilly a gown, a barf bin, and some ice chips. Tilly changed, sat up on the bed, and waited.

"Now what?"

"I don't know, now you wait for more pains?"

The nurse came back in and told us a doctor would check Tilly shortly. Tilly sat on the edge of the bed. "Thanks, Liz, for everything. I mean *everything*. I'm never gonna forget ya, and I'm gonna call ya, I'll even call you at the facility sometime." The nurse came in and told me to leave. She told me if Tilly wasn't ready, she'd be released back to the facility. I reached over and hugged her sweaty neck and kissed her head.

I sat down again on the bench outside the hospital. I looked up at the warm sun, and then saw someone standing directly in front of me. I put my hand up to my forehead to block the glare.

"I need my lighter," Jill said, looking at me with a smile on her face.

"What the hell? How did you get out of there?"

"You're kidding, right?" She sat down next to me. "I told them I was so inspired by the confession lecture, I'd be at confession a long time."

I reached in my pocket and handed her the lighter. She pulled out the cigarettes and handed me one. "So what happened—is Tilly okay?"

"I don't know. They have to check and make sure she's ready to stay there and have the baby. If she's not, she'll be coming back."

"So we wait and see?"

"Yeah."

"What did Dr. Dick say about *your* baby coming?"

"He thinks I have three more weeks."

"Well, that's gonna suck for me." She turned and looked at the hospital. "Fuck it, let's go check on her." She stepped on the cigarette and we headed to the hospital door. We made it to Tilly's room without getting stopped. Tilly was sitting on the bed, dressed again.

"I'm not ready yet, I'm at a two, you have to be like a seven or eight."

"It comes out at a ten. . . . Can you come back to the facility till you're at a seven?" Jill said.

"Yeah, they're calling Alice right now."

Jill rushed out the door, said she'd be right back. Tilly and I waited.

Jill came back in with the nurse, who said, "Okay, Tilly, these girls are going to escort you back to the facility. We'll see you soon, hon."

Tilly hopped off the table and turned to Jill. "Whatdya do?"

"I just pretended I was Liz, who can go anywhere she wants. I told the nurse to tell Alice I'd bring ya back." I marveled at how scrappy and adult Jill really was.

She snuck off to the church on the way back, to make it look like she'd gone to confession. Tilly and I watched the line of over-eighteen girls on the path back to the facility.

"I thought I had it bad," she said.

"Yeah, me too," I said.

"You? Jesus, you're the luckiest person in the world! You're lucky on top of lucky." Tilly was smiling a sad smile. "My mom used to say some people in this world are lucky, and some people aren't, and you gotta know which one you are. She reminded me every day *I'm* not one of the luckys."

I thought about that for a while as we walked. And then I asked her, "Did your mom ever talk to you about the good people in the world, and the not-so-good people?"

"No . . . why?"

"'Cause you're one of the good ones . . . and that might even be better than being a lucky."

chapter 13

Tilly had an expression on her face I'd never seen on anyone before. They were one person together, Tilly and her baby. Even in her jeans with the holes in the knees and her floppy shoes, she was breathtaking. She shined in the kind of way I'd forgotten it was possible for people to shine. She smiled and knelt down by my chair in the lounge. I was almost too big by now to hoist myself up.

"You gotta hold him." I shook my head. "Pleaaseeee, Liz, just smell his head, you'll fucking die." I looked a long moment, and then reached my arms out and took Tilly's little baby boy. He had a light blue cap on his head and a round rosy face. He smelled like all things good in the world. My heart rose up through my chest and into my throat.

"He's perfect, Tilly, just perfect," I said. And he was.

I gave her back the baby, hugged them both for a long time, and she left. To go back to her life—with Rick, and the baby, and everything that came next. A raw sadness filled me as I watched her walk out. Every ounce of me was happy for her, but at the same time, I was horrified and petrified for myself. I had to lean into her joy at that moment, instead of falling into my own darkness. She navigated her way to the cab with her big sneakers, her baby, and her bag. I smiled and touched the window as she waved goodbye and shut the cab door behind her. Tilly had saved me in a way that she may never know, but that I would never forget. Wren, Alice, Jill, Amy, Deanna, and the new girl were all staring at me. Alice cleared her throat.

"She's a good egg, that Tilly," Alice said.

"Yeah, you don't meet people like Tilly in a place like this," Jill said. I stared out the window and watched as the cab disappeared.

* * * *

Ms. Graham sat behind her desk in the tweed suit. She had a slight sparkle to her that I hadn't seen before.

"Thanks for coming in, Liz, I know it's not the regular day. How are you doing?"

"Fine."

"You're finally in the homestretch. How does it feel?"

"Good."

"Are you looking forward to going home?"

"Yeah." I'd been looking forward to leaving almost every day since I arrived, but as the reality approached, it felt different. Was I looking forward to beginning this new phase? To living the lie that would become branded into the core of who I was? Was I prepared to give birth to a baby like Tilly's, a baby that smelled like heaven, and give it away to people I would never meet?

"You know that baby of yours will be in very loving, caring hands," said Ms. Graham. It was like she could hear my thoughts. "The adoptive parents are so looking forward to the delivery. You'll be coming back up to the city soon after to sign off in court on the adoption."

"I know."

She smiled at my huge belly. "You *look* ready." Just as I was about to tell her how much it sucked to be so hugely pregnant, there was a knock on the door. Ms. Graham called out, "Come in." I looked up at her door and saw my mom's face.

"Liz, *dear!*" she said. She had on a light blue cotton sweater with several thick strands of pearls around her neck. Her golden sun-tanned skin against her big white smile lit up the gloomy room.

"*Mom?* What are you doing here?" She came over to hug me, but stopped short to take in my enormous stomach. She stepped back for a moment and then hugged me sideways away from my belly. She put her black patent leather bag down on Ms. Graham's desk and sat in the chair next to me.

"She called early this morning," Ms. Graham said to me. "I assured her this was a good day to come."

My mom held my hand. "I feel *terrible* about Easter, after saying I would come up and see you. I feel just awful. I am so, so sorry. So . . . here I am." She threw her arms up in the air. Ms. Graham smiled at us.

"While I have you both," Ms. Graham said, "I want to share some very good news going on around here." She was as close to excited as I'd ever seen her. "Believe it or not, *two* of the resident girls have decided to also give their babies up for adoption.

"There have been *no* adoptions in all the time I have been here. We are thrilled and relieved that the girls are beginning to see adoption as an option to keeping their babies. They're so young, and so many of them ill-equipped. Honestly, Liz, we believe most of this is due to the influence you've had."

I looked down at the floor. I didn't know what to say. Ms. Graham said to Dorothy, "Mrs. Pryor, you should feel deeply proud. Liz has impacted the girls in so many positive ways. They respect her, they listen to her, and they feel close to her, which is rare. Remarkable, really."

My mother didn't say a word. She turned her head and looked out the window in silence. What the hell? Why was she not saying anything? After a long moment, Dorothy stood up and straightened out her skirt. "Liz has an *enormous amount on her plate* right now, Ms. Graham," she said. "She is here to *have* this child, and get home as soon as possible to resume her life. The well-being of the less fortunate girls here, well, that is not something Liz should be taking on. It is difficult enough that she has had to immerse herself and live here. I don't want her saddled with their problems and lives. *My* concern is for *Liz,* and her ability to get through this difficult time. You can understand that, no?"

"Mrs. Pryor, all I meant to say is that you have a kind and impressionable daughter. . . ."

"I see," Dorothy said. She was terribly uncomfortable. My mom rose from the chair, picked her purse off the desk, and headed for the door. She turned around and waited for me to get up. But I remained seated. I looked at Ms. Graham.

"Who else is giving up their baby besides Amy?" I asked.

Ms. Graham smiled a real smile. "Wren, and Jill has asked some questions. And as time goes on, there will be more. I just know it. Amy is ready with a family in place and set to return to high school. And we're working on some things for Wren as well."

I got up from my chair and walked around the desk toward her. "Thanks for saying those nice things." For the first time ever, I hugged Ms. Graham. She pulled me close, stomach and all, and whispered, "Thank you, Liz." I turned back and followed my mom out of the room and through the guard gate door. The click, click, click of Dorothy's heels against the linoleum floor rang loud in my ears.

The trees outside had almost all their leaves now, and the grass covering the grounds looked like a fresh green carpet. Dorothy started the car and rolled down the window. That meant she was not going to drive. She couldn't stand the wind blowing her hair while she drove. Window down meant she was going to talk.

"I'm happy to see you, honey," she said.

"Thanks, Mom."

"I'm an ass, aren't I?"

"Yeah . . . you kind of are."

"Liz, I . . . I don't want to hear about the girls in there. I just don't, damn it. Does that make me an awful person? It is *ridiculous* to me that you would be even slightly burdened with their problems. You aren't supposed to be *impacting* them, you are to be focusing on yourself, on getting through this and out of here."

"She wasn't saying that, Mom, you don't get it. I've been living here for five months now." Tears were falling down her cheeks. "Mom, please, it's fine, don't worry, it's just . . . *Damn it,* Mom. Ms. Graham was trying to tell you something nice about *me,* and you didn't want to hear *it. That's all . . .*"

She brushed some lint off her coat and answered, "Fair enough, you're right, really you are. I apologize . . . I don't know what's wrong with me. This whole mess has been difficult, I mean very, very difficult, for me. All of it. You are my *daughter,* I love you, and I *worry so* about you. And I desperately want it to be *over.*"

She continued in a more surrendered tone. "I know you're disappointed about Easter . . . maybe I made the wrong decision in going to Sea Island. It's just that I have the twins to consider also. I feel very guilty now about it. . . ."

"It's fine, Mom."

"It's not fine." She looked out the window. "And then there's your father *of course.* He had *quite* a bit to say about his visit here with you. His royal highness believes I've made another *rotten* decision sending you here." She paused. "I need to sell more houses, Liz, I'm out of money. I'm *always* out of money. While that *ass* travels the world with his . . . wife."

"*Mom . . .*" I said. She was full-on crying at this point.

"*I'm* sorry, honey, it just *never* seems to get easier." She looked up at the ceiling of the car. "I'm doing the best I can, I just can't seem to get a break!" She wiped her eyes. "Forgive me, Lizzie, I'm falling apart." I scooted over in my seat and put my hand on her shoulder. It was torture to watch my mother so desperate—she had tried so hard and done so much to keep it all together for us.

"It's okay, I'm glad you're here, so glad, Mom. And you're not falling apart. You never do, you've held it together for so long." She was likely the best winger-of-life on the continent. I could see sitting there next to her, she really was doing the best she could.

We decided to go to the movies that day. Dorothy *loved* the movies. We walked into the small, musty theater in town and sat down to watch *The Great Train Robbery*. She whispered to me at least a dozen times, in a dozen different ways, how flawless a *specimen* of a *man* Sean Connery was. All I could do was laugh. We ate grilled cheese sandwiches and ice cream afterward. We talked about the twins, and her work, and the coming of spring. Dorothy loved springtime, the hope it brought and the chance for new beginnings. "You have your new beginning coming up here soon, Liz," she said.

When we pulled back into the facility parking lot, both of our spirits were better. "I almost forgot, I brought you something," Dorothy said.

"You did?"

"Well, I felt so terrible, but I didn't know *what* to get. So here . . ." She reached under the car seat and pulled out a carton of cigarettes. I burst out laughing.

"Mom, are you kidding me?"

"What? You didn't think I knew you smoked?"

"Well, I mean, I don't know but . . ." For Dorothy to have brought me cigarettes meant that she obviously felt beyond horrible. I was a kid, and I was pregnant, and she thought nicotine was a wretched burden—she'd recently quit herself. The gesture was so absurd, it somehow made me feel better.

"Thank you, Mom."

"One more thing, Liz." She looked out at the sky and then dramatically turned and asked me, "Is there *anything* you can think of, *anything at allllllllllllllll* that I can do to make this easier on you? Other than *not* go on vacation again?"

"Well . . . there is one thing that's been on my mind."

"What is it?"

"I'm worried you won't make it here to be with me when it comes time to have the baby. I'm very worried, actually."

She put her hand on her forehead and moaned.

"I'm not saying that to make you feel bad, Mom. I'm just, I'm scared."

Dorothy sat up straight and enunciated her words. Which is what she did when she was trying to make a *point*. You never wanted her point to include the w-h words. She'd blow the sound hard and long: whhhhhhhhat, whhhhhhhhere, whhhhhhhhhy. She spoke loudly and clearly: "I will be here, no matter *whhhhhhat*. I will *not* miss it. You have my *word of honor*." Her word of honor? She'd never given her word of honor to me. A person's word of honor was the highest and most valued statement of promise in our family. She ingrained the concept in our heads when we were very young. It began when she and my dad went out at night, leaving the seven of us kids with some poor sitter. When she *needed* to trust us to do what she said, she'd put us on our word of honor. She'd make us say it back to her, and it always worked. It actually pissed me off when she asked for my word, as the years passed, because it meant I would have to do whatever it was I said I'd do. It was nonnegotiable.

"Wow, okay, I *know* you'll be here. Thank you, Mom."

She smiled. "I do love you, Liz."

I got out of the car and looked back at her. "Hey, Mom, next time I see you, this will almost be over," I said. And I shut the car door. My heart was lighter as I walked back inside.

. . . .

It happened on a Thursday afternoon, almost three weeks later. I was sitting in my chair in the lounge watching the same card trick I'd seen a dozen times. I couldn't figure out how Jill did it. I asked her to do it again and again and again, hoping I'd catch it. As she pulled my card out of the deck for the umpteenth time, I felt my stomach tighten. I put my hand on it. It tightened again super hard, as though there were a vise-grip turning too far in one direction, and my stomach was caught in it. I didn't say anything at first, but after a while the gripping began to hurt, badly, and I started to freak out. It was here. This baby was finally coming. I leaned over the chair with an intense pain and held my breath, as though that might somehow relieve it.

Jill calmly got up and led me to our room, where she tried like hell to keep me distracted. I was a shockingly *horrific* patient. She did everything she could to occupy me: cards, concentration, hangman, tic-tac-toe. By midnight, the pains were twelve minutes apart. The closer they got, the clearer it became. There was no way out. I was going to give birth to a person out of my vagina. I was scared to death. I told myself to get a grip, to calm down, to have faith, but it was completely useless.

Jill had a pad and pen and moved the Snoopy clock onto the floor where she was trying to get me to play Battleship. She tracked, timed, and documented the labor pains like a statistician.

"Liz . . . you're okay!" she said every time I shrieked from the pain.

"No, I'm not, it *fucking* hurts, Jill. I'm not kidding."

"I fucking believe you, but it's supposed to hurt."

I winced.

"Okay, you know what? You should pack your shit. Let's pack it up, you're almost outta here. You want outta here, remember that? It'll give us something to do."

"Grab my suitcase," I said. We began gathering my things. Jill was emptying the drawers until I said, "Wait . . . here. Just keep this stuff." I handed her the maternity clothes, the towels, and the burner and pointed to the food.

She smiled big. "Shit, I hit the jackpot."

"Yeah, people just *kill* for towels and maternity clothes, Jill." She laughed. Then the pain got worse.

"Owww, owwwww," I said. She stroked my hair.

"You're okay. Hey, I might have so much stuff I'll have to get a new bag."

"Really? You'd actually get a new bag? Please let me give you my bag, my suitcase?"

"No, you need it."

"Owww. No, I don't. I can use the shopping bags from my dad. I'm gonna throw a fit right now if you don't say yes."

"Okay, fine, fuck yes!" She put my suitcase down near her trash bag.

A big pain came and I screamed, "FUCK SHIT FUCKING MOTHERFUCKER."

"Jesus, Liz. Try and breathe." She sat me down on the bed. "You okay?"

"NO, *stop* asking me that."

"*Mean* pregnant bitch."

The pain waned. I relaxed for a second and managed a smile. "Sorry."

"No problem. You're a good reminder to not have fucking sex." She pushed her bangs out of her face and her little red heart tattoo caught my eye. It was between her pointer finger and her thumb.

"What's the deal with the tattoo, Jill?" I asked.

"Oh, it was just a stupid thing I did one night when I was kinda drunk. I'd just broken up with another asshole and got this idea to get a heart there to remind me that I don't need a fuckin' guy to love me. I don't need anyone to love me. I guess it's there to remind me just to like myself."

"Geez, Jill, that's kinda deep."

"Well, I'm a deep person, Liz P." She calmly got up and checked the clock on the floor. "I can't believe you're going. You're gonna have this kid and leave here. I'm gonna miss the shit out of you."

I leaned over again and tried breathing loudly, but just ended up full-on shrieking in pain.

"I'm getting Alice," Jill said. "She has to call your mom. I'll be right back." I looked at the bags and guitar case leaning against the wall. The bed, where I'd cried myself to sleep so many nights. I scanned the room and took a photograph in my mind. It was a place, no matter what happened in my life, I knew I was never going to forget. I looked and saw my stuffed dog Henry's ear sticking out from underneath the pillow. I grabbed him and held on to his leg. Alice and Jill came through the door. Jill was holding on to her stomach laughing.

"Like her sleeping hat?" She pointed to Alice's purple-and-black plastic hat that looked like a shower cap. Her pink polka-dotted robe had a zipper all the way up the front. On her feet she had what looked like rubber rain boots that were covered in terry cloth. "She works at the circus at night, did you know that, Liz?"

Alice folded her arms. "Well, this is what I get for gettin' woken up at one in the morning. I already called your mom. She's on her way."

"How long will it take her?"

"Don't you worry, she'll be here. Looks like you're ready to go." Another pain hit hard. I squeezed the shit out of poor Henry. Alice and Jill came and helped me up off the bed. Alice stroked my hair and said, "Yeah, you're ready."

When the two paramedic-looking nurse guys arrived with the wheelchair, I was suddenly overtaken with fear, to the point of wanting to throw up. Jill put her hands on my shoulders and said, "You can do this." Then she grabbed a pen from the table and picked up my hand. She drew a little heart on it between my pointer finger and thumb and colored it in, so it looked just like hers. I looked down and smiled a little, and then hugged her hard. Just as I was about to leave, Wren came walking in in her pajamas, rubbing her eyes.

"You're going, aren't you?"

"Yes, she is, Wren, it's time," Alice said.

"I'll never see you again, I know it. So bye," Wren said.

I smiled. "Bye, Wren, good luck with everything."

"Gonna suck without you, Liz," Wren mumbled.

Jill looked over at her. "Thanks a lot, Wren."

"See you, Jill . . ." I said.

"Later, bitch," she said, smiling.

The nurse men wheeled me out of the lounge and headed through the dark tunnel toward the hospital. It felt like I was heading to the burning fires of hell. I was brought to a small room with no windows and told to change into a gown. My nausea took over and I threw up on the floor. A small, curt nurse with short blond hair handed me a barf pan and said, "Next time hit that." She told me the doctor would be in to check me in a while. I sat on the plastic sheet covering the hospital bed with the gown on backward, so I could cover myself up. There was nothing I could do but scream when the pains came. I'd brace myself and try to breathe, and the breath would lead to a grunting, guttural shouting. I didn't recognize what the hell was going on inside me. It felt like I'd hit a panic button I didn't even know existed, and there was no shutting it off. My whole body was involved. The nurse came in and nearly yelled at me to be quiet. She turned the lights down, checked the barf bin, and said that I should try to sleep. I asked her for some water, and a while later she came in with ice chips in a plastic cup. She said if I drank water I might throw up again. I sucked on some ice chips and dozed in and out of my screams, convinced I might actually pass out from the pain. Pass out or possibly *die.* I prayed to God like I was on my deathbed, prayed to God to let me and the baby live. The clock on the wall read two-thirty; I was sure I would die by three A.M. At three-fifteen someone came in the door. I turned and saw Dorothy. She was wearing her blue peacoat with a red scarf. Her hair was messy, and she looked tired. I burst into tears.

"I can't do this, Mom, and I mean it, I can't," I said. And then a pain came. She threw her stuff on the chair and held my hand as I screamed through it. She rubbed my forehead, left the room, and came back with the nurse, who took my hand and tried to shove a thick needle into a vein on the top. She finally got it in, and I shrieked.

"You need to calm yourself, young lady," said the nurse. "That kind of shouting gets all the other women on the wing agitated." I hated her, I hated me, I hated everything, and I didn't care. The needle was to hook up an IV so I wouldn't dehydrate. Dorothy sat in a chair next to the bed and held my hand, her other hand holding her forehead, staring down at the floor. Dr. Dick finally wandered in after a few more pains.

"How far apart are they?" he asked. Dorothy attempted to introduce herself, but he ignored her. He sat down and put his gloves on. Dorothy answered for me. "About six minutes." His hands went up me while I was having a contraction; I screamed and squeezed the shit out of Dorothy's hand. "You could wait until the contraction is finished, Doctor," Dorothy said. The doctor continued to try to kill me.

"She's at about four centimeters," he said. "She's got several more hours to go until this baby is ready, maybe six or even ten. Get her to quiet down, put a muzzle on her if you have to." He turned toward me, "You need to get ahold of yourself."

Several more *hours*? Dorothy stepped in front of the door blocking him from being able to leave. He stood right in front of her, but she held her five-foot-two ground like a lion.

"She is a young, frightened *girl* in *enormous* pain. Your behavior is *inexcusable.* Whhhhhhere were *you* when they taught *bedside manner* in medical school?" I winced and tried to stay quiet. "I hhhhhighly suggest you figure out a way to relieve her pain, so the screaming can cease, or she will have not only this floor but your *entire* hospital wondering which doctor is caring for the pregnant teenager who has been given nothing to help manage the *pain.*"

Dr. Dick smiled arrogantly and left. When the next pain came, Dorothy stood up and said, "*Scream, scream all* you need, sweetheart. Do it, scream *bloody murder* if it makes it feel better." The pain came on and I screamed bloody murder a few times. Dorothy covered her ears, and the nurse came running back in.

"I suggest you *get the doctor* and give my daughter some drugs,"

Dorothy said. Finally Dr. Dick came back in, several minutes later. He looked at my mom with surrender.

"I am reluctant to give your daughter drugs. There is a chance they will slow down or even *stop* the labor. She doesn't want to be here for three days, does she?"

Dorothy suddenly resembled a wild dog. "*YES . . . YES, she does* if it will *lessen* the pain. SHE DOES! LOOK AT HER!" The doctor pointed to the IV and told the nurse to begin a flow of some drug and left the room. I started to feel woozy, and five minutes later I was convulsively throwing up. The nurse and Dorothy couldn't get the barf pans in front of me fast enough. After an hour or so the vomiting stopped, and the pains felt slightly more manageable. I tried to breathe through them. Dorothy fed me ice chips and blotted my sweaty forehead. She dozed off a few times but was awoken every time the doctor checked me and I wailed in pain.

By four P.M. the next day, almost twenty hours after the labor started, I had finally dilated to nine. The nurse and doctor stood at the end of the bed. The nurse was opening bags, readying the baby scale, and shaking bottles on a tray she'd wheeled in. They both had cloth masks over their faces. The doctor sat on the stool, pushed my legs apart, and said, "It's time to push." The nurse pulled a lever that made the bed fold up. My mom stood next to me and gritted her teeth. I couldn't believe that I hadn't passed out from the pain yet. The pressure down below was so intense it felt as though it was going to blow the insides out of my body. I pushed as hard as I possibly could, again and again and again. And then I hit a point where my choice became to either push harder into what felt like a burning rage of fire, the kind of pain that is impossible to choose, or to ease up on pushing and return to the contractions that assured me I was going to die anyway. I chose to push one last time toward the fire. My eyes and face filled with blood and pressure.

My mother kept her eyes on me and screamed, "Push, Liz, PUSH FOR GOD SAKES. Get it ouuuuuuttttt!"

I heard the doctor say, "There it is, keep pushing."

I shrieked in pain as I felt the raging burn of fire, and then the baby's body as it thrust out of me.

"Okay, that's it. It's out, healthy . . . little small, but good," Dr. Dick said. I looked down and saw something small and gooey-looking. I whispered with the greatest relief I'd ever felt, "It's over, Doctor." The doctor turned, handed the baby to the nurse, took the rubber gloves and mask off, and headed toward the door. The nurse walked over to the little table with the light. I could hear the baby crying. I lay back down, looked up at the ceiling, and smiled. My mother grabbed my hand.

"Well done, Liz. Thank God, it's over. Now, don't look over there."

All I could think is: I didn't die. Dorothy looked over at the nurse and in a slight Kate Hepburn voice asked, "Could you *please* go out of the room with the child now?"

"I'm getting the vitals, ma'am. We'll be out in a minute." The baby was still crying. I looked over at the small steel table with the light and saw two little feet sticking up in the air. I smiled and knew I'd never see more than that, but it was enough. And then I burned the image in my mind, to stay with me forever.

The nurse rolled the steel table toward the door. She turned toward me and said, "This one's a real cutie." And she left. I placed my hand over my stomach and stayed quiet on the bed for a long time. When I opened my eyes again, Dorothy was standing over me in her coat and scarf, with a tired smile.

"You've been asleep awhile, honey."

"Mom, are you leaving? Why do you have your coat on?"

"I wish I didn't have to," she said, "but I have to get back to the twins, and while you rest here I'll rest at home. I'll come right back first thing in the morning. There is a nurse who works upstairs on the third floor. Her name is Annie. She's going to take you to a private room with a lot of space and big windows, where you can eat and rest and sleep tonight. Will you be okay?"

"Yeah."

She leaned over and kissed my hair. "Goodbye, sweetheart, I'll see you very soon." She walked away and then closed the door behind her.

. . . .

The room was completely quiet. The tears slipped out the sides of my eyes, down my cheeks, as I lay perfectly still. And felt the inside of me begin to lighten. I did it. The baby *lived* and I *lived*. It was over. I lay alone for a long time in the dark quiet.

. . . .

"Liz?" A youngish-looking nurse peeked her head in the door. "How you feeling?"

"Fine."

"I'm Annie. I'm going to roll you out of here and take you upstairs, if you're up for it? We can get you settled in a nice room, get some food in you."

I gingerly made my way off the table and into the wheelchair. She handed me my clothes and Henry. We rolled through the dark hallway, where I could hear low, muffled labor pain sounds coming through the doors of the rooms. Hearing them felt like seeing someone with a sliced-open wound. It was too fresh and painful. The wheelchair headed down another hall. It was quiet for a moment and then I heard the sounds of babies, crying and cooing. A sweetly painted sign that read Nursery was placed above a large viewing window. We wheeled slowly by the window; I looked in and saw the cribs lined up with tiny new babies sleeping in them. The nurse sped up and headed for the elevator. We got off on the same floor and wing where I'd visited Nellie six weeks ago. Annie wheeled me into a large room with two beds. There were a few bouquets of flowers on the windowsill and table. The sun sprinkled in through the big windows, and I felt something inside me begin to warm. Annie helped me out of the chair and onto the bed. "Your mom asked us to get your things from the facility, so here you are." She opened the closet door wide where my guitar and the shopping bags were sitting on the floor.

"Thank you," I said. "Um, are the flowers for me?"

"Well, of course they are. Here." She took the cards from each bouquet and handed them to me. "I'm going to go find you some food. Are you hungry?"

"Mostly thirsty."

"I'll be back," Annie said.

I opened the first tiny envelope and read, *"Love you loads, Dad."* There were more than a dozen white and yellow tulips in a glass bowl. The next card read, *"Happy New Beginnings. Love you, Mom."* I took a whiff of the beautiful bouquet and smiled. Annie came back in with a plate full of nasty-smelling hospital food, a Coke, a lemonade, and a Squirt soda.

"I didn't know what you liked to drink, so I brought everything."

I looked at the green Jell-O and turkey-looking mush and sipped on the soda instead. I felt like I could breathe, like my entire body could finally feel the oxygen coming in and going out. I was sore and exhausted as I dozed off. Then I was awoken by something in the room. I opened my eyes.

"Hi, Diz." Lee was standing over the bed. He wore a crisp, light blue button-down shirt and a navy blue blazer. He leaned down and kissed my forehead. The familiar smell of shaving cream and Beeman's gum made me smile.

"Wow, I didn't know you were coming. Hi, Dad," I said.

"Well, of course I would come." He smiled down at me. "So . . . you okay? Everything went all right?"

"Yeah, but it wasn't fun."

For some reason he thought that was funny. "Well, I can imagine it wasn't *fun,* but it is over."

"I wasn't very brave, Dad. At all."

"Are you kidding? You had a baby, for Christ sakes. I don't care how you did it, that's brave."

"I thought it would never end," I said.

"I can imagine. I'm so sorry you had to go through all this." He handed me a white paper bag from behind his back.

"What is this?"

"Just some edible food."

I reached in and pulled off the wax paper around a perfect ham and Swiss cheese sandwich on rye and started chowing down. Lee walked around the room, looked out the window, and smelled the flowers. As I watched him, I wondered when was the last time he and I were completely alone. There were so many of us, and we were always in a crowd. It was almost strange to be just the two of us. I thought back to the Sunday mornings I'd had with him as a little girl, the pastries and newspaper at the French bakery. He pulled the chair over to the bed and sat down.

"I wanted to tell you something," he said. He took off his blazer and laid it over the chair.

"Okay," I said.

"I, well, I want you to know I'm proud of you. . . . You've handled this very difficult time incredibly well." He waited a moment, then went on. "Diz, this doesn't define who you are, it just becomes a *part* of who you've been. Okay?"

"Okay."

"It's important . . . that you know I love you, and I'm here for you. You really are all the things people need to be to live a great life. I'm not worried about you in the *least*."

He was so sincere. We both sat quiet until he smiled big and said, "And what does adversity do, anyway?"

"Makes you stronger." I laughed with a mouth full of ham sandwich. He used to tell me that all the time, growing up.

"That's right, don't forget it. So your mother was here for the whole thing?"

"Yeah."

"Well, that's good."

"Dad, I thought I was going to die. Mom yelled at the doctor and got me drugs and . . . she had to listen to me scream for like two days."

"I'm glad she was here. When is she coming back to get you?"

"Tomorrow morning."

He was standing up again, looking out the window, getting the lay of the land, I guessed.

"I've got the college stuff mostly handled," he said. "There's a great small school in Denver; we'll go over everything when you get home. Don't worry about any of it." He asked if I wanted to work at Pryor Corporation over the summer to earn money to bring to college. I had almost *forgotten* about college. My mind was still trying to catch up to what was happening. I'd just had a baby. I looked at Lee, and it was like he was standing at the doorway to the safe, comfortable world I'd always known. And then I thought about the baby, and the facility, and the girls. This was the last time I would be straddling the two worlds, and I had to wonder if both of them would now become one inside me.

My dad smiled at me. "Got to go, honey. Just needed to see your face." He grabbed his blazer, kissed my cheek, and was gone.

I made my way to the shower. I was still tired and sore. I stepped in and let the warm water wash away the IV tape, the iodine, the breast milk, and some of the shame I'd held on to so tightly. I closed my eyes as the birth rinsed off me and swirled down the drain. I thought about my dad coming to visit, how surprised I was by it. Very few people would ever understand the depth of the complicated mistrust and disrespect that defined the combat of Dorothy and Lee—and know the impact that dynamic had on the children they brought into this world. But for a moment, *this* moment, I let go of all I knew about the two of them. Instead I held in my mind who my dad was to *me*. I was suddenly aware how lucky I was to have him, *specifically,* as my father. I felt it clearly and fully. Over the last five months I'd looked for the judgment from him, for the shame and disappointment I was so sure I deserved. But it never came.

For a girl to look into the eyes of her father at her lowest moment in life and see faith and love shooting back—it felt like a miracle. A miracle I needed at that very moment. If the great all-powerful Oz—my dad—knew I would be okay, then *I* knew I would be okay.

I stepped out of the shower and looked at my wounded body in the mirror. I saw beyond the rock-hard boobs, the stretch marks on my stomach, and the broken blood vessel on my cheek. Instead I saw the body and face of the girl I remembered myself once being. I smiled and noticed a hint of something familiar in my eyes. And then I began to ready for a different kind of battle. I was going home. I changed into a clean pair of sweats and a T-shirt, walked over to the window, and looked at the rooftop of the facility as the sun sank into the horizon. I looked down at my hand and saw the last fading trace of the heart Jill had drawn. Annie, the nurse, showed up at the door.

"Was *that* your dad? That handsome man who just left?" she asked.

"Yeah."

"What a sweetheart."

She smiled as she fixed up the bed. "He stood in front of the nursery window just staring at that baby for such a long time."

chapter 14

A candy striper volunteer was rolling another awful-smelling meal into the room. Out in the hall I saw a baby in a wheeled crib at my door.

I pointed. "There's . . . a baby at the door."

She smiled. "Yes, it's feeding time for the little ones. I'm rolling that angel to the room next door. Did you want me to bring you your baby?"

"No . . . that's okay." The woman set a plate of dinner in front of me, quietly made big faces into the tiny crib in the hall, and rolled it next door. I was exhausted. I couldn't keep my eyes open. When I woke up again, the room was dark, the sun low and rising through the trees. It was early morning. I felt something filling my eyes. It was over. I made it. It was still sinking in, that I was on the other side of the event that had defined my entire life for the past five months. The relief sang through me.

I sat up and looked out at the facility roof, hiding behind the trees, when a blaster headache almost knocked me over. The nurse said that might happen from the drugs. I popped the aspirin she'd put on the table and downed the melted ice water in the plastic cup next to me. I was bleeding, badly, down below, but they said that too was normal.

As the sun rose higher in the sky, the day beginning, the sound of the babies out in the hall grew louder. A nurse brought me some orange juice and breakfast. I cleaned up, got dressed, and waited for Dorothy, who was coming to take me home. I watched the clock move from seven-thirty to eight to eight-fifteen. The back of my sneakers tapped the metal bar on the bed over and over. Finally, I heard a light knock. Ms. Graham was standing in the doorway, wearing a long tan trench coat, her glasses resting on top of her head. She was carrying a Styrofoam cup.

"You like hot chocolate?" she said, offering it to me.

"Yes, thanks," I said.

"So how are you? Are you okay?"

"Yeah. Yeah, I really am. I'm ready to go home."

"Good. I can't stay. I just wanted to say goodbye."

I hated saying goodbye to people. Dorothy once told me you don't have to say goodbye, you can say *see you later,* or *see you soon,* or *see you next time.* But there would be no soon, or later, or next time—not with Ms. Graham, or with anyone here.

"Thank you for everything, Ms. Graham."

She smiled. "I see great things for you and your future, Liz." She reached over, patted my hand, and in a quiet voice said, "You just keep doing what you're doing. Everything is going to work out." Ms. Graham believed in me, I mean really believed in me. I wondered if she knew how much she'd mattered to me in these past months.

I got up, walked over, and hugged her for the second time in all the time I'd known her. Then she quietly walked out. Neither of us said goodbye.

Annie came in a minute later. She said, "We have to go over home care for your healing over the next few weeks.

"So, I have a few different medications. Here you go. This one is twice a day to stop lactation, dry up your breast milk." Holy crap. "This one is a stool softener in case you have trouble going to the bathroom, and this big one is an antibiotic to make sure you don't get an infection." I looked inside the bottles. They were like horse pills. I probably wouldn't even be able to swallow them. She went on. "Oh and here, this is a cushion, you blow it up and sit on it at all times. It will help your bottom heal." *What?* A cushion? For how long? She continued. "You should sit on it as often as possible, especially the first week or so."

"Okay," I said. This all seemed so strange.

"Oh, and, Liz, you know it is very common to get the blues after you give birth. If that happens, there isn't much to do, but it *is* normal if it does." *The blues?* I'd already had the blues, I didn't want them anymore. "Are you feeling blue now?" Annie asked.

"Well, no, I don't *think* so."

"Good. Here are some pads to put in your bra so the milk doesn't leak onto your shirt." Leak on my shirt? "And I think that's it. Looks like you're ready to go. You can keep all this stuff in this bag. I'll check in later when your mom gets here." And she was gone.

I sat down on the bed and thought about how I was going to hide sitting on a cushion for a week. I counted the trees outside the window, between the hospital and the facility. I strained to see the windows on the side of the facility building, but the brush was too thick. Just around twelve-thirty, the door finally opened.

"Bonjour, my love," my mom said. Dorothy was wearing her cream-colored St. John knit sweater set with her hound's-tooth pants and black zip-up leather booties. "Sorry I'm so late. The twins needed to be dropped off at a birthday party and traffic was horrendouuuuuuus. How are you feeling, sweetheart?"

"Pretty good."

"You look *wonderful* except . . ." She pointed. "Do you have any actual *clothing* here?" Dorothy considered sweats and T-shirts *and* sneakers non-clothing.

"Mom, I don't have any of my regular clothes here, no."

"Well, that's okay. We'll just be in the car."

Dr. Dick arrived at the door. Dorothy turned around and got a hard look on her face. "*Maaaaay* we help you?"

He ignored Dorothy and approached me.

"Having any irregular pain, young lady?"

"I don't think so, but I'm bleeding pretty badly and having some cramps, and my boobs hurt."

"Sounds about right. And the nurse went over the home-care instructions with you, the meds I prescribed?"

"Yes."

"All right, then." Both Dorothy and I looked at him. I secretly hoped my mom would remain quiet and let it go, but this was Dorothy.

She took a step closer to him and asked, in her most sarcastic of Katharine Hepburn voices: "Is that *coooooncerrrrn* for your patient I detect, Doctor?"

"Just doing my job."

"Your *jooooob*? Is it your *job* to wait until a patient is in a healthy state to behave in a reasonable professional manner? Don't answer that, actually. You can be assured I will be making a formal complaint to whoever is in charge here. And you can expect consequences for your reprehensible behavior." I smiled slightly, knowing she would never really do that. Dr. Dick looked at my mother a long time, like he was about to fire back, and then appeared to change his mind. He didn't say a word as he turned and left the room. Dorothy watched him until he was gone.

"Wow, Mom. Good stuff," I said.

"What an *incredible* ass."

"At the facility we called him Dr. Dick."

"Well, that's vulgar, but appropriate, I suppose."

We said goodbye to Annie and made our way to the elevator. I glanced one last time down the hall at the nursery with the viewing window and then headed out the door. The air was crisp, and the sun was high in the sky. Before I stepped in the car, I took one last, long look over at the facility.

"What are you doing, Liz?"

"Nothing." I thought about going back up and saying goodbye, but there was no one really left. Nellie and Tilly were gone. I'd said goodbye to Wren, and Alice, and Jill before I left. And Ms. Graham I'd seen early that morning. I scanned the grounds for the last time.

"Well then, come on, get in!" my mom said. I got in the blue car and closed the door. We drove away from the facility for the last time. I couldn't stop myself from smiling. It was over, I was out . . . I was free. I wondered how long the feeling of relief would remain; maybe it would be there forever. Dorothy was tapping her fingers on the steering wheel. I listened to the coffee mugs roll beneath us and thought how strangely comforting it is that moms never really change. She let out a long breath, looked at the road ahead, and said, "It's over, sweetheart. You'll see, everything will go right back to normal."

I was pretty sure nothing was ever going to feel like the kind of normal I'd once known. I imagined Dorothy would never really understand that, and that was okay, because it had to be. We pulled onto the interstate. Frank Sinatra came on the tape deck; of course he did. He was singing "That's Life." Dorothy lifted up her shoulders in her car-dance kinda way, turned it up loud, and shouted, "Honey, you hear that lyric? Listen!" She sang along and swayed back and forth,

I just pick myself up and get back in the race
THAT'S life, ahhhh that's life

She took both hands off the wheel to snap her fingers.

"MOM!"

"We're fine, I got it, I got it." She put her hands back on the steering wheel. When the song was over, she turned the music down and looked at me.

"Just have to get back on the horse, Liz, the horse of life."

The trees along the interstate were beautiful, lush and green. Spring was here. I wondered what Dorothy was thinking. She often looked so lost in thought. And then, with as much indifference as I could muster, I asked her, "What did you tell people, Mom? I mean about what was wrong with me?"

She threw one of her hands up in the air and replied, "Nothing, *nothing*, you're back and *that's it*."

"No, I mean, when they ask what *sickness* I had. What *did* I have, Mom?"

"You were ill, Liz. That's it." That's it? That's the cover-up? That's the lie I'm going to tell and live with for the rest of my life?

"And how did I get better?"

"You, you were at the *Mayo Clinic* with the best doctors in the country, they made you well. End of story." She *still* didn't know what sickness I had. She hadn't thought about this at all. "No one will ask the specifics, Liz. You just need to put this behind you right now and you mustn't speak of it again, to *anyone*. Honey, are you listening?"

"Yeah," I said. But it wasn't over. I was bleeding, my boobs leaked, I was sitting on a goddamn cushion, and I was certain I would think about this chapter in some form most of the days of the rest of my life. I watched the Indiana farms whizzing by. So this was the grand plan. It had a lot of holes, and I knew it.

"Have you heard from your father?" Dorothy asked.

"Yes."

"When?"

"Yesterday."

"Well, that was nice, he called the hospital?"

"He came to visit."

"*Really*, he actually drove up and you saw him?"

"Yes."

"Did he bring his bride?"

"*Mom* . . . nooooo. He came alone."

She went into her sad, surrendered voice. "Well, there are truly very few people on the planet for whom Lee would go out of his way, and you have always been one. You are one of his chosen few." We were both quiet. Lee had crushed my mom when he left, there was no denying that. But it was his blatant disregard for her existence ever since then that made it so difficult for all of us. She turned to me with a knowing look.

"And did he stay longer than twenty minutes?"

How did she know that? "Well . . . I don't know, maybe thirty."

"Don't be fooled by your father, Liz."

We drove along and listened to more Frank and Bing Crosby. And without thinking, the words came out of my mouth. "Did you look at the baby, Mom?"

"*What?* Did I look at your child?"

"Yeah."

"God, no." She mumbled something under her breath. She looked almost angry. "I don't know why you would ask that. . . . Why would I look at it?" Dorothy cleared her throat. "Do not think about the child, Liz. I'm telling you, not seeing it was the best choice, for both of you. That baby is about to begin a great life with two parents who are ready to have a family. You must try to move on and forget about all of this."

The lying had begun. We exited and made our way through the Winnetka streets. I looked out at the enormous houses passing, one after another. Four-car garages, circular driveways, kids on shiny new bikes, beautiful groomed dogs prancing on fresh lawns. I'd truly almost forgotten what it was like here. We finally turned in to the familiar gravel driveway, and I saw our big white house. Dorothy smiled, and I smiled back. The lion statue sat crooked on the path, the bikes leaned up against the garage, and our old croquet game was strewn all over the front lawn.

We stepped onto the shiny hardwood floor at the front entrance of the house. I saw the big yellow couches in the living room, and the brass dictionary stand with the two-ton dictionary opened to some word Dorothy probably made the twins look up. In the dining room was the glass table with the ten chairs neatly pushed in around it. And then I looked up at the staircase and saw my little sister Jennifer flying down the stairs, Tory right behind her. The sight of them put my entire body at ease. I hugged them and drilled them with questions about school and friends. Neither of them asked a word about where I'd been, or what had gone on. Only the present mattered. It was as though I'd just come home from summer camp. We talked about all kinds of everyday things. Tory grabbed the peanut butter from the cabinet in the kitchen; Jen got the bologna out of the fridge. They made sandwiches while we talked.

"You want one?" Jen asked me. But tears were rolling down my cheeks, and it was too late to stop them. Tory gently asked, "Did Jen say something?"

Jennifer looked at Tory. "I didn't *say anything,* maybe *you* said something." The two of them began bickering about who made me cry, until I tried to laugh.

"Nobody said anything. It's just me, you guys . . . I'm sorry." I couldn't place what was going on, maybe it was seeing the twins after being gone so long. Or maybe it was the food, the edible normal food inside our amazingly beautiful home. I dried the stupid tears and ate the bologna and mustard sandwich that my little sister made for me.

Eventually I made my way upstairs to my room. I stared for a long time at the brass bed with the white down comforter and swan mobile hanging above it. I'd thought about that bed a thousand times in the last five months. I bent down and ran my hand over the soft blue carpet. My Madame Alexander dolls sat on the shelf above my desk. On the dressing table, my puzzle ring and puka shell necklace sat untouched. I turned and saw my mom standing behind me at the door. "Laurie has called you several hundred times," Dorothy said. "That's an exaggeration, but you get what I mean. You must call her at school. Lauryn has also called several times and so has Daniel."

"Okay, thanks."

"Glad you're home, sweetheart."

"Me too." Maybe they *had* noticed I was gone, after all.

"And, Liz?"

"Yeah?"

"Stop saying yeah, the word is *yesssss* . . ."

It was official. I was home. I unpacked, played around on the piano, ate Lay's potato chips, and read the titles of the dozens of books on the shelf in the living room. I wandered around the house, feeling the familiarity I had so longed to feel. And then I sat down on the yellow couch in the living room and thought of Papa for the first time in a while, and his tiple, and the music, and I realized how far away the years now felt since I was a little girl. Just as the sun was disappearing from the sky, I made my way out to the big wooden tree swing in the backyard. I sat on the swing for a long time and watched the willow tree branches swaying back and forth over the pond. I looked up at the star-filled sky and searched for the tiniest one of them all. I found it and quietly said, "I see you."

. . . .

The next morning I woke up to my wet, hardened T-shirt stuck to my boobs. It stank of sour milk. I reached for my stomach, but there was nothing in there. I looked up at the ceiling, sighed, and remembered: I was home. I spent the next day and a half in a mild fog, getting used to it all.

. . . .

On my third day home, Dorothy reminded me that I needed to go to court to finalize the adoption papers.

"Today?" My heart began beating fast against my chest.

"Yes."

"Are you coming with me?"

"No, I can't make it, I have to work."

"Mom, I can't go *alone*, it's court." I was nervous. "I'm a kid, you *have* to come with me."

"No, I signed everything that needs signing; you just have to go do this last part. It's a formality, Liz. You will *literally* sign a document and come home."

. . . .

The green VW bug was sitting in the driveway. The car I'd driven to school every day that year till my life as I knew it stopped. I'd waited forever for that car to be mine, for my older sisters to go off to college. It was once the only thing I thought about. I looked at the passenger seat next to me and saw my dirty hiking boots, a sweater, and my friend Jen's coffee mug. I tried to remember the life behind those things, but couldn't. There was a green ribbon from the last football game tied to the rearview mirror. I turned the key and pushed the stick shift into reverse. I drove past the beautiful homes on our street and was reminded just how much more than enough the people around us had.

I merged onto the interstate and headed for the courthouse. The little farms and cornfields felt almost familiar as they whooshed by. There was an undercurrent of something brewing inside me. Maybe survival mode had ended, and I needed to deal with what was now in front of me, but I didn't want to. I drove, listening to the Bee Gees on the radio, ignoring everything beckoning. An hour later, I looked down and saw my hands beginning to tremble on the wheel. I was short of breath. The more I watched my hands shake, the harder it was to breathe. I pulled over onto the shoulder of the highway and stopped the car. It was dead quiet. Something inside wanted me to listen, but I didn't want to hear it. The baby was out, I was home, I'd had enough. I stared ahead at the empty road—and then suddenly I felt the need to scream, at the top of my lungs. Again, and then again . . . bloodcurdling screams. And then I whispered, "Somebody help me."

The image of the two tiny feet sticking up in the air flashed into my mind. Would I live with the worry and fear and wonder if the baby was safe and loved for the rest of my life? Or would I believe that my parents, the adoption place, God, and life could all be trusted—that the baby would have a warm, loving home and be just like my adopted cousins, happy and cherished? I took a big breath and decided there in the car that I had to choose *faith* over fear. I had to believe with all that I was that the baby would be safe and loved. I seared that belief into my soul and promised myself I would never go back on it.

I closed my eyes and clutched the steering wheel. I thought about the fabricated lie, the lie with a thousand holes, the lie that was forced upon me for my own good. That would become a part of who I was, until the end of time. It had begun. The rest of my life was right now, and I couldn't fathom the amount of lies I would have to tell in the years to come. I couldn't wrap my head around the number of people I loved who would never know the truth, never know why or how I'd come to be the person I am. I was scared that over time, even I would begin to wonder what was the truth and what was a lie. I sat in the shit of it all, feeling trapped and helpless. I didn't want to *survive* life. I'd been doing that for the last five months. I needed to be able to *live* it. I knew I couldn't erase any of this or let time cloud the truth. I *wanted* to remember it. And so I told myself I would seal my truth about the baby—the girls, the facility, everything that happened to me—in a place inside where I knew it could live forever. I had to, no matter what was said, or done, or told on the outside. No one could stop me from holding that knowledge safe and alive on the inside.

I started the car back up. I had a strange, lonesome feeling— knowing it would just be me, by myself, the only person who knew the *whole* truth. I drove another long hour and a half, so-lidifying all the promises I'd made to myself. Finally I pulled into the underground parking structure of the court building in Indi-ana. I was wearing my blue cotton skirt with a white button-down sweater and my pearl necklace. I looked in the rearview mirror at my puffy eyes and tried to smile.

Room 302 was at the end of a long hall. I entered a crowded

courtroom. A bailiff told me to sit and wait for my case name to be called. I took a seat in the back. A judge sat at a high desk in the front of the room. More than an hour later the judge shouted, "Pryor baby 443671."

My heart began to pound. I stood up and meekly raised my hand. He looked over his glasses and summoned me to his desk up front.

"Are you Elizabeth Knight Pryor?"

"Yes, sir."

"You are here to sign off on the adoption of a child born"—he looked down at the papers—"three days ago?"

"Yes, sir."

"You have identification?"

"Yes, sir."

"Step over here." I stepped around to a different desk and was handed some papers to read and sign. I made my way to my seat in the back. And then craned my neck to see what was going on up by the judge. I saw a few different people and then noticed a man and a woman with their backs to me, standing together. The woman was holding a baby wrapped in a blanket. I could see a baby's head resting on the woman's shoulder. Was that them? Was that the baby? They looked kinda nice from the back. The judge called my name again and dismissed me. I whispered *goodbye* to the little baby. I stood outside the door in the hall and etched my faith for the baby to live a safe and loving life in stone in my soul.

◦ ◦ ◦

I was going to wear my sister's graduation dress from a few years ago. New Trier High School didn't follow cap and gown protocol, and girls wore long white formal dresses of their choice. They also received a dozen red roses upon receipt of their diplomas. There were more than eight hundred graduates, which meant an insane amount of roses. The packet sitting on my desk said I had to arrive two hours early for a talk-through rehearsal and placement instructions. At the bottom of the paper it gave details for the party and dance following. Five and a half months suddenly felt like five years. I couldn't believe this used to be my life.

I pulled the long white eyelet dress over my head and squeezed my boobs into the sweetheart neckline. I zipped it up and faced the mirror on my door. Dorothy shouted from the hall.

"I can loan you some makeup if you like!"

"No, thank you, Mom." She was always trying to get me to wear makeup.

"Do you need shoes?"

"No, I have them." I reached in the closet and found my old white Converse high-tops.

"I have beautiful white strappy heels if you'd like to try?" Dorothy said.

"No, Mom, I got it," I shouted back. I took the brush from the dressing table and scowled at my long, curly hair. Then I took two pieces from the front on both sides, pulled them to the back, and clipped them together with a tortoiseshell barrette. I found my silver chain necklace with one single pearl in the middle and fastened it around my neck. The sapphire ring Lee gave me for Christmas sat in my ring box. I opened it up and put it on my finger. Dorothy shouted at me to get moving, I was going to be late. I threw on my high-tops and double tied them. The dress was just too long, so you couldn't see the shoes at all. Dorothy knocked, and opened the door. Her eyes went wide.

"My God, sweetheart. You are *truly stunning*."

Dorothy's eyes started to well up. "I am proud of you, Liz." She took a long pause. "This can't be easy, *any* of it, and I know it." That was the first time she'd ever said anything like that. I couldn't believe she'd finally acknowledged what this might be like. I needed someone, so badly, anyone to say that out loud—that they knew it was hard. I kept my eyes wide open, hoping she wouldn't see the tears welling up. She came over and put her hands on my face. And said in her best, low, I-mean-it voice, "Now you go to that *high school,* you keep your head high, *ignore* those brats, and *gradddduuuuatttte. . . .*" She hugged me close. Dorothy knew what I knew. The firing squad would be brutal at school. There would be gossip about the truth, and rumors, and nasty things whispered behind my back. But my mom didn't like to give attention to the bad stuff. She let go of me, headed out of the room, and then turned back around.

"I mean it, I am proud of you. I'll see you there, sweetheart." I knew that Dorothy loved me completely. I felt the safety of that in my bones. I knew that *both* my parents, in their markedly different ways, believed and expected I would make it through all of this. They had been like two odd bookends throughout my life, leaning on either side of me, helping to hold me up with their own versions of strength, love, and encouragement. Maybe that had helped me more than I realized, because I was starting to believe I was going to be okay.

* * * *

The parking lot was crowded with kids and their fancy cars. Heads turned as my conspicuous bright green VW bug pulled in. I took a deep breath and prayed my boobs wouldn't leak. I made my way toward the gym. Kids were gathered in small groups in their graduation outfits. Many of them looked my way and whispered; several pointed and murmured. A couple girls I knew in our grade said hello. But no one asked *where* I'd been. No one asked *anything.* Everyone stayed clear, as though they might catch whatever I had if they came too close. Mom's words from three and a half years ago were echoing loudly in my head. "Mark my words, sweetheart, you will have nobody your senior year if you insist upon hanging around the girls a year older than you." She was right.

I felt a thousand eyes watching as I made my way up the outside stairs and into the gym. The entire room had been transformed; enormous barrels of white flowers laced the aisles and podium. I gazed up at the basketball hoops and banners near the ceiling.

I made my way through the crowd to an open spot against the bleachers. I did everything I could to ignore the growing buzz and stares. I thought about the world I lived in before I left, the things that used to matter so much that didn't matter now. The whispers were turning into outright comments. Three girls I didn't know approached and then turned back around, laughing. This was bad—but bad had changed its meaning for me. I waited for myself to feel something awful, to feel the heat and shame, but somehow I was okay.

I kept my head steady, waiting for the few teachers to tell us what to do. I caught eyes with a girl across the room. It looked like she was going to wave, but instead she pointed to her stomach and made a big circle with her hands. I looked away, up at the podium where we would be receiving our diplomas. I didn't feel like crying or running. Instead I felt something strong, something that was stopping the hurt from seeping in. I didn't know until that very second that I even had that strength.

A few teachers finally began lining us up. I made my way to my section. I sat in a seat on the end of the row and began to scan the room for my parents, but didn't see either of them. Families and guests were filing in, waving and smiling to their kids. The ceremony speeches began. There was no sign of my dad, but I finally saw my mom walk in. She sat down near the back of the middle aisle. Dorothy spotted me, waved, and did her uncomfortable open-mouthed-smile thing. After a long time, the names were finally being called for diplomas. I was worried about my now incredibly sore bleeding bottom, and my boobs leaking onto my dress. I discreetly adjusted the cloth pads in my bra and then waited. Name, after applause, after name, after applause, until I heard *Elizabeth Knight Pryor*.

I slowly stood up. And heard the searing sound of a few boos around the section where I was sitting. I couldn't seem to hear anything but the boos as I tried to make my way to the aisle. There were a few muffled laughs. My heart fell hard as the unbelievable reality hit. My classmates were booing me. I could only hope my mother didn't hear it. She was way far back, and I was glad about that. As I made my way to the podium, I felt everything in my body settle. And a surprising feeling of triumph swept through me. A woman in a white suit handed me the dozen red roses. I turned to the dean, took the diploma, and smiled. As I turned around, I looked up one last time at the New Trier Indians banner and the American flag hanging from the ceiling. I knew I was never coming back. For the first time since I returned home, I could feel the ground beneath my feet. Instead of heading down and back to my row, I decided to continue down the aisle toward the double-door exit. I felt the newfound strength tenderly guiding me as I walked past Dorothy, in her pearls and yellow suit. I could feel her heart pouring out as she smiled—sad, but proud.

I knew I would live with a version of the judgment and malice from the gym for the *rest* of my life, and that no one would ever know about the time I'd spent on the other side of the world. But I also knew I would be able to *live* my life. That with the truth alive locked inside, I would forever be able to see what *truly* mattered.

I stepped outside into the cool summer air. The football field across the street was empty and quiet. The sky had just finished growing dark. I glanced up at the stars and searched for the smallest one of them all.

Liz at New Trier High School graduation, 1979

afterword

Thirty-six years ago I made a promise to my mother that I would never tell anyone about this story. I kept that promise my whole life. I never told my siblings or my friends, until this book. In 2011, before my mother died, I asked her what she would think about me writing this story. And she answered, "Well, you do whatever you want, sweetheart. Look at you now."

I'd always thought about writing this story, but wasn't sure I would actually ever do it. As the years passed, it felt more and more unlikely. But then a few things happened. Around the time when my mother passed away, my three children were approaching the age of sex and love, the age I was when I went through this. It was time to tell them, and deep down I knew that telling them might change something inside me—and it did. Their remarkably loving responses, and their unwavering lack of judgment, were why I began to know I could write this story.

I outlined the major events, and I began writing. It was shocking how vividly it all came back. There must be something about a story that has never been told, an unusual preservation of the imagery and emotions. I began with the emotions, and then the colors, people, scenes, voices, faces; all of it came back so fast that I'd have to stop typing and take notes before getting back to writing.

A lot of people seem to want to know why I wasn't angry with my parents. I think I was just too angry with myself. Getting pregnant was all on me—that's what I felt at the time. I didn't question the decisions and authority of my mom and dad, and I don't exactly know why. I think I needed them. I was a child, and I felt completely alone. They were the only two people in the world who knew where I was. However, during the writing of this book I did look back with a different view, and all these years later, I questioned many things. But by now it is sadness that I feel, not anger. There was a point in my late twenties when I confronted my mother about why she asked me to lie to everyone I cared about, and we had a long conversation about it. My siblings and friends surely heard rumors over the years, but only one of them ever came forward and asked me directly. None of them learned the entirety of this story until this book. My parents were my only touchstone to this reality, but even they had no idea of my life inside those walls. Surprisingly, my relationship with my mother deepened after I left the facility and through the years that followed; like an unspoken bond, it kept us tied together.

When asked what it's like to keep a secret for so long, I have to answer that I don't know what it's like *not* to keep a secret for so long. In time the lie became a part of me, like an appendage that no one could see. But there's a loneliness to it that forced me to navigate and understand certain aspects of myself on my own. I developed an inner strength that no one knew why or how I had. Those months changed everything about how I saw the world. All of it lives with me every day in the work I do and the life I live. But it wasn't until the writing of this book that I was able to see the path my life has taken to get where I am today.

The most difficult part of this journey has been hiding the truth. It created an unspoken space and distance between me and the people I love. If I could change that, I would. If I could give my seventeen-year-old self any advice, it would be difficult not to mention the obvious: don't have unprotected sex. But I also might tell my seventeen-year-old self that you are not defined by what happens to you in life; you become who you are by how you choose to carry on. And it may have helped to hear, back then, that the toughest times in life do not happen without the gain of something truly valuable—even if it takes decades to find.

acknowledgments

I'd like to thank my children, Conner, Augie, and Luca, for supporting me in the telling of this story and for their boundless faith in me as a person. They are the reason and the hope behind everything I do. To Augie, for taking the time to read every page along the way, I thank him from the bottom of my heart. Thanks to my brother Bill, for believing in my writing and allowing me to entrust him with this work so early on. To my brother John, for his incredibly passionate support of this story and his unwavering love and friendship throughout my life. To the women who power and feed my soul every day, Laurie Sykes, Kristen Trucksess, Sara Gooding, Laura Dunn, Deb Williams, Laurie Wenk Pascal, and Beth Ewing. To my lawyer, Cindy Farrelly Gesner, for standing by me through every step I take, always. To Carisa Hays, for her constant support and guidance. To my true angel of an agent, Jennifer Gates, whose kindness goes beyond description. I thank her for her faith in me and this story, and for guiding me with such profound compassion and effort. To the great Kate Medina, I thank her for believing in this book, in these characters, and in me. I can barely contain the gratitude I feel. To the phenomenal team of people at Random House, I am in awe of the professionalism, talent, and confidence they have shown my story. And to Anna Pitoniak, I thank her for everything about her. For her thoughtfulness, kindness, and skill. And for making the editing process so seamless and safe. To my parents, Dorothy and Lee Pryor, for being the perfect recipe of strength and love in my life, and for providing me with such abundance and opportunity. To my four sisters, Kiley, Alex, Jennifer, and Tory, I have valued and loved each of them more than they'll ever know. And finally, to Peter O'Fallon, I thank him for convincing me to write this book, for helping me to go so deeply, and for being all that he is to me in my life.

What lies behind us and what lies before us are tiny matters compared to what lies within us.

—Henry Stanley Haskins

about the author

LIZ PRYOR is an author, speaker, parenting columnist, and life advice expert. Her book about female friendship, *What Did I Do Wrong?*, was a finalist for a Books for a Better Life Award. In 2011, ABC's *Good Morning America* conducted a national search for an on-air life advice guru, and out of fifteen thousand applicants, Pryor was chosen for the position. She lives in Los Angeles with her three children.

lizpryor.com

@lifewithliz

Find Liz Pryor Advice Guru on Facebook